Routledge Revivals

Lu Hsün and his Predecessors

Originally published in 1980, Alber's translation of Semanov's study aimed to contribute to the studies of Chinese literature and the knowledge of Lu Hsün's work to an English-speaking reader. Lu Hsün was an influential democrat and humanist in the early twentieth century and his work had a great influence on literature in China. Semanov therefore attempted to place his life and work in the context of his literary predecessors as well as commenting on his world view, his teaching and place in history. This title will be of interest to students of Asian studies and Literature.

Lu Hsün and his Predecessors

V. I. Semanov
Translated and Edited by
Charles J. Alber

First published in 1980
by M.E. Sharpe, Inc.

This edition first published in 2016 by Routledge
2 Park Square, Milton Park, Abingdon, Oxon, OX14 4RN
and by Routledge
711 Third Avenue, New York, NY 10017

Routledge is an imprint of the Taylor & Francis Group, an informa business

© 1980 M.E. Sharpe, Inc.

All rights reserved. No part of this book may be reprinted or reproduced or utilised in any form or by any electronic, mechanical, or other means, now known or hereafter invented, including photocopying and recording, or in any information storage or retrieval system, without permission in writing from the publishers.

Publisher's Note
The publisher has gone to great lengths to ensure the quality of this reprint but points out that some imperfections in the original copies may be apparent.

Disclaimer
The publisher has made every effort to trace copyright holders and welcomes correspondence from those they have been unable to contact.

A Library of Congress record exists under LC control number: 80050885

ISBN 13: 978-1-138-64752-7 (hbk)
ISBN 13: 978-1-138-64753-4 (pbk)

Lu Hsün and his predecessors 鲁迅

V. I. SEMANOV

Translated and edited by Charles J. Alber

M. E. Sharpe INC., WHITE PLAINS, NEW YORK

Copyright © 1980 by M. E. Sharpe, Inc.
901 North Broadway, White Plains, N.Y. 10603

All rights reserved. No part of this book may be reproduced in any form without written permission from the publisher.

Library of Congress Cataloging in Publication Data

Semanov, Vladimir Ivanovich.
    Lu Hsün and his predecessors.

    Translation of Lu Sin' i ego predshestvenniki.
    "Titles of Lu Hsün's works":
    Bibliography: p.
    Includes index.
    1. Chou, Shu-jen, 1881-1936—Criticism and interpretation.
I. Alber, Charles J. II. Title.
PL2754.S5Z82813   895.1'8509   80-50885
ISBN 0-87332-153-7

Printed in the United States of America

Contents

Introduction by Charles J. Alber	vii
Author's Note	3
Chapter I The Beginning of the Century	5
Chapter II A Caustic Sense of Values (1918-36)	42
Chapter III The Innovator	75
Some Conclusions	120
Appendix: Titles of Lu Hsün's Works	123
Notes	133
Bibliography	155
Index	161

Introduction

BY CHARLES J. ALBER

The works of Chou Shu-jen (1881-1936), the most important Chinese writer of the twentieth century, were rather slow (though no slower than elsewhere in the West) in coming to the attention of Soviet scholars and critics. In fact, it was not until the spring of 1925 that Ts'ao Ching-hua, a Chinese slavicist, introduced Leningrad academician B. A. Vasilev to Chou's—Lu Hsün's—first collection of short stories, entitled *Outcry*. Fortunately, a record of that meeting has been preserved, and it is extraordinarily revealing.

"Comrade, I am a foreigner and my reading ability in Chinese is limited, so explain to me as a foreigner and a nonprofessional what I ought to select first. Tell me, in your new literature, whose work should I look at first? What sort of works? The most important..."

Without waiting for him to finish, I continued his sentence. "The most important work you had best read first is 'The True Story of Ah Q.'"

"'The True Story of Ah Q'?"

"Right, Lu Hsün's 'The True Story of Ah Q.'"

"Lu Hsün? Where is he from?"

"Let's discuss this again later in detail. First read over 'The True Story of Ah Q' and then we'll talk..."

On returning to the Dragon Pavilion I took a volume of *Outcry* at hand and presented it to him: "'The True Story of Ah Q' is in here."

A few days later in the lounge of the place where he worked, as soon as we came face to face, Vasilev clapped and cried in surprise: "Marvelous! Marvelous! Lu Hsün... I see, is just... like our Gogol, Chekhov, and Gorky. Marvelous!"

Obviously he was holding 'The True Story of Ah Q' just like someone holding a ball of fire, and sat, letting it burn, but could hardly rest. He went on anxiously: "Such a pity! Such a marvelous writer like this, such

> a marvelous work, and we hadn't an iota of an idea. I am determined to use my spare hours, to translate it into Russian and to spread it to the Soviet Union. Only there are still quite a few places in the book that I do not understand; for this I want to ask for your help."[1]

Vasilev did indeed become enthusiastic about Lu Hsün and, with special assistance from the author, became the first to introduce Ah Q to the Soviet public.

Lu Hsün's reaction to Vasilev's efforts was quite favorable, as indicated by his special preface dated May 26, 1925.

> Something I should feel grateful for and even very delighted about is that my short story, owing to the translation of Mr. B. A. Vasilev, who deeply understands Chinese literature, has at last been spread before the Russian reader....
>
> The first thing that I received following the publication of my short story was a rebuke from a young critic; later there were some who thought it was sick, some who thought it was comical, and some who considered it satiric. Perhaps there were others yet who thought it was cold ridicule, until I too was forced to suspect that my own heart was really storing a dreadful ice cube. But again I thought, no author looks at life the same, and no reader looks at a work in the same way, so perhaps in the eyes of the Russian reader without any trace of "our traditional thought" this work will appear in a different light, and this really aroused my interest.[2]

Little did Lu Hsün realize that a few years later he would be branded an "anarchist" and a "petit bourgeois radical." In a flagrant misinterpretation of "Ah Q," the once humble Vasilev himself wrote:

> Lu Hsün's work, like that of Dickens, is based on laughter, humor which mitigates the sharpness of class contradictions. If laughter can expose, then laughter can sometimes quiet and reconcile. Lu Hsün's petit bourgeois types of beggars are created with love, but a sympathetic laugh prevents one from seeing the difficult conditions in which they exist, prevents one from noticing their limitedness. Like Dickens in his *Tale of Two Cities*, Lu Hsün flinched from revolution, which for him was folly. As an ideologist of petit bourgeois radicalism Lu Hsün captures neither the pathos of industrial capital nor the psychology of the proletariat.[3]

But this was only the first contribution to the long debate over Lu Hsün's own "grand finale." Opinions of the writer were destined to change drastically within a relatively short span of time.

By 1934 (or perhaps even earlier) Lu Hsün's name had come to the attention of the Comintern. That year *International Literature* sent out a questionnaire asking various left-wing foreign authors how in particular the revolution had affected their lives. The July 5 edition of *Pravda* contains a group portrait of some authors who sent in replies—Henri Barbusse (1874-1945), Theodore Dreiser (1871-1945), Upton Sinclair (1878-1968), and other, lesser-known authors. Lu Hsün's portrait was not included in this gallery of famous left-wing writers, but his answers to the questionnaire were printed, albeit in the bottom right-hand corner of the page. Later his name continued to be listed on the international advisory board of the journal. None of this notoriety is very surprising in light of Lu Hsün's reputation and his shift in views after 1930, but it is remarkable just how great a cultural hero he was to become. In 1938, two years after his death, a special commemorative volume was published both in Moscow and Leningrad, and as the lead article (signed by the Academy) shows, his name was already highly revered.

> It is completely natural that the untimely death of the great contemporary Chinese writer Lu Hsün, this true Humanist, best friend of the Soviet Union, friend of the working people and the Communist Party of China, irreconcilable and passionate enemy of fascism, and fearless fighter for a better future for his motherland, evoked in the hearts of the peoples of our great socialist country a feeling of sincere grief and deep sympathy for the Chinese nation which has lost its great compatriot.[4]

Nevertheless, despite this lavish display of affection and esteem, the articles and translations were very poorly done! One undoubtedly competent reviewer wrote:

> Examples of syntactical unclarity combined with sheer grammatical blunders could be cited *ad infinitum*. Such is the language in which all of the short stories are translated. One must be surprised that the editorial staff approached so carelessly the editing of translations of the great Chinese writer's first published works.[5]

Undoubtedly these difficulties reflect the growing pains in the "new sinology," including the forced reorganization of the Academy, but there were other complicating factors. Stalin had come to power, and by the year of Lu Hsün's death the "purges" were reaching their peak.

The record shows that not even sinologists were immune from Stalinist terrorism. As a now deceased Soviet member of the profession recalls:

> In the summer of 1925 many Soviet students gathered in Peking. There were representatives from all the centers of Soviet sinology—Moscow, Leningrad, and Vladivostok. The Muscovites V. L. Gamberg, I. M. Oshanin, A. P. Rogachev, and V. I. Melnikov had come earlier and were, so to speak, old timers. But the recently arrived alumni of the Far Eastern University in Vladivostok were in the majority.... Among the Leningraders we met Ye. S. Yolk, S. M. Okoneshnikova, and later P. Ye. Skachkov and E. M. Abramson. Scholars as well as student probationers were visiting Peking. The Leningrad sinologist V. A. Vasilev [undoubtedly B. A. Vasilev—C. J. A.] was there at the time....
>
> It is with sadness that I write most of these names, remembering the terrible years of Stalinist repression (the end of the thirties). How many young and talented China specialists perished, men who were loyal to the party and their work, and who laid the foundation of Soviet sinology, thereby contributing so much to the cause of Sino-Soviet friendship. Melnikov, Vladimirova, Bokanenko, Voyloshnikov, Yakovlev, Perlin, Yolk, Abramson, Vasilev, Novoselov are no more. Dubasova and Skachkov spent many years in exile.[6]

Some of the names on this list belong in the permanent Who's Who of Soviet Sinology (Skachkov, for example), so one can understand why B. A. Vasilev might not escape persecution. In any case, his name is conspicuously absent from the list of contributors to the 1938 commemorative volume.

Aside from political and organizational problems there were others facing the new Institute of Oriental Studies (1930), which was forced to submit to planning and charged with covering the whole of Asia, including the Soviet Far East. Needless to say, the Academy's holdings had to be improved, even more so than before. Fortunately, there was already a remarkable network of book exchanges with Chinese and foreign organizations in Peking, Nanking, Shanghai, Tientsin, Kunming, Hong Kong, and Harbin. But here again there were complications. Not to mention internal strife, the Chinese were at war with Japan (1931-45), and this in turn merged into a worldwide conflagration. Because of their special linguistic skills, Soviet sinologists were called upon to serve in the Far East, and many, it is said, gave their lives in defense of their nation. World War II may even have left the ranks of sinologues depleted, but for whatever reason, the decade from 1937 to 1948 proved to be "comparatively unproductive."[7]

In September and October of 1949, the noted writer Alexander

Fadeev (1901-56) led a Soviet delegation to China, and this was to herald a new era in Sino-Soviet cultural relations. In a speech entitled "The Worldwide Significance of Chinese Culture" delivered to the Soviet Friendship Association in Peking on October 5, 1949, Fadeev declared:

> I was still a very young man when Lu Hsün's works were first translated into Russian. It is very difficult to reproduce the force of his mother tongue; (and) we still do not have that many people who know Chinese. (But) I can assure you that we will in the very near future. I had the chance, as someone a bit familiar with the standard speech, to work out a literal translation of Lu Hsün's works with the help of the Chinese poet Emi Siao [1896-?]. Don't get the idea that we did so in the interests of the so-called "artistry" of this great Chinese classic. On the contrary, we tried to find the most exact expressions in the Russian language capable of translating Lu Hsün's genius. This was my modest reply to the fact that such a world-renowned writer as Lu Hsün spent his time on a translation of my youthful novel, *The Rout*. I can give my promise to Chinese literary workers that we will do everything possible to translate the magnificent works of Lu Hsün, one of the world's most noble humanists, as closely as possible to the original.[8]

Here Fadeev gives us reason to suspect that he too worked on the Lu Hsün commemorative volume (1938). This would explain his insistence on "accuracy" as opposed to "artistry" in the translation. And yet, the noted writer's reminiscences undoubtedly reflect his own as well as the Party's frustrations. The above statement seems very much like a public apology for Soviet sinology's remissness over the previous two decades, as well as a declaration of its firm purpose of amendment.

Several studies (1953, 1954, and 1956) and translations (1954-56) of Lu Hsün's works did appear in the early part of the next decade, but unfortunately they were of poor quality. Since the Academy's reorganization there had been a "definite gap"[9] between the sinologues of the old school (who dealt mainly with philology and classical literature) and those of the younger generation, whose research was to center on contemporary China. Would-be contemporary specialists, therefore, were forced to produce dissertations in classical poetry! This was true of L. Z. Eydlin (Po Chü-i), N. T. Fedorenko (Ch'ü Yüan), O. L. Fishman (Li Po), and L. D. Pozdneeva (Yüan Chen). This generation did not have the preparation to study *pai-hua* (vernacular) fiction. As a result, those studies of contemporary fiction that were produced in the early fifties (chiefly by Eydlin and Fedorenko) were sketchy and inaccurate, and their oversimplified ideology was most apparent. All these inadequacies are reflected in Gustav Glaesser's review of Fedorenko's *Chinese Literature* (1956), which serves not only as a review but as a commentary on the scholarship of the time.

> In the whole of his book the A[uthor] shows himself to be—be it said without the slightest thought of offending the great scholar, Fedorenko— a "great simplifier" who tries to reduce this exceedingly complex world of the Chinese *corpus poeticum* and Chinese literature, to little more than an unceasing "social protest," harping on a single string, undoubtedly a most important one, but not the only one in the great symphony of Chinese literature.... If only the Author had entitled his book "The Social Idea"—or better still, "The Social Protest in Chinese Literature"! Then he would have avoided this charge of one-sidedness from which no reader who can distinguish politics from science can acquit him.[10]

Of course Stalinism undoubtedly had some effect on the discipline (Lu Hsün, for example, was idealized as "the Chinese Gorky"), but the scholarship *itself* left much to be desired.

By 1956 the Soviet hierarchy must have viewed the situation in oriental studies with alarm.

> Speaking to the point, Anastas Mikoyan asked the Twentieth Party Congress: "But whom do we have, after all, to engage in a serious study of these questions? ... The Academy of Sciences does have an institute that studies the problems of the East, but all that can be said of it is that although in our day the whole East has awakened, that institute is still dozing."[11]

The Soviet satirical magazine *Krokodil* (Crocodile) printed a full-page color cartoon of the Oriental Institute "at work." A number of turbaned Academicians, spread out on a cushy Turkish rug, are indulging in chess, the water pipe, and tea. One individual sits reading the *Thousand and One Nights*, while another sits in a couch enjoying a snooze. All in all it is a hilarious glimpse of the Academy, though the intent, to be sure, is deadly serious. The results were predictable.

In his 1958 study of Soviet oriental studies Roger Swearingen pointed out that the Soviet Union had "very recently launched a major training and research effort designed to fill in research and personnel gaps in their total national resources on Modern Asia" and that "China and India appear to be the focal points of this intensive effort." His conclusions were based on observations of the growth and extensive reforms taking place in research institutions.

> A new Institute of Chinese Studies was set up in Moscow in November 1956 by detaching and expanding the Chinese Department of the Oriental Institute.... The Institute now has about eighty specialists whose task is "to study all things bearing on modern China." Institute work is organized into six main divisions or sections: (1) History, (2) Economics, (3) Literature and Culture, (4) Modern State Structure [Contemporary Public Law and Government], (5) Languages, and (6) Publications....
>
> The Literature and Culture section of the Institute has eight staff members: five working on Chinese literature, two studying the problems of Chinese culture (not clearly defined), and one Chinese staff member who assists with difficult translations and otherwise serves as a sort of "troubleshooter."[12]

The effect of this reorganization was immediately visible in the area of publications. According to R. V. Vyatkin, 242 books on Chinese problems were published from 1957 to 1959 as compared with 447 from 1950 to 1957. Certainly there was an enormous new effort as well as a commitment to the "eternal friendship" between China and the Soviet Union.

The more relaxed atmosphere of the Khrushchev era made it easier for scholarship to flourish, and sinologists were quick to take advantage of this new flexibility. Several studies of Lu Hsün were published in the late fifties, and each reflected a somewhat different ideological orientation. L. D. Pozdneeva, whose doctoral dissertation (1952) had won a Lomonosov prize, produced a ponderous study (1959) of Lu Hsün's work nearly six hundred pages in length. According to one Japanese reviewer (1964), this work far outstripped other Western studies and even exerted some influence in China and Japan.[13] But that opinion is certainly subject to debate, as the following comment on the story "Soap" demonstrates:

> In this story Lu Hsün stands before us as a master of detail. It might seem there is nothing special in a husband bringing his wife a small cake of soap. But this package, the color of an unripened sunflower seed, with a scent similar to olive, helps the writer to lead us to serious conclusions. Soap has appeared for the first time in Ssu-min's family. Only the scoffers' sneers at the beautiful beggar girl ("if someone would only wash her!")

made this guardian of "national purity" aware of his own wife's dirty neck and sent him to the perfume shop.

The writer's battles against the defenders of the old ideology, Confucianism, are here crowned with the exposure of their physical uncleanliness. The writer makes a good piece of soap the first prerequisite in the struggle with zealots of antiquity. Rather than moralize and defame the young, the writer tells us, the bombastic moralists should wash, and scrub off the dirt behind their own ears.[14]

Pozdneeva attempts to prove that artistically and ideologically Lu Hsün developed from a "revolutionary romanticist" to a "critical realist" and from a "critical realist" to a "socialist realist," but in order to find a "positive hero" entirely worthy of the name she is compelled to go beyond the writer's short stories to his essays and, more specifically, to his real-life student Miss Liu Ho-chen. Among the unarmed student demonstrators during what Lu Hsün called "the darkest day since the founding of the Republic" (March 18, 1926), Pozdneeva discovers a feminine "revolutionary," a supposedly "conscious participant in the antifeudal, anti-imperialist movement unfolding under the leadership of the Communist Party."[15] What the critic neglects to point out is that in this instance Lu Hsün was not "depicting" anything; he was simply reporting. And even at this late date he *flatly denied* the effectiveness of demonstrations, especially unarmed ones. But I need not belabor the point; the record is clear to all who have read Lu Hsün, whether in the original or in translation. Pozdneeva's study can be viewed as a vain attempt to defend Mao's Yenan thesis (1942) that Lu Hsün was "a national hero on the cultural front, the most correct, the bravest, the firmest, the most loyal and the most zealous hero who stormed and broke into the enemy's front."

Two other studies of this period were produced by younger, less conservative sinologists. One (Petrov, 1960) portrays Lu Hsün as a "revolutionary democrat" and the other (Sorokin, 1958) as a "revolutionary humanist." In comparison with Pozdneeva both sinologists are more literary than ideological in their orientation, despite the fact that they adopt either a sociohistorical or sociopsychological approach to the problem. V. V. Petrov was really the first to venture an analysis of Lu Hsün's more melancholy prose poems in the collection *Wild Grass*, and he does so with keen insight. He is unwilling to accept the vision of Lu Hsün as an eternal optimist, and despite a Marxist orientation, he frankly admits the *"inevitability* of man's loneliness in contemporary society" (italics mine—

C.J.A.). As a result, a more realistic portrait emerges, that of a bona fide nonviolent revolutionary who, as Pozdneeva herself acknowledged, "suffered through" Marxism. V. F. Sorokin's study, written a couple of years earlier, is more optimistic than that of Petrov, who concentrates on the more somber aspects of Lu Hsün's works, his problematic view of the people. Sorokin is entranced with the image of the "rebel theomachist" in Lu Hsün's stories, and occasionally he does capture the fire of this hero, the *Übermensch* who stands out above the crowd and dares to challenge Heaven itself. Then, too, Sorokin deliberately separates Lu Hsün's narrator (or persona) from the writer himself, something all other Soviet sinologists, including Semanov, fail to do. He is careful to distinguish fact from fiction, which in my opinion gives this early study of *Outcry* more validity than any of those previously attempted (i.e., Fedorenko, Eydlin, Pozdneeva). In the final analysis, the critical studies of Petrov and Sorokin are encouraging. They are the first that can reasonably be recommended to the Western critic and the first that make a truly literary contribution to the study of Lu Hsün.

As mentioned above, the Khrushchev era was one that encouraged exchanges in scholarship, so that Leningrad once again, so to speak, reopened its window to the West. V. I. Semanov was one of the first students of Lu Hsün to take advantage of the new spirit of inquiry. This is evident, for example, in his review (1959) of Sorokin's study *The Evolution of Lu Hsün's World Outlook* (1958). Most of the review is favorable, although the critic does have a few admonitions.

> It is a shame that the author writes about much that was already well known in the tone of one who is the discoverer. V. Sorokin, of course, was familiar with Pozdneeva's [1957] book, the works of N. Fedorenko and V. Rogov, but in vain do we search in his monograph for references to works preceding his or debates with their authors. To us it seems that this is not the way to bring about cooperation among scholars in Soviet literary criticism. One hopes that each new work will move Far Eastern Studies ahead, not by the mere fact of its appearance or the character of its appreciation, but by an active, energetic attack against those things that were erroneous in previous works as well as by support of the valuable scientific discoveries made by Soviet and foreign scholars.[16]

Semanov was born in Leningrad in 1933. In 1955 he completed his work in Chinese philology for the Far Eastern Department

(*Vostočnyj fakultet*) of Leningrad University. After graduation he studied for three years as a graduate student (*aspirant*) of the Academy of Sciences Institute of World Literature in Moscow. The last of these three years (March 1957—March 1958) was spent in China collecting material for a master's (*kandidat*) dissertation dealing with Lu Hsün and Chinese literature of the nineteenth and early twentieth centuries. After completing his work abroad, Semanov remained at the institute as a junior researcher and defended his dissertation in 1962. In 1967 he became a senior researcher in the same institute and head of its Asian and African section. He defended his doctoral dissertation (*The Evolution of the Chinese Novel from the Late Eighteenth to the Early Twentieth Century*) in December 1968, and the work was published two years later.[17] Most recently (1973) Semanov was appointed chairman of the Department of Asian and African Literature at Moscow University. The Soviet scholar already has an impressive list of publications to his credit, and one can only hope that he represents a new breed of sinologists and intellectuals. L. Z. Eydlin, editor of *Lu Hsün and His Predecessors* (1967), commented that this was the first book to deal with this particular subject and that it was based on a "painstaking analysis" of the works in question.

Throughout *Lu Hsün and His Predecessors*, apparently an extension of the author's master's thesis (1957-62) as well as a product of later research, we find evidence of that spirit of debate which Semanov himself advocated. In preparation for this study the author apparently familiarized himself with the majority of recent publications on Lu Hsün, including various studies by B. Krebsová, J. R. Průšek, J. Last, Huang Sung-k'ang, H. Mills, J. Chinnery, Liu Chün-jo, and others. But we also find him debating with his own colleagues, senior and junior. The author is careful to point out, for example, that Lu Hsün did not "introduce simple folk into Chinese literature" (a thesis upheld by Pozdneeva and others), that domestic problems do not play a major role in "Diary of a Madman," and so forth. The reader will find many such instances of rebuttal throughout the study, and in chapter II the author even challenges such noted Chinese critics as Cheng Chen-to and Liu Ta-chieh. It has always been my conviction that without such an open and frank exchange of views, scholarship in general, and sinology in particular, will inevitably become impoverished.

Nevertheless, there are certain views expressed in the work that reflect the prejudices of the past. In some cases the bias seems quite blatant, as, for example, when the critic flatly asserts that Lu Hsün was a "consistent" revolutionary and that he "always" evaluated popular movements from a "progressive" standpoint, or that he wrote "for the sake of" the nation as a whole. This compulsion to find something "positive" or "optimistic" in Lu Hsün's works (e.g., "numerous optimistic endings," see *infra*, p. 109), I regard as a holdover from the past, because only in the most complex sense could the writer be characterized as a *narodoljubec* (Petrov's neologism), one who "loved" the nation (*narod*) or "the people." If Lu Hsün did love the peasant or the "common man," surely it was *in spite of* the latter's notorious apathy and lack of political conviction, for undoubtedly the image of the gaping crowd forms a constantly recurring motif in the writer's essays and short stories. Semanov is more accurate, therefore, when he recognizes that Lu Hsün's love of the people only intensified his criticism of them and that this critical approach to the national psychology is somewhat reminiscent of Chekhov.

Semanov would even have us believe that in the period following *Outcry* (1918-22) there are "far fewer satirical images of the common people," but I can find no proof of such an assertion. On the contrary, in the collection *Hesitation* (1924-25) there are the stories "An Example" and "The Eternal Lamp"; in *Wild Grass* (1925-27) there is the devastating prose poem "Revenge (I)"; and in Lu Hsün's essays the images are even more explicit. I refer, for example, to the essays "What Happened to Nora after Her Departure?" (*The Grave*, 1923), "Some Notions Jotted Down by Lamplight" (1925), and "In Memory of Miss Liu Ho-chen" (1926). But perhaps a citation from the first of these three essays would be in order.

> The masses, especially in China, are always spectators at a drama. If the victim on the stage acts heroically, they are watching a tragedy; if he shivers and shakes, they are watching a comedy. Before the mutton shops in Peking a few people often gather to gape, with evident enjoyment, at the skinning of the sheep. And this is all they get out of it if a man lays down his life. Moreover, after walking a few steps away from the scene they forget even this modicum of enjoyment.
>
> There is nothing you can do with such people; the only way to save them is to give them no drama to watch. There is no need for spectacular sacrifices; it is better to have persistent tenacious struggle.

> Unfortunately, China is very hard to change. Just to move a table or overhaul a stove probably involves shedding blood; and even so, the change may not get made. Unless some great whip lashes her on the back, China will never budge. Such a whip is bound to come, I think. Whether good or bad, this whipping is bound to come. But where it will come from or how it will come I do not know exactly.[18]

This, I think, is rather typical of Lu Hsün's attitude toward the masses, even after 1922. Moreover, it was because of such passages that many of the essays and short stories were deleted from the 1956-60 edition of Lu Hsün's "selected" works published by Peking Foreign Languages Press. Of this admittedly subtle form of censorship there can be little doubt. Fortunately, however, some of these works have been published elsewhere, and to some extent this will help set straight the record.

Unlike previous studies, however, Semanov's monograph is neither an apology for Lu Hsün nor a defense of the Chinese populace. In fact, he realizes the necessity for Lu Hsün's critical attitude, and is even concerned with the validity of the term "nation." What is striking, I believe, is not the degree of distortion, but the extent of the author's objectivity. In portions of the study, particularly the literary analysis of chapter III, one is hardly aware that a Soviet critic is at work. His analysis throughout is technique-oriented, i.e., he attempts to show *how* Lu Hsün created his short stories and *how* they differed from the literature of the past. Of particular interest is his comparison of story-telling fiction (*huapen*) and its offshoot, the so-called "multi-chapter" novel (*changhui* or *ch'ang-pien hsiao-shuo*), with the more modern, European-style short-story form used by Lu Hsün. Many sinologists have been intrigued by this contrast. In form and in content the two genres may seem totally different, yet there are areas of resemblance, and vestiges of tradition can be found even in more recent literature. Many other portions of the study are, of course, provocative—the allegorical interpretation of Lu Hsün's "Travel Notes" (1911), for example; but then, most of the analysis comes to the attention of the English reader for the very first time.

There are a number of implicit assumptions in Semanov's analysis that seem to require an explanation. For example, he rather takes for granted the similarity between prerevolutionary France and prerevolutionary China. And actually, the comparison is not that new nor farfetched.[19] With the so-called "invasion" of Western ideas in the late nineteenth century, China was thrust into its own age of "enlightenment." "Reason" did not always triumph over traditional morality, but certainly the "discovery" of Western civilization opened new vistas to the Chinese. Eventually China was to send its students abroad to learn from the technologically more sophisticated West (including Japan) so that the nation could generate its own industrial revolution, but the impact of the new ideas was not limited strictly to military or industrial technology. The humanities and social sciences also played an important role. Darwin, Huxley, Spencer, Mill, Montesquieu, and Rousseau—all were to be introduced to China in the late nineteenth or the early twentieth century.[20] And later still, the more revolutionary works of Marxism-Leninism would follow. This whole "school" of evolutionary and revolutionary thought was to influence China in a relatively short span of time. We know its collective impact on the West, and we are beginning to understand its impact on the East.[21]

In one of the early works on Western influence in China, E. R. Hughes gives a colorful illustration of the history of ideas, one that seems particularly relevant to this study.

> Reference was made to Jesuit works on China and the influence which Chinese humanist and naturalist philosophy came to exercise in Western Europe, particularly in France of the eighteenth century. Amongst others, Montesquieu, and then later Rousseau, betray this influence. In the latter it shows itself as fitting in with his romanticism and leading him to his theories on natural rights. Now through the translation of the *Contrat social* these ideas were to reach China. They were highly attractive to those who felt the Manchu sway as a tyranny.

Hughes also mentions the influence of Montesquieu and goes on to explain why his *De l'esprit des lois* was "exactly calculated to excite admiration" among the Chinese. Then he cites this graphic example.

> The idea that law existed primarily not to strengthen the arm of the government but to protect the governed came as a revelation, as also did Montesquieu's sections on the types of perversion to be found in the various forms of government. Take the following statement as coming from the pen of a Westerner, famous through two centuries: "The emperor of China is not taught like our princes that if he governs ill he will be less happy in the other life, less powerful and less opulent in this. He knows that if his government be not just, he will be stripped of both empire and

life." Liang Ch'i-ch'ao, writing in exile after 1898, quoted: "Montesquieu also says, 'All autocratic rulers misleadingly say that they unify the people. Actually they cannot do this for the reason that they steal the people's right of liberty and make them afraid.... What is called Great Peace in countries under an autocracy always contains in it the seed of disorder.'" Liang also described the American system of government, the abolition of slavery, and the movement for penal reform, winding up each paragraph with the words, "Who is the creator of this blessed state of affairs? Montesquieu!"[22]

Semanov refers to Liang Ch'i-ch'ao and other Chinese thinkers of the late nineteenth and early twentieth century as "enlighteners" (*prosvetiteli*) or "popularizers." And this is precisely what they were: intellectuals who spread knowledge of the new ideas. But if the word "popularizer" sounds vulgar, the word "enlightener" sounds even more pompous. I prefer the term "philosophe," which implies someone with a less systematic approach to knowledge than the theory-oriented philosopher. (Nietzsche, for example, was more philosophe than philosopher.) What is interesting and, I believe, valid about Semanov's analysis is that he ferrets out certain vestiges of the philosophe in Lu Hsün himself, *viz.*, his at times marked tendency to teach, instruct, or otherwise persuade. And this, I think, is no less true of Lu Hsün at the beginning of his career (1906-08) than it is at the end, the only difference being that the writer moved from academia into the world of journalism. He never really abandoned the war of ideas.

One other analogy from the Age of Enlightenment carries over to *Lu Hsün and His Predecessors*. In the seventeenth (and eighteenth) century authors like Madeleine de Scudéry (1608-1701) and her brother George wrote romances even more lengthy and episodic than their Chinese counterparts!

> In 1649-1653 their joint labors resulted in the ten parts of the celebrated *Artamène ou le Grand Cyrus*. Here, beneath the thin veil of the Persian war, the entire aristocratic world—from the Grand Condé (Cyrus) to Voiture (Aristhée) and Chapelain (Callicrate)—found itself reflected in detailed "portraits." The stir that this work produced can be imagined. Tallemant des Réaux affirms that a key to the romance was in circulation; and we may be sure that more than one key was used. Meanwhile, however, Madeleine de Scudéry had begun her own *samedis* [get-togethers or meetings—C.J.A.] where *précieux* gallantry rose to melodramatic proportions in the form of maps and indices of sentiment, like the well-

known *Carte de Tendre* in *Clélie* and the so-called *Conversations galantes*. Once more, it is a question of whether it is sweeter to be loved than to love, of love via friendship, of absence as a cure to love, and so on.[23]

I will not bore the reader with a description of the Scudérys' third romance, *Clélie, histoire romaine* (10 vols., 1654-60), except to note that here, as far as the literary critic is concerned, "the long-winded heroic romance attains its summit, and fortunately its term." In addition to being lengthy romances, these novels are some of the earliest examples of the so-called *roman à clef* or "novel with a key," and in some respects they seem remarkably similar to the "novel of censure" (sometimes more loosely translated "novel of exposure") described in Lu Hsün's own *Brief History of Chinese Fiction*. In both instances, it is said, prominent persons easily identified by the reader became the targets of sensationalist, rumor-mongering writers. The authors of the above-cited excerpt go on to comment that "the ridicule that they [i.e. Mlle de Scudéry's works] evoked came near destroying the genre they represent," and Lu Hsün levels the very same charge against the novel of exposure.[24]

The problem with this comparison of the Chinese and the French novel, of which I am well aware, is that even after excluding cultural and historical factors, there are far too many variables. To what extent did either or both "expose" the evils in society? To what extent, if any, did they contribute to the "enlightenment" of society? Which works were written purely for entertainment? Which for some even more sordid motive? After all, philosophes were not necessarily novelists, nor novelists philosophes, whether in China or in France. So there are some serious questions that deserve to be answered before any comparison of the two genres or periods can be readily accepted. Indeed, "any interpretations in terms of Western history cannot avoid missing certain critical points and causing misunderstanding."[25] Perhaps that is why Semanov has at times strenuously objected to the rendering of *prosvetitel'* (*ch'i-meng chu-i che*) as "philosophe" rather than simply "enlightener." I personally have no interest in perpetuating the comparison, but I have not found a more acceptable translation.

The problem of comparison is no less complex when extended to Lu Hsün and his immediate literary predecessors. To some extent one can agree with Semanov that in *Outcry* Lu Hsün is more an "exposer" than a satirist, and that his short stories are simply a higher expression of that art. This is brought out, for example, in his essay "How 'The True Story of Ah Q' Was Written" (1926), where the author tells about some of the reactions to his "satirical" short story:

> I used the pen-name Pa Jen [rough, uncouth fellow—C.J.A.] to show that I was not refined, little thinking this name would get me into trouble again. I did not realize this until this year when I read Mr. Kao Yi-han's "Idle Chat" in *Modern Review*. He wrote much as follows:
> "I remember that when 'The True Story of Ah Q' was being published as a serial, many readers went in fear and trembling, dreading lest an attack on them should follow. One friend actually told me that he was sure the installment published the previous day had been an attack on him, and therefore he believed the author was So-and-so, the only man who knew about this incident.... After that he grew hypersensitive, imagining all his secrets were being attacked in 'Ah Q,' and suspecting everyone connected with the paper that published the story of being its writer. When he finally learned the author's name and realized that he had never met him, a great load was lifted from his mind, and he went about telling everyone that the story was not an attack on him after all."[26]

Evidently this reader reacted to the "True Story" as if it were a "novel with a key" or a "novel of exposure." What more vivid proof could there be of its relevance to modern times? And yet, as the author himself testifies, the story was not "true" in the literal sense of the term. There simply was no "key."

Of course there is a sense in which Lu Hsün "exposed" the ills of his society, and it is this characteristic which has earned him the title of "revolutionary humanist." Rather than totally rejecting this thesis, which as I see it must be carefully qualified, I would simply stress that Lu Hsün's works, and particularly his early short stories, are as much personal as social, and probably as much lyrical as critical. In that respect I share the views of Jaroslav Průšek, who sees "the larger proportion of subjective elements" as the "most characteristic feature" of postrevolutionary literature.[27]

To what extent, if any, were Lu Hsün's short stories "traditional" in form and to what extent "contemporary"? Once again, there is no easy answer. Basically, there were two forms of traditional "short story"—the literary (*ch'uan-ch'i*) and the vernacular (*huapen*); and yet the contemporary "colloquial" (*pai-hua*) short story falls comfortably into neither category. I have always thought of "Ah Q," for example, as a contemporary parody of the traditional "story script." Not all of the conventions are there, but some are, and this is the only story that Lu Hsün wrote in serial form. Here again, however, "Ah Q" is the exception, and the *wen-yen* (literary language) influence in Lu Hsün's works seems to predominate. It is evident not only in his polished language but in his haunting lyricism. Perhaps no one can or will ever pinpoint this influence, i.e., determine whether it stems primarily from classical prose or from classical poetry; but surely these are questions that deserve to be studied.[28] Semanov's contribution to this analysis is scattered throughout this monograph, yet I have no doubt that he finds the problem of the evolution of genres as perplexing and intriguing as I do. It is not enough to say that the New Culture Movement ushered in a period of experimentation in literature. The problem is, *how* is that literature experimental?

* * *

The text of Semanov's study came into my possession in Japan in the academic year 1968-69. That year and the following one at Indiana University I researched my doctoral dissertation, entitled *Soviet Criticism of Lu Hsün*, an attempt to describe and evaluate the views expressed in all major Soviet studies devoted to Lu Hsün. Much of the early material that I covered was discouraging, as I have already hinted, and the study became more ideological than literary. As the work progressed, however, the critics began to show more promise. I found myself reading Semanov's monograph with enthusiasm, and later in Indiana some of my own thoughts on Lu Hsün's style began to solidify. (What proved most valuable to me as a critic was Semanov's observations on the usage of time and time sequences within the apparently "simple" structure of Lu Hsün's short stories.) It was at that time that I decided to complete this translation. I believed then, and still do now, that the work could be done in such a way that the American reader would be pleasantly surprised, and that the translation itself would make its own contribution to the study of Chinese literature.

I feel obliged, however, to offer some words of caution to the unsuspecting reader. No translation, however accurate, can substitute for the original, and one is always wise to consult it when doubts arise. Some necessary, and hopefully permissible, liberties with the original have been taken, and they are as follows: a) The author's use of the editorial "we" has been deleted in most cases, especially where it clearly substitutes for the first person. This gives the critic direct responsibility for his own statements. b) The length of many paragraphs, though admittedly a matter of taste, has been altered, particularly if the original paragraph was comprised of a single sentence. Though an exception in English, this occurs rather frequently in the original. To maintain the paragraph divisions intact would have been extremely unorthodox. c) Additional footnotes have been provided when necessary and, occasionally, existing ones have been rearranged or deleted, so there is no "one-to-one" correlation between the original and the translation. Not only has the number of footnotes been changed, but their order is also different. d) As an authority for the transcription of Russian, I have chosen J. Thomas Shaw's *The Transliteration of Modern Russian for English-Language Publications* (Madison: University of Wisconsin Press, 1967). System I is used for all personal and place names, whereas System III, the more professional variant, is used for information, i.e., words as words, and *all* citations of bibliographical material. This is the least awkward of the systems or mixtures of systems that I could choose, but there are still a few unfortunate results. The Russian names, for example, will now be intelligible to the average reader, but the system in which they are written no longer corresponds to that used for bibliographical entries (hence "Vasilev" rather than the more desirable "Vasil'ev"). On the other hand, the Russian *narodoljubec* ("narodolyubets") must then be written in System III, because, says Shaw, System I "is *not* satisfactory for transliterating words as words or citations of bibliographical material." As it happens, this is no more awkward than the Polish names Slowacki (Slôväts'ki) and Mickiewicz (Metskyĕ′vich) in which the *letter* "ts" is transcribed "c." For the sake of consistency, I have avoided the use of intervocalic "y," hence Alexeev, not Alexeyev; Fadeev, not Fadeyev or Fadayev; and Dostoevsky, not Dostoyevsky. The reader should be aware, however, that these spellings are in common use elsewhere.

The most extensive emendation has been in the translation of titles, particularly those of the novel and the short story. In most instances I have elected to use titles already known to the English reader, i.e., those found in the translations of Gladys Yang and Yang Hsien-yi. This includes not only the titles found in Lu Hsün's

Selected Works (English) but all works of traditional fiction mentioned in the writer's *Brief History*. (To facilitate identification an Appendix has been provided.) There are, of course, both advantages and disadvantages to such a solution. For one, the use of ready-made titles ensures the continuity of research; and this is important, if knowledge is to be useful rather than ornamental. Secondly, it has eliminated several ungainly titles, despite their potentially greater accuracy. Thus, *Notes of the Yüeh-wei Hermitage* substitutes for *Notes from the Hut for Observing the Minute* or some similar variation. Let the reader decide if there is a net loss or a net gain. The first, though less accurate, is at least partly familiar; the second is unrecognizable. Nevertheless, some grievous errors have been perpetuated. There is no doubt, for example, that *Lives of Shanghai Singsong Girls* is utterly devoid of symbolism, while *Flowers by the Seashore* (*Hai-shang hua*) is more accurate! For this we can only thank Chinese "idea-ology." But I am hopeful that (in this instance at least) the utility of the former will outweigh the artistry of the latter. Fortunately not every "translation" is as horrendous as this.

I have endeavored to make the translation as readable as possible by using the most appropriate and attractive English possible. This has not always been accomplished without taking some unwanted liberties. But after all, who will read a critic's views—any critic's views—if they are not attractively presented? In this particular instance, however, there was an added incentive. Much of the existing Chinese and Soviet "literary" criticism reads like either undiluted propaganda or an eight-legged essay. This is something I felt compelled to avoid at all cost, without either diluting the original author's work or compromising his beliefs. Of course, these are rather demanding ideals; and that is why I am doubly grateful for Semanov's own assistance, wherever and whenever it could be given. His painstaking corrections, as well as those of my colleagues Frank Miller and David Danow, have already saved me considerable embarrassment. If there are still more errors that have managed to escape detection, I will be more than happy to assume the responsibility. But no doubt someone will feel that I have "ignored the Chinese point of view" or otherwise "falsified the record." To him I would simply say: "Please, be generous! Criticism is not something we *accept* lightly; it should not be something we *give* lightly."

This is something I myself learned the hard way, for I set out to identify Soviet prejudices and in the process discovered some of my own.

It has always astounded me that there has been so little systematic research on Lu Hsün in English, and above all no index to his writings. The problem is that there is none in Chinese either, despite the numerous editions of his collected works. Let us hope that these difficulties will eventually be remedied. This year an extensive, month-by-month chronology of Lu Hsün's life and works was published, *Lu Hsün nien-p'u* (Ho-fei: An-hui ren-min ch'u-pan-she, 1979). The two-volume work was compiled by students from two universities, Fu-tan and Shanghai Normal. Still, there is much to be done in the study of this great writer, and I am proud to make even a modest contribution.

I cannot conclude this introduction without some mention of the scholars who, directly or indirectly, have assisted me in this undertaking. Ono Shinobu put his library at my disposal and spent many long and pleasant hours with me discussing the topic. His help was invaluable. Kawakami Kyūjū sent me a very rare collection of essays (1938) as well as his own research on the subject of Soviet sinology. Takeuchi Yoshimi consulted with me and gave me the pleasure of addressing the Friends of Lu Hsün Association. Kazuo Enoki of the Tōyō Bunko was a most gracious host; and without the help of Kozen Tachibana of that same institute my work would have doubled. I am indebted also to scholars from other countries, to members of the Czechoslovak Academy of Sciences who initially offered their assistance and to Jaroslav Průšek in particular for his inspiration. Without the earlier help of Semanov, who also sent me many out-of-print books and articles, my thesis would have taken much longer and undoubtedly would have been much less complete. To my advisor, Professor Liu Wu-chi, I owe most of all. Without his inspiration, encouragement, and direct assistance this monograph would never have been written. His love of Chinese literature has truly been infectious. Some of my own colleagues, Harriet Mills, Leo Ou-fan Lee, Jerome P. Seaton, William Schultz, Patrick Hanan, and others have offered their encouragement when it was most needed. William Lyell read the manuscript in its entirety and made some valuable suggestions. All of these scholars and many friends have contributed something to this manuscript, though I alone must take responsibility for its contents. I also wish to thank the Department of Health, Education, and Welfare for the Fulbright-Hays award which enabled me to do research in Japan, as well as the University of South Carolina for the faculty research grant which freed me for a summer to complete the rough draft of this manuscript.

Charles J. Alber

Lu Hsün and his predecessors

Author's Note

The creative work of the father of modern Chinese literature, the outstanding democrat and humanist Lu Hsün (1881-1936), has attracted the attention of literary critics from the most diverse countries. Many monographs and an enormous number of articles have been devoted to Lu Hsün; nevertheless, such problems as the evolution of Lu Hsün's world view, his artistic technique, and his place in the history of national and world literature have not yet been sufficiently studied. There is almost no research on the relationship between Lu Hsün's work and that of his direct predecessors and elder contemporaries, i.e., Chinese literature of the nineteenth and early twentieth centuries. Of all the existing monographs on the writer, only those of Ozaka Tokuji and V. V. Petrov[1] contain sections dealing with the literary climate in the years when Lu Hsün began his career, and it is even more unusual for his creative works to be compared with those of the previous century. In Chinese there is only Kuo Mo-jo's article "Lu Hsün and Wang Kuo-wei"[2] (though here the author hardly chooses the best subject for comparison), a small chapter on "Lu Hsün and Late Ch'ing Literature" contained in one of the memoirs written by the writer's younger brother Chou Tso-jen (pseudonyms: Chou Hsia-shou and Chou Ch'i-ming),[3] a few notes on Lu Hsün's attitude toward traditional theater, and an equal amount on his relationship with Chang Ping-lin (Chang T'ai-yen).

During the twenties and thirties, when the writer was still alive, many researchers tended to underestimate Lu Hsün's innovative role in Chinese literature. Native spokesmen for the so-called "left" wing thought that Lu Hsün was merely rehashing old motifs. In 1924, for example, Ch'eng Fang-wu, a well-known critic and member of the Creation Society, wrote: "Except for 'My Old Home' (a story in the collection *Outcry*—V.S.), it seems to me that I am reading the works of an author who lived a century or, at very least, a half-century ago."[4] Similar ideas were expressed in 1928 by Ch'ien Hsing-ts'un (pseudonym: A Ying), a leading critic of the Sun Society.

> No matter how great Lu Hsün may have been, how deeply a certain portion of the public may have admired him, or how subtle and witty the style of "The True Story of Ah Q" may be, Lu Hsün never was, in fact, a spokesman for our era.... The era which he depicts allows him to be placed alongside of Li Pao-chia and Liu O.[5] Lu Hsün's ideas took shape before the May Fourth Movement, and they were the very same ideas that prevailed at the end of the Ch'ing dynasty, or even at the time of the Boxer Rebellion. The journal *New Citizen* would willingly have subscribed to them.[6]

Eventually this critical tendency disappeared from the pages of works devoted to Lu Hsün, and after 1936 Ch'ien Hsing-ts'un himself recognized the writer as an innovator. Reproaches for mimicking tradition became a thing of the past, but so also did most attempts to trace Lu Hsün's ties with his immediate literary predecessors. Meanwhile, this is a very important problem. To solve it means, by and large, to discover the relationship between the old and the new literature, and this is the goal that the author of the present work has set for himself.

CHAPTER I

The Beginning of the Century

By now there are a number of specialized works that deal with the early years of Lu Hsün's creativity, and relevant chapters are contained in studies on the writer. Nevertheless, the creative development of the young artist, as reflected in his literary works, translations, and articles on aesthetics, has still not been sufficiently explored. It is on this problem, therefore, that I will concentrate, not repeating what other researchers have already said, but referring the reader to their works when necessary.

First impressions and experiences

When recounting Lu Hsün's childhood experiences (prior to leaving the small town of Shaohsing for Nanking in 1898), critics usually stress the youth's alienation from the social and cultural life of China at that time.[1] But this alienation was only relative. The folklore of late nineteenth-century China, and particularly folk drama,[2] which contributed to the spiritual moulding of other modern Chinese writers as well, left clear impressions on the young boy's memory. Moreover, it was during this period that Lu Hsün became acquainted with a number of works from the nineteenth century.

Contemporaries recall that the young Lu Hsün read not only ancient and medieval prose, but also Li Ju-chen's novel of satire and fantasy *Flowers in the Mirror*, as well as other tales of the nineteenth century (Chi Yün's *Notes of the Yüeh-wei Hermitage* and Wang T'ao's *Random Notes from Shanghai*). In the year 1894 Lu Hsün gained access to the library of one of his relatives, a great admirer of fiction, and he became acquainted with the nineteenth-century picaresque novel.³ He became fascinated with illustrations for *Suppression of the Rebels*,⁴ where the heroes of the insurgent novel *Water Margin* (fourteenth century) were "punished." As one can see, Lu Hsün, in his enthusiasm, was not very discriminating. Only in one instance is there evidence that he was critical of his predecessors: even in youth he had no special sympathy for the T'ung-ch'eng school, the orthodox school of eighteenth- and nineteenth-century Chinese literature.⁵

Nevertheless, this evidence does not seem very reliable in light of Lu Hsün's own recollections regarding the development of his views in youth. "After the Reform Movement an elder of the clan admonished me, saying, 'K'ang Yu-wei wants to usurp the throne; no wonder he bears the name Yu-wei [Possessor of Power]!' ... 'Isn't it the truth,' I thought. 'How detestable!'"⁶ In other words, initially Lu Hsün judged the reformers (as did other figures of nineteenth-century Chinese culture) from an ignorant, conservative standpoint, although the youth's thirst for knowledge and independence of thought ensured an eventual rapprochement between the future writer's views and the progressive ideas of that era. This rapprochement gradually became more and more apparent, and it is no accident that the Japanese literary critic Shiga Masatoshi calls the period of Lu Hsün's study in Nanking "a time of apprehending translations,"⁷ i.e., European books (mostly in the exact sciences and sociology) which were published at that time by the reformers.

The writer himself later recalled how great a discovery these translations were for the youth of China in the late nineteenth century.

> At the time the new books started to become the rage, and I discovered that there was a treatise in Chinese entitled *The Completion of the Heavens*.⁸ On Sunday I set out for the southern part of the city after it and for 500 cash bought a thick book printed by a lithographic process on white paper. It was written in a clear script and began as follows:
>
> "Huxley lived alone in the southern part of London, England. Behind his house rose a hill, in front lay a ravine. Sitting at a desk and observing the scene revealed from the window, he began to wonder what had been there two thousand years ago, even before the great Roman general Caesar. At that time, the grass grew naturally and wildly . . . ."
>
> So that's it! ... It seems there was a man named Huxley, who sat in his study, meditated, and actually discovered something new!
>
> I turned page after page. Further on emerged the struggle for existence and natural selection, and afterwards Socrates, Plato, and the Stoics.⁹

Even in his prime the writer did not forget and could recite from memory many excerpts from the translation of *Evolution and Ethics*.[10] It was this translation which helped him to comprehend the theory of evolution, a theory that remained an essential part of his philosophical views right up until the end of the twenties. Nevertheless, in my opinion, the Czechoslovakian sinologist J. Průšek is justified in taking issue with the Western European critics J. Chinnery and Huang Sung-k'ang, who attribute Lu Hsün's world view entirely to the theory of evolution, a world view which only a few years later could be characterized as revolutionary-democratic.[11] Soon after the translations of Yen Fu, books published by the Chinese reformers in Japan began turning up in Lu Hsün's library. The émigré journal *Translation Magazine* (*I-shu hui-pien*), which Lu Hsün read while in Nanking,[12] printed such works as Rousseau's *Contrat social* and Montesquieu's *De l'espirit des lois*. From his native city Shaohsing Lu Hsün brought to Nanking a philosophical treatise entitled *On Humanism* (*Jen-hsüeh*) by the left-wing reformer T'an Ssu-t'ung, and concurrently he read two works by Liang Ch'i-ch'ao, *A Letter on Freedom* and *The Chinese Soul*.[13]

To the extent that Lu Hsün actually took part in China's social life after the "Hundred Days,"[14] he became exposed to revolutionary as well as reformist ideas. In the early twentieth century Lu Hsün, in his own words, "could not tear himself away"* from Chang Ping-lin's *A Letter on Oppression* (1900) "although I did not understand everything in it."[15] Even prior to departing for Japan, he "knew something about anti-Manchu teachings, cutting off the queue, and literary inquisitions."[16] Along with other students in Nanking he rode past Manchu officials on horseback, thereby demonstrating his enmity toward them. But all this, of course, is far from the revolutionary convictions that many researchers ascribe to Lu Hsün as early as the Nanking period.[17] Furthermore, V. V. Petrov's observation that Lu Hsün summarily dismissed the Reform Movement as "superficial and ineffective"[18] is not supported by concrete evidence. On the contrary, while in Nanking Lu Hsün considered it a sign of independent thinking[19] to read the journal *Current Affairs* (*Shih-wu pao*), which was published in 1896 and

---
*This is apparently a mistranslation in the Russian *Selected Works*. The Yangs' version (IV, 266-267) reads: "I remember over thirty years ago, when his *Chiu Shu* was first printed, I could not even punctuate the sentences let alone understand them."—C.J.A.

1897 by Liang Ch'i-ch'ao, the poet Huang Tsun-hsien, and others, and he did not see anything "wrong" in the works of K'ang Yu-wei and Yen Fu.[20]

In addition to works on sociology, Lu Hsün read Lin Shu's translations of Western literary works: *La Dame aux camélias* by A. Dumas *fils*, *Cleopatra* by H. Rider Haggard, the short stories of Arthur Conan Doyle, and others. These translations bolstered Chinese interest in "popular" (*hsiao-shuo*) fiction* and contributed to the rise of the novel of censure** in the early twentieth century.[21]

In the years from 1898 to 1902 traditional authority had already been shaken for Lu Hsün. One of his biographers mentions that in Nanking the future writer was "not very interested in the classics"[22] and his attention was focused mainly on European science and literature. Nevertheless, in his own first attempts at original creation the youth turned to the officially sanctioned forms of "refined" prose and poetry, and did not as yet attempt to express his thoughts in the guise of "popular" fiction, as did many Chinese writers at the end of the nineteenth century. The first of Lu Hsün's works that have come down to us ("Notes of a Warrior,"[23] "Plant Sketches," and several other verses of a personal nature) belong to the Nanking period. His prosaic sketches, which develop various impressions (about being away from home, tasty dishes that he first tried in Nanking, various plants, etc.) are still very naïve, although in them Lu Hsün did utilize successfully several stylistic devices of classical Chinese literature.[24] Interesting also is the inclination to enlighten, which the majority of passages show. Here the young Lu Hsün utilizes his new knowledge of "Western" sciences, botany and chemistry. When describing a beautiful flower, he is no longer satisfied with the Chinese nomenclature ("late aromatic jade") but looks for its "real" (international, scientific—V.S.) name, the tuberose. Elsewhere Lu Hsün clarifies the origin of a certain English word: "Foreigners call *ch'a* 'tea,' the same as in Fukien. The Fukienese were the first to sell

*The Russian *nizkaja* (literally, low-class, inferior, trivial, etc.) *proza* calls attention to the traditional contempt shown by scholars for the genre. In other words, the Russian translates *hsiao-shuo* ("small talk") quite literally.—C.J.A.

**It is tempting to translate *obličitel'nyj roman* (novel of censure or exposure) as *roman à clef*, which it resembles (c.f. Introduction, pp. xx-xxii). For the sake of clarity, however, I will stay close to the Chinese (*ch'ien-tse hsiao-shuo*).—C.J.A.

tea abroad, and so foreigners began to imitate their dialect."²⁵ It goes without saying that Lu Hsün's early prose sketches cannot compare either in depth of thought or social impact (at the time they were not even published) with articles written about the same time by Sun Yat-sen or Liang Ch'i-ch'ao, but obviously they held vital significance for the future writer's creative growth.

Participation in the enlightenment movement (1903-06)

The main significance of Lu Hsün's first impressions and experiences lies in the fact that they encouraged him to become involved in the actual work of enlightenment. Almost ignorant of the language, Lu Hsün came to study in Japan in April 1902, and in July of the following year he had already published in the journal *Chekiang Tide* (*Che-chiang ch'ao*) works that were based on Japanese books and the press. This was a journal created for Chinese student circles by the revolutionary Restoration Society (Kuang-fu hui). But even before leaving Tokyo for Sendai, i.e., prior to 1904, Lu Hsün had become acquainted with participants in the anti-Manchu struggle. It was then that he learned how the Manchu authorities had taken reprisals against Chang Ping-lin, one of the leaders of this movement, for his "Reply to K'ang Yu-wei's *Letter on Revolution*" and the preface to Tsou Jung's *Revolutionary Army*.²⁶ In the newly created journal *Chekiang Tide* Lu Hsün read poems that Chang Ping-lin wrote while in prison, and under their influence he composed the poem "Inscription on My Portrait," promising "to give my blood for my native land." All these facts, it would seem, support the claims of sinologists who assert that Lu Hsün was already a "staunch revolutionary" in 1903-04.²⁷ But the writer's own appraisal of his activities at this time differs. He enrolled in Sendai Medical Institute because he wanted "to relieve the suffering of the wounded" and because he "dreamed of convincing fellow countrymen of the value of reforms."²⁸ As we see, Lu Hsün spoke of reforms and not of revolutionary upheavals.

In the years 1902 to 1906 Lu Hsün maintained his interest in the émigré reformist press and followed the journals *Public Opinion* (*Ch'ing-i pao*), *New Citizen*, and *New Fiction* (*Hsin hsiao-shuo*), which were published in Japan by Liang Ch'i-ch'ao. Lu Hsün tried to buy every translation published by Yen Fu: Jenks's *Principles of Politics*, Spencer's *The Principles of Sociology*, Montesquieu's *De l'Esprit des lois*, and Mill's *System of Logic*.[29] And all this was entirely natural. The enlightening works of the reformers were still rather close to Lu Hsün's heart. In fact, he himself promulgated the sciences in a series of articles: "An Outline of Chinese Geology" [1903], "On Radium" [1903] and others. Although, according to the testimony of Hsü Shou-shang,[30] by 1904 Lu Hsün already expressed a certain dissatisfaction with Yen Fu's pompous style, nevertheless Lu Hsün still had a great deal of interest in his translations.

Lu Hsün also welcomed with great pleasure the *literary* translations published by the reformers. During the years 1902 to 1906 he read in Chinese some of the works of Victor Hugo, Jules Verne, Walter Scott, and H. Rider Haggard.[31] Many of these translations were those of Lin Shu, whose authority in Lu Hsün's eyes was still quite high. At the time Lu Hsün was especially fascinated by the Chinese translations of Byron. "I remember how my heart caught fire when I first read Byron," he later wrote.

> I was even more deeply shaken when I saw his portrait with the bandaged head, done at the time of the Greek war for national independence....
>
> Unfortunately, I did not know the English language and read exclusively translations. Not long ago an argument flared up among us here whether or not translations were worth a plug nickel, even if they were good. But at the time we weren't so particular.... Everyone memorized passages from the piece "New Rome,"[32] even though the translator put them into the *tz'u* genre[33] and the name Sappho was changed to "Sajipo" —proof that the translation was made from Japanese.
>
> Mr. Su Man-shu also translated several poems. At the time he was not yet trying to "appease people" with his verses, and so the soul of Byron was still rather dear to him. Nevertheless, his translations were uncommonly obscure and refined... so the poems approximated those of the classics.[34]

As we see, basically the young Lu Hsün read literature in translation published by the Chinese emigrants in Japan. "He did not pay much attention to original works produced in his own country," recalls Chou Tso-jen. "It was only later, apparently, when preparing lectures on the history of fiction that he really read the novels of Li Pao-chia and others."[35] Nevertheless, more precise evidence is needed. At that time original works of *belles lettres* were not published solely on the mainland. Lu Hsün was familiar, for example, with Wu Wo-yao's novels *Strange Events of the Last Twenty*

Years and *A Crime Involving Nine Lives*, which were published in the journal *New Fiction*. He was also familiar with the poetry of the reformers and the revolutionaries, that of Chang Ping-lin, Chiang Chih-yu, and Ch'iu Chin.

It is not surprising, therefore, that Lu Hsün's own publications in the years 1903 to 1906 were very similar in nature to other works of enlightenment literature in China. Lu Hsün's first important publication was the story "The Spartan Spirit" in which the author enthusiastically told his countrymen of the brilliant feat of the Spartans, who barred the path of Xerxes' hordes. In this tale the characteristics of the literature of enlightenment are quite apparent: an obvious political bias, didacticism, pathos, authorial addresses to the reader, and so forth. "Even now while reading this story I am seized with trepidation," writes Lu Hsün in the introduction to his first story. "I tell it here in order to inspire our youth. Alas! Can it be there are no more heroes in this world whose bravery surpasses that of women? If there are, let them throw away their pens and come alive. The translator of this story is untalented and cannot reproduce even a thousandth part of its heroism. Oh, I stand guilty before you, reader, guilty before the Spartan spirit!"[36] "The Spartan Spirit" is based on facts from Greek history which Lu Hsün drew from Japanese sources. Possibly the story is even a translation or a recounting of some passage written in another language, but there is no doubt that Lu Hsün reworked the material. It is no accident, for example, that he included "The Spartan Spirit" in the *Collection of Uncollected Works* (1934), which does not incorporate translations.

The large quantity of purely Chinese images in the story is the first indication of Lu Hsün's manipulation of the material. It is the "translator" himself (Lu Hsün) who addresses the reader. "Have you ever seen a man who has failed in the official examinations? When his name does not turn up on the golden list, his wife sits at home and cries. You always sympathize deeply with such women. How can they not feel sad or angry when their husbands have been put to shame but still do not contemplate suicide?" writes Lu Hsün,[37] attempting with the aid of an analogy accessible to the reader to justify the sternness and even cruelty of the main heroine, Helen. Here authorial digression, as often happens in early twentieth-century Chinese fiction, replaces psychological motivation for the characters' deeds. Even more often authorial remarks resound with a direct reproach or an appeal: "Victoriously the banners flutter, lighting with their brilliance the faces of the heroes.... Readers, are there any such men among you?" Sometimes Lu Hsün puts his own thoughts about the present into the mouths of his heroes. "You should be proud. You, apparently, have not seen countries where base slaves kill their fellow countrymen and fawn on foreigners, become spies and traitors! How would you react to such people?" asks a Spartan general of his troops.[38] In a tale of heroism this allusion to Manchu China seems just as deliberate as an open authorial reproach to the reader. The better Chinese prose writers of the early twentieth century (Li Pao-chia, Tseng P'u, Liu O) avoided such frontal assaults.

The publicistic element in "The Spartan Spirit" is so apparent that sinologists have even referred to this work as an article. As far as I am concerned, however, it is a short story. This not only coincides with the title of the section (*hsiao-shuo*) of the journal in which "The Spartan Spirit" was placed but is justified in substance. The clearly defined plot, broad usage of dialogue, and various descriptive techniques[39] provide a basis for incorporating "The Spartan Spirit" among the works of creative literature.* Moreover, it should be regarded as one of the first modern Chinese short stories (in the usual sense of the term) as opposed to the traditional short story (*ch'uan-ch'i*), which usually contains an element of the fantastic, or the "multi-chapter novel" (*chang-hui hsiao-shuo*),[40] constructed along the lines of a popular oral tale with its traditional beginnings and endings. Like the majority of early twentieth-century stories, "The Spartan Spirit" is written in classical language (*ku-wen*), proof that the author was striving for brevity and stylistic richness, hallmarks of the ancient language.

It would seem, however, that in the years 1903 and 1904 Lu Hsün's choice of a genre that was new to Chinese literature was still unpremeditated, i.e., made under the influence of a classical education and a propensity for "refined" prose. At the time his main objective was the promulgation of the natural sciences. And so, following "The Spartan Spirit" Lu Hsün wrote an article "On Radium" for the journal *Chekiang Tide* and translated two of

---

*Even "broad use of dialogue" by itself does not warrant this conclusion. The technique was used in historical works (very much like "fiction") as early as the *Tso Chuan* and in other more "literary" works, such as Ssu-ma Ch'ien's biographies. —C.J.A.

Verne's science-fiction novels, *From the Earth to the Moon* and *Journey to the Center of the Earth*. It was in these translations, and in the preface to the first in particular, that the young Lu Hsün's views on literature, similar to those of the reformers, became apparent. With an enlightened, and sometimes even romantic, fervor he writes of man's constant struggle with nature and cherishes the dream that his people will take heart:

> People are ashamed that on account of the elements they are forced to vegetate in a gloomy underworld, close eyes and ears, deceive one another, and glorify their own nonexistent virtue. Mankind always strives toward progress, and so the best of the species, hardly catching a glimpse of the light, ceases to be satisfied with what has been achieved and is filled with a great sense of hope. They want to destroy the force of gravity, conquer the atmosphere, and fly like spirits that know no obstacle.[41]

Like the majority of progressive Chinese essayists of the early twentieth century (Liang Ch'i-ch'ao, T'ui Yen, Yün Shu-chüeh, and others), Lu Hsün takes note of the achievements of European prose and utilizes them to criticize China's imitative literature:

> Verne fully deserves to be called the most prominent of nineteenth-century writers who described interplanetary travel. In contrast to the windbags who, without the least bit of sense, describe rivers, mountains, animals, and plants [in outer space—C.J.A.], his each and every word is based on facts or scientific conclusions. He doesn't need to get into abstruse discussions and make derogatory statements to the effect that nature is too mysterious and the human mind limited. Unlike the majority of prose writers, he does not use feminine charms to allure the reader. The main heroes are three men who do not allow a single woman into their company, yet the novel retains its brilliance and is not at all boring. This makes the work exceptionally original.[42]

Here we see the typical cautious attitude of the Chinese philosophe toward descriptions of nature and love conflicts, as if such things detracted from the main problems art ought to solve.

At the time, Lu Hsün's factual knowledge of foreign literature was quite negligible. Sometimes he calls Verne an "Englishman," sometimes an "American"; and only in the choice of novels itself does he prove more perspicacious than many contemporaries.[43] As a rule Lu Hsün turns to more serious works as opposed, for example, to detective novels, which exercised an influence on the majority of early twentieth-century Chinese writers. Hence, the young writer is quite straightforward in his reproach of the Chinese philosophes:

> In our country one can find a multitude of novels that portray human emotions, tell of antiquity, expose the present era, or describe marvels. A purely scientific novel is rare, like the horn of a unicorn. This is one of the reasons for the decline of our knowledge. And if we want to fill the gap of contemporary translations, to move the Chinese masses forward, then we ought to begin with science fiction.[44]

Nevertheless, this dissatisfaction still rested on a very shaky foundation: an unqualified acceptance of science fiction and an underestimation not only of the novel of fantasy (and this was characteristic of the majority of progressive intellectuals in early twentieth-century China) but of the novel of manners, the historical novel, and the novel of censure.

At this stage Lu Hsün's method of translation followed the guidelines laid down by early twentieth-century Chinese translators. He did not so much translate as rework the original, or to be more precise, not even the original, but Japanese translations, which continued to help him master Western literature. Lu Hsün turns the twenty-eight chapters—in the Japanese translation by Inoue Tsutomu there were that many—of *From the Earth to the Moon* into fourteen, and in addition translates Verne's novel into a relatively archaic form of Chinese. In the preface to the translation of *From the Earth to the Moon* he justifies this as a necessity to reduce the volume of the work,[45] but the real reason is more deeply rooted. From an aesthetic standpoint the translator was not yet in close touch with the democratic strata of Chinese society.

Like many Chinese literati of the early twentieth century, Lu Hsün writes almost exclusively in the classical language (*wen-yen*) right up until the year 1918. True, in the years 1903 to 1906, when translating foreign works, he attempted to shift to a more colloquial, medieval style (*pai-hua*), the language used by many writers of that time (Tseng P'u, for example). But Lu Hsün the translator was also attracted to the classical language, as shown by the abundance of archaic expressions in the Verne translation and in a work Lu Hsün prepared for press, *Expedition to the North Pole* (1904),[46] where he preferred "description in the classical language, and dialogue in *pai-hua*."[47] This experiment undertaken by the young Lu Hsün (a combination of classical and medieval language within the confines of a single work) was completely lacking in foresight and did not interest the publishers. "At my request," he recalls later on, "Mr. Chiang Kuan-yün [Chiang Chih-yu] recommended the translation to the Commercial Press. Despite my hopes, the book was not only not accepted, but I was upbraided besides for an absurd method of translation."[48]

By 1906 Lu Hsün had long since rejected the medieval colloquial style in favor of the classical, a paradoxical fact, but understandable. To him the epigonic, imitative literature of the previous centuries was distasteful. Following the example of his teacher Chang Ping-lin, he turns to more "ancient and glorious" traditions and at the same time revives (though at first uncritically) the classical language. The translation of *Expedition to the North Pole* can be regarded as a kind of watershed along the way toward resurrecting antiquity.[49]

Attempts and failures (1906-09)

After returning to Tokyo (1906) from Sendai Medical Institute Lu Hsün established closer ties with the revolutionaries. By this time the Alliance Society (T'ung-meng hui), the first pan-Chinese revolutionary organization, had been established in Japan, and it was joined by the Restoration Society, which was already familiar to Lu Hsün. According to some sources, the writer joined this society in 1908.[50] At any rate, Lu Hsün sided with the revolutionaries in their struggle against the liberals, which says a great deal about his attitude toward contemporaries and immediate predecessors.

Only after 1906 did Lu Hsün cease paying homage to the leading Chinese translators of the early twentieth century. "We were so enthused about Lin Shu's translations," recalls Chou Tso-jen,

> that no sooner had his next work reached Tokyo than we dashed over to a store called "The Forest of Chinese Books" and bought it. Moreover, having finished the book, Lu Hsün took it back to the bookstore and exchanged it for a hardbound copy.
>
> But this was only true for Lin Shu's earlier translations.... We had already read *Mr. Meeson's Will* and *Nada the Lily*[51] without any great sense of pleasure, although, as usual, we provided them with hard bindings and added them to our library. Lin Shu was beginning to translate

too freely and reading them made no sense. Swift's *Gulliver's Travels* and Irving's *Sketches*[52] are good books, but in translation they were distorted beyond recognition. As far as the translation of *Don Quixote* (which Lin Shu called *The Tale of the Mad Knight*) is concerned, it was out and out bad, literally riddled with errors. At first, with such works as *Ivanhoe*, it seemed Lin Shu had done a magnificent job of conveying the humor. Who would have guessed that with genuinely humorous works he would suffer complete failure? Honestly speaking, some of Lin Shu's last translations, for example *David Copperfield*,[53] were done rather well, but once a man has choked on a certain dish, he no longer wants to try it again.[54]

In reality, it was not so much a matter of Lin Shu's degeneration (he had "reworked" originals earlier) as Lu Hsün's growth, which may also explain the great attention he paid to Chang Ping-lin's writings. The writer intently followed Chang Ping-lin's articles directed against Liang Ch'i-ch'ao and enthusiastically attended the lectures he gave in the office of the journal *The People* (*Min-pao*), an organ of the Alliance Society. Having learned much from his teacher, Lu Hsün on one occasion earnestly came to his assistance. In 1908, when the Japanese, at the request of the Manchu court, banned the journal and fined the publisher 150 *yüan*, Lu Hsün handed over to Chang Ping-lin the honorarium he received for editing a translation of a Japanese book entitled *A Sourcebook on Chinese Economics*.[55] In certain statements on this subject[56] Lu Hsün makes clear what attracted him most in Chang Ping-lin: his revolutionary zeal, his battle with reformers and reactionaries. It is useless, however, for Lu Hsün to deny any interest in Chang's "enigmatic classical style."

The story of Lu Hsün's relationship with the poet Chiang Chih-yu is an interesting example of Lu Hsün's relationship to the reformers and his break with them in the years 1906 to 1909. From 1903 to 1905 Lu Hsün often visited the poet and even attempted, with his help, to publish the translation of *Expedition to the North Pole*. At that time Chiang Chih-yu was quite progressive and Lu Hsün often recited his insurgent poetry. After returning to Tokyo from Sendai, Lu Hsün continued to call on the poet, but one day Chiang Chih-yu declared that "Manchu caps with red tassels look very impressive." "Hearing this, we were very surprised," recalls Hsü Shou-shang. "On the way back Lu Hsün said: 'So Kuan-yün has changed his way of thinking!' I nodded my head. From that time on we no longer went to see him." Soon afterwards Chiang Chih-yu along with Liang Ch'i-ch'ao actually created the Political News Society (Cheng-wen-she), which fought for constitutional monarchy, and then Lu Hsün gave him the nickname "the uninspiring one" (*wu-wei-i*).⁵⁷ This episode with Chiang Chih-yu shows that in the years 1906 and 1907 Lu Hsün was more preoccupied with the ideological positions of the early twentieth-century Chinese poets than with their poetry. Lu Hsün's views, however, were not in complete accord with the views of present-day revolutionaries. In the article "On Extremes in Culture" written in 1907, for example, he indicts both the reformers and the revolutionaries for their coarse "materialism" (pragmatism).* Thus, he was one of the first in China to understand the limitations of the bourgeois revolution.

The writer considered the suppression of individuality by the crowd and the dominance of material factors over the spiritual as "extremes."⁵⁸ This led him to the idea of the necessity of struggling for the emancipation of the individual and of the enormous role of art. "I imagine that if the whole world valued only knowledge, human life would become more and more dry and uninteresting, and if this continued for too long, the sense of beauty would become deadened and so-called science would disappear along with it," writes Lu Hsün in the article "A Chapter from the History of Science" (1907).⁵⁹ This point of view is fundamentally different from a view of art as something practical, intended only for the popularization of politics and science, and it was shared by most Chinese philosophes of the early twentieth century, Lu Hsün included, as shown in the preface to the translation of Verne's novel *From the Earth to the Moon*. Now, in 1908, in the article "On the Power of Demoniacal Poetry" the author declares: "There is no direct connection between literature and the fate of the individual or the State. Literature is far from being of practical benefit, and it is not governed by objective laws. Hence, it cannot broaden our knowledge as successfully as historical treatises, caution like proverbs, make us rich like industry or trade, or create a great name like diplomacy."⁶⁰ It was this very "uselessness" which Lu Hsün at

---

*In my own view, it is quite clearly "materialism" that Lu Hsün denounces. "Are material goods really enough to satisfy human life to the core?" asks the writer rhetorically, and the answer is: "Quietly considering it, definitely not" (I, 41 and 45, 1938 ed.).—C.J.A.

the time thought made literature valuable. "Its essence, like all art, lies in the fact that it gives man enjoyment."[61] Here the writer's views are quite similar to those few Chinese philosophes who fought against overestimating the social function of literature—the reformer Hsia Tseng-yu, the revolutionary Huang Jen, and Wang Kuo-wei, the propagandist of European aesthetics. Nevertheless, the ostentatious and mystic traits in the views of Wang Kuo-wei were alien to Lu Hsün.

The main purpose of the article "On the Power of Demoniacal Poetry" was to celebrate the writer as a rebel who hurled challenges at society.

> The word "demoniacal" (*mara*) comes from India and in European languages it corresponds to the word "satanic," often used in reference to Byron. In the present article I extend it to all poets who consciously put up resistance, did not shun involvement, and were not greeted by the world with any special joy .... Each of these poets [Lu Hsün selects the literature of Byron, Shelley, Pushkin, Lermontov, Mickiewicz, Slowacki, Krasinski, and Petöfi—V.S.] had his own point of view, though their basic goal was the same. They did not want to utter a sound that would delight the world, and they let out a howl that shook the living. They battled with heaven itself and stood up against human mediocrity. Their energy infected the hearts of later generations and has not run dry to this very day. There is no one among those yet to be born or those already dead who would not find it worthwhile to listen to the voice of the demoniac poet. To all those whose feet are pinned to the earth, who are tormented and cannot get free, the sound of his voice is most brave and beautiful.[62]

This is not the first time that a romantic note has been sounded in Lu Hsün's work. Recall, for example, the story "The Spartan Spirit." Ch'en Ming-shu calls it (and not without some justification) a "romantic tale," suggesting that it was written under the influence of Byron, who absorbed Lu Hsün's attention in 1902.[63] Soon afterwards he translated an extract from Victor Hugo's *Les Misérables*,[64] and later, poetic extracts from a work by the late romantic H. Rider Haggard. And finally, in 1908, this article on early nineteenth-century European poetry was written. In the early 1900s romanticism had not developed into an independent school in Chinese literature, but Lu Hsün undoubtedly belonged among those writers of the early twentieth century (Su Man-shu, Tseng P'u) in whose works the romantic motif could most readily be discerned. The Japanese sinologist Ozaka Tokuji rightly notes that although in content the articles "On Extremes in Culture," "Against Evil Voices," and others were directed against the enlightenment movement, they clearly show the influence of the philosophe's style, particularly the "new style" of Liang Ch'i-ch'ao. One other feature of the article "On the Power of the Demoniacal Poets" is that here there is no strict logic, no attempt to organize ideas—a characteristic of Liang Ch'i-ch'ao's essays. And though the narrative may seem more confused, it is also more intense.[65] It is quite possible that Lu Hsün imitated the style of the very romantics of whom he wrote.

Lu Hsün's interest in mythology and fairy tales, something uncharacteristic of the majority of Chinese philosophers, who were battling against superstition and rejected fantasy as well, testifies to his romantic propensities during these years. In the article "Against Evil Voices" (1908) the author becomes enraptured with the myths of India, Greece, Eastern and Northern Europe, and sees in them proof of the richness of popular fantasy,[66] a situation similar to that in the article "On the Power of Demoniacal Poetry."

At the time Lu Hsün had a rather harsh attitude toward Chinese literature, especially contemporary literature, and, generally speaking, he focused on its negative features. "One only need walk along our streets to encounter soldiers who march dandily along singing at the top of their voices martial ballads that criticize the servility of India and Poland.[67] Some of these songs have almost become national anthems.... Now we will no longer be able to figure out who has degenerated further—the countries mentioned or China. Beneath the Heavens there are still a fair number of treatises that glorify the beautiful and express the thoughts of the people, and yet never have I seen the spirit of autocracy flourish to such an extent."[68]

The article "On the Power of Demoniacal Poetry" is interesting not only as a philosophical work and as an essay that ushered in a new era of Chinese aesthetics, but also as an attempt to expand China's literary ties. Nevertheless, Lu Hsün's role as a popularizer of foreign writers should not be exaggerated.[69] Many other translators in the early 1900s were more productive and more influential. In the summer of 1907 Lu Hsün founded the literary journal *New Life* (*Hsin sheng*), but because the writer had too few collaborators and, consequently, money and manuscripts, the journal did not survive for very long.

The balance of Lu Hsün's literary career was to constitute a whole chain of attempts and failures, because from this time onward he began to depart from what was widespread and conventional in national literature. In the beginning of this century Chinese literary journals in Japan and China (*New Fiction, Illustrated Fiction, Fiction Monthly*, and others) concentrated on "multi-chapter novels" [i.e., serial novels—C.J.A.] and novels in translation. After 1906, however, Lu Hsün was interested primarily in essays (political, scientific, and literary) and foreign short stories, which he translated into the classical language, as opposed to the semiconversational style of the Chinese novel. Lu Hsün managed to publish the material intended for *New Life* in the revolutionary journal *Honan* (i.e., the 1907-1908 articles) and in *Short Stories from Abroad* (1909), but the writer's audience had shriveled. If the journal *Chekiang Tide* reached the remotest provinces, the journal *Honan* is mentioned almost exclusively in Lu Hsün's biographies. When the young author translated Jules Verne, his books "went like hotcakes at 30 *yüan*,"[70] but when he turned to Vsevolod Garshin and Leonid Andreev, he could hardly get twenty copies off his hands.[71] Of course, the conservatism of the reading public and the limitedness of its interests played no small role in this regard. The Romanticism and Realism which Lu Hsün championed eventually made headway and gained acceptance, but prior to 1919 examples of such artistic techniques were limited mostly to his own works and those of others like Su Man-shu or Tseng P'u.

In the preface to the second edition of *Short Stories from Abroad* (1920) Lu Hsün recalls that in order to truly popularize Eastern European literature, which was his main interest after 1906, he would have needed, at very least, knowledge, collaborators, time, money, and readers. None of these did he have in sufficient quantity.[72] As a result, Lu Hsün was able to publish a grand total of two small volumes of short stories in translation (March and August, 1909). Included among them were the works of Guy de Maupassant ("Claire de lune"); Oscar Wilde ("The Happy Prince"); Edgar Allen Poe ("Silence. A Fable"); Anton Chekhov ("At a Country House" and "In Exile"); Vsevolod Garshin ("Four Days"); Leonid Andreev ("Lie" and "Silence"); S. Stepnyak-Kravchinsky ("The Story of a Kopeck"); Henryk Sienkiewicz ("Yanko the Musician," "Jamiol," and "The Lighthouse Keeper of Aspinwall"); a story by the father of Finnish realism, J. Aho ("New

Village"); and two stories by a Serbian writer[73] whose name I have not been able to identify. The contents of this collection show the translator's inclination toward realism, but this advance in his development was partly a result of his previous work, including the aforementioned article "On the Power of Demoniacal Poetry," where along with the poetry of Byron, Shelley, Mickiewicz, Slowacki, and Petöfi the author analyzes works by Pushkin, Lermontov, and Gogol, and quotes Korolenko.[74]

Lu Hsün was not the first to acquaint China with examples of critical realism. By 1909 there had already been translated into Chinese several novels by Dickens, Pushkin's "The Captain's Daughter," an excerpt from Lermontov's *A Hero for Our Time*, L. Tolstoy's "Popular Tales," Chekhov's "Ward No. 6," Gorky's "Kain and Artem," and Tokutomi Roka's "It's Better Not to Live." Nevertheless, his was the first "real" attempt to do so, i.e., to regard the popularization of realism as his prime objective and to decide to translate world classics precisely, without the adaptation that so often degraded the original to the level of didactic literature. In addition, Lu Hsün attempted to bridge the gap between early nineteenth-century writers and his own contemporaries. "From the very moment that our collection appears in China the best works of modern foreign literature will begin to penetrate.... Let us hope that from now on Chinese translations will no longer seem outdated."[75]

This transition to late nineteenth- and early twentieth-century Western literature, through which modern ideas spread, was brought about, of course, not so much by a mere curiosity about contemporary life as by the fact that Lu Hsün discovered in them contemporary sentiments that were in harmony with his own. His attention to Nietzsche testifies to this as well as the fact that of the sixteen named short stories, Lu Hsün himself translated only three: L. Andreev's "Lie" and "Silence," and V. Garshin's "Four Days." Sinologues explain Lu Hsün the translator's choice in various ways,[76] but none of them mentions an essential feature of the stories that was of special interest to Lu Hsün, *viz.*, their pessimistic spirit. And yet, it was this very characteristic which set V. Garshin and L. Andreev apart from many other writers of the nineteenth and early twentieth centuries. Otherwise, would not Lu Hsün have chosen to translate the works of Gogol, Turgenev, Chekhov, and Gorky, whose "humanistic character" and "exposure of the false morals of a class society,"[77] etc. are no less apparent? Many of the works of these authors were already accessible to Lu Hsün at that time in Japanese and German translations.[78] Agonizingly aware of the oppressed position of his people and the people of other countries, Lu Hsün saw no way out of the crisis. Hence, his sympathetic attention to the creative work of Garshin. "He suffered so deeply for the world that he went out of his mind," wrote Lu Hsün, for example, in a commentary on the story "Four Days." "His last works are particularly melancholy, but for now we will only translate one of them. Both the language and the plot are unusual."[79] As one can see, Lu Hsün was attracted not only by the content of these stories, which was in keeping with his own mood, but by their unusual form. Of Andreev Lu Hsün writes: "His works are deep and mysterious; he forms his own independent school."[80]

Lu Hsün read the stories of Garshin and Andreev in translation, which means that to a certain extent they were already distorted. Let us, therefore, attempt to trace which changes came from the "intermediary" and which came from Lu Hsün. "Four Days" is written in short, pulsating phrases. "I remember how we ran through the woods, how the bullets droned, how the branches torn off by them fell, how we forced our way through the hawthorn bushes."[81] A similar tone is preserved in all German translations known to me that were completed prior to 1908.[82] Lu Hsün's rendition of this passage is calm and objective, because in the classical language groups of four characters are most common, and even groups of six characters would be considered long. In addition, Lu Hsün moves the words "I remember how" to the end of the sentence ("... all this I remember even now"),[83] thereby eliminating Garshin's nervous repetition. On the other hand, in the translation of L. Andreev's story "Lie" the majority of changes come from the German intermediary.[84] Thus, in striving for a precise translation (*chih-i*), Lu Hsün did not fully achieve his objectives in the years from 1907 to 1909, because he did not translate from the original and also because where style was concerned he unwittingly adapted the translated text (though to a much lesser extent than either he or his contemporaries did earlier) to his own tastes and sympathies.

A number of other inaccuracies in the translation result from the fact that the archaic classical style was not always capable of translating complex sentence constructions. There is no such thing as a subordinate clause in classical Chinese, so Lu Hsün found it necessary to break large passages into parts. For example, Lu Hsün divides L. Andreev's sentence "And when I lifted up my eyes, I saw his profile—so white, austere, and upright, like some pensive angel over the grave of a forgotten man,"[85] into two, and the passage turns out as follows: "And when I raised my eyes, I saw his cheeks, as white as ivory, and his magnificent locks. I was sure that only an angel, kneeling beside a lonely grave and mourning a man forgotten by the world, could look like this."[86] The pompous comparison of the cheek to ivory, which replaces Andreev's terse epithet "white, austere, and upright," was borrowed from the German intermediary; but now the syntactical smoothness is lost in the transition from German to Chinese. Lu Hsün could not help feeling disturbed by this situation, and in a number of instances, attempting to capture the uniqueness of the original (or more properly, the German translation), he breaks the rules of the classical language. "And so I fell (and though I do not remember this, I do recall how everyone was running ahead, while I was unable to run, and the only thing left before my eyes was something dark blue), and I fell in a clearing on top of a hill,"[87] writes Garshin. Lu Hsün chooses the appropriate Chinese word with great skill, but he leaves the construction of the sentence the same as in the original and in the German translation. The result is a long introductory clause, completely atypical of the classical Chinese language.[88]

Like Tseng P'u and other translators, Lu Hsün used European punctuation marks (exclamatory and interrogatory) in *Short Stories from Abroad*. For literary allusions and historical facts he added footnotes. All this undoubtedly enriched the text, though it still impressed readers as something foreign. And to some extent the readers were correct. For example, the long European names which Lu Hsün, in contrast to his contemporaties, transcribed in full did not harmonize with the laconic style of the classical language and the archaic forms of the characters.[89]

The principle of precise translation, which Lu Hsün advocated from 1907 to 1909, was progressive and necessary for Chinese literature. Lu Hsün wanted to advance Chinese literature to an understanding not only of the plot of a translated work but of the individual style of the writer, the multiplicity of details, and the psychological characteristics. However, the classical language interfered with the realization of this plan. In the translations of grandiloquent verses from the novels of H. Rider Haggard and A. Lang (1907) such contradictions are not yet apparent. They only become apparent after the transition to works of late nineteenth- and early twentieth-century Russian authors. It is not surprising, therefore, that later on, after 1918, Lu Hsün began to confine himself primarily to the colloquial language.

On the eve and the day of the revolution (1909-13)

The young writer's first failures were painful, and yet on returning to his native land he not only did not curtail his creative work, he even joined the Yüeh Society, a branch of the Southern Society (the first society of revolutionary Chinese literati) in the province of Chekiang. There is some evidence that Lu Hsün actually belonged* to the Southern Society, whose headquarters were not far away, "although, it seems, he did not approve of this organization's programs, since he never showed up there at all. Many members of the society were not even aware that he was their comrade."[90] Nowhere, however, does Lu Hsün mention his participation in the Southern Society; nor does his name appear on any lists of the members of the society.[91] If, on the other hand, Lu Hsün did join the Yüeh Society in the early part of 1911, perhaps the reason lies in certain changes that occurred in the writer's views immediately prior to the revolution and, possibly, under the influence of the Canton Uprising (March 1911).

Lu Hsün did a great deal for the Yüeh Society. For example, the first issue of the *Yüeh Society Miscellany* contains his "Travel Notes of the Year 1911," which, judging from its contents, was completed prior to the 1911-13 revolution. At first glance the "Travel Notes" seem very similar to "Plant Sketches," written while he was still in Nanking. Here too there are descriptions of nature, the names of flowers are explained, and the impressions of the author are only tenuously linked together.... Now, however, one senses in this fragmentation more an artistic freedom than any lack of mastery. The mood of the writer is pensive and lyrical. Several episodes convey the feeling of allegory: "We descended to-

*Liu Wu-chi, Liu Ya-tzu's son, assures me that "Lu Hsün was not a member of the Southern Society"—C.J.A.

gether along the side path. By the direct path only ascent is easy, so people, without hesitation, have trampled down the transverse slope. So often has it been used that it has turned into an actual road."[92] The allegorical meaning of this passage (simple landscape sketches would hardly have been of any interest to an anthology of the revolutionary Yüeh Society) is contrary in spirit to the future optimistic conclusion at the end of the story "My Old Home": "There is no road, but people will pass and a road will be paved." The writer seems to be saying: Alas, the direct path is only fit for ascent, and having climbed to the summit, people choose roundabout, crooked paths.

Apparently the critic Shen P'eng-nien is correct in asserting that in the poems, articles, descriptions of walks, and scenes of nature published in the *Yüeh Society Miscellany* Lu Hsün "unconsciously poured out his sorrow for the nation."[93] But perhaps in this instance the word "nation" sounds a bit too general. Lu Hsün was far from any conception of the nation as a monolithic unity, and this is borne out, in my opinion, by other passages from the "Travel Notes":

> About one hour after midday a patch of white waves appeared on the sea. Drawing closer, it rocked the boats more and more forcibly, and suddenly it was right before our eyes.... The main portion was like a chain of clouds, but hitting the shore and carrying away clay, it turned black. "Oh, black tide!" sighed an old man and looked about fearfully. According to local belief, black waves portend misfortune. But the tide always carries away clay; the waves cannot remain white....[94]

Quite possibly this passage reflects Lu Hsün's partial lack of faith in the oncoming bourgeois revolution, characteristic of his 1907-08 articles, as well as his attempts to justify it [i.e., the revolution—C.J.A.] ("the tide always carries away clay," but this does not ensure misfortune).

One should remember that landscape allegory in general was rather widespread in Chinese art. For example, the early seventeenth-century essayists whom Lu Hsün admired also resorted to it. And take note of the last of the "Travel Notes":

> Finally I succeeded in getting one large flower. I would certainly have planted it in my garden had I not already known that a zizania grows only on the root of a rush and, once transplanted, dies.[95]

Is the appearance of this beautiful plant-parasite a coincidence?

One senses in all of the above-cited passages some of Lu Hsün's uneasiness over the fate of the revolution and a desire to warn his contemporaries not to distort revolutionary ideas. I will not insist on my own interpretation of individual passages, but it is difficult to believe that the "Travel Notes," which were written on the eve of the revolution, following the vivid publicistic articles of 1907-08, and printed in an anthology of a revolutionary society, are nothing more than landscape sketches. Doubt about the purity of revolution is "shameful" to a revolutionary and, therefore, the allegorical form is completely natural.

On returning to his native land, Lu Hsün's interest in national folklore and classical literature was once again reawakened. Proof of this, for example, is the collection *Neglected Ancient Tales* (*Ku hsiao-shuo kou-ch'en*), which he compiled, and the preface to it, which, like the "Travel Notes," was published in the same *Yüeh Society Miscellany*. Enamored of folklore, Lu Hsün writes: "Legends grow out of a profound insight into life, and stylistically they are sometimes reminiscent of magnificent flowers."[96] The entire preface is directed against the contempt for fiction so prevalent among the literati of China[97] and against the narrow, pragmatic attitude toward it.[98] Now Lu Hsün seems closer to the view that literature can enlighten than in his 1907-08 articles. Perhaps this is because the preface to *Neglected Ancient Tales* was written on the eve of the revolution and printed right after it. Legends are "quite capable of enriching civilization and dispelling dreary solitude,"[99] asserts Lu Hsün, and he concludes his work in the following manner: "Since I am not averse to discussing lofty matters either, I repeat: the duties of the scribes (designated to record legends—V.S.) were about the same as the duties of the ancient officials who collected ballads. From these tales rulers could learn of the habits and customs of their people as well as their own successes and failures." This thesis reflects the ancient Confucian view of "popular" genres, which to a certain extent is contrary to the later contemptuous attitude toward fiction; and, in fact, it was the view espoused by the Chinese philosophes.

* * *

For Lu Hsün the years of the Hsin-hai revolution (1911-13) marked even greater creative activity. It was during this time, for example, that his story "The Past"[100] appeared, a story depicting scenes of popular uprising* associated with a recent rebellion in Wu-ch'ang. In both content and artistic technique "The Past" differs strongly from Lu Hsün's first short story. Authors of the early twentieth-century novel of censure, and Lu Hsün himself in "The Spartan Spirit," often expressed their attitude toward events openly, avoiding understatement and indirect descriptions of characters; but in "The Past" Lu Hsün employs a more subtle technique. He depicts the "revolt" sympathetically and ridicules the reactionaries and their parasites, but no longer in overt editorial digressions.

The various characters in "The Past" have different opinions of the uprising. We do not, of course, trust those of the pedant Yang Sheng or the avaricious landowner Chin Yao-tsung. On the contrary, their negative attitude toward the rebels evokes an opposite reaction from the reader. The tale of the servant Wang is contradictory: on the one hand, we learn of the cruelty of the Taiping rebels, who at times killed innocent villagers, and on the other, how adept were members of the ruling classes (Third Master from the neighboring town, for example) at using the conduct of the Taiping rebels and the ignorance of the peasants to suppress the rebellion. The most sincere of all in his sympathy toward the "rebels" is the young boy, the main hero of the story. His faith in the triumph of justice and, simultaneously, deliverance from the wicked teacher is quite touching. The young boy is not intimidated by the dreadful incidents that the nannie and the servant Wang relate to him. He continues to be attracted by the romantic life of the rebel and is unwilling to come in off the street when it starts to rain. Tomorrow tedious rote memorization and the teacher's ruler may once again await him.

In this child's portrait and in that of the servants from "The Past" one senses for the first time that genuine Chekhovian warmth and gentleness which is characteristic of the mature Lu Hsün's short stories. Here there is not a hint of the sentimentality or pomposity found in "The Spartan Spirit." And in the depiction of the negative characters there is the seed of that subtle, caustic irony

---

*This is at best misleading, because the tale only concentrates on *rumors* of revolution. Rumor is a classical theme not only of Chinese but of Western literature, and Lu Hsün's works are no exception. It is difficult to believe, as Semanov asserts, that Lu Hsün depicted the so-called popular uprising "sympathetically." The story strongly resembles "Storm in a Teacup" (*Feng-po*). —C.J.A.

which later became such an important feature of Lu Hsün's talent, a talent seldom encountered in early twentieth-century literature of enlightenment.

In this story there are no long authorial diatribes, and very few explicit evaluations, only that of Chin Yao-tsung, whom Lu Hsün characterized as "stupid" and "miserly," and whom L. D. Pozdneeva compares with Plushkin.*[101] Generally speaking, the author's viewpoint is established indirectly, through the aid of satiric details (having learned of the appearance of the rebels, Chin Yao-tsung hastens to give them evidence of his loyalty), verbal expression ("Being nearsighted, he almost touched the book with his teeth, as if he intended to bite it"[102] —said of the teacher-bookworm), and unexpected juxtapositions. For example, in his "elegant" style Lu Hsün tells in detail how "wisely" the eminent ancestors of the teacher Yang Sheng conducted themselves in time of rebellion. "They did not sacrifice themselves in the struggle against the rebels, nor did they destroy themselves chasing after them."[103] And then, the author deliberately, casually, and with one phrase, reveals that, owing to the efforts of such a "renowned" ancestor, his descendant has been turned into a simple domestic tutor who is obliged to drum Confucianism into the head of a playful boy! In this comic episode there is more of literature than any didactic tirade. The reader understands that "wise circumspection" brings a man neither tranquility nor prosperity. At the same time, gibes at "sagacious gudgeons"** demand from the author no less strength and belief in man than the doleful cries of Liang Ch'i-ch'ao or the revolutionary pathos of the novelist Tseng P'u.

This masking of authorial attitudes toward characters and events shows Lu Hsün's refusal at this stage to express his political opinion openly (a characteristic of the novel of censure) and is, to a certain extent, a reversion to classical traditions. Thus, critical realism, a more progressive and complex literary technique, found its way into Chinese literature and took the place of enlightened didacticism. By calling the story "The Past" (literally "Reminiscences of the Past")*** and basing it on other than contemporary

---

*A character in Gogol's *Dead Souls*.—C.J.A.

**The name of a small fresh-water fish that is easily caught, hence someone easily ensnared.—C.J.A.

***According to V. F. Sorokin, the title was supplied by Lu Hsün's brother Chou Tso-jen (*Lu Hsün's World Outlook*, p. 64). For confirmation of this see *Lu Hsün hsiao-shuo-li te jen-wu*, p. 139. See also J. Průšek's provocating article "Lu Hsün's 'Huai Chiu': a Precursor of Modern Chinese Literature," *Harvard Journal of Asiatic Studies*, no. 29 (1969), pp. 169-176.—C.J.A.

material, Lu Hsün initiated a silent debate with early twentieth-century novelists. True, they too turned to events of the past. One of the most prominent writers of the time, Wu Wo-yao, for example, wrote several historical novels. But the basic trend in Chinese literature of enlightenment was devotion to the issues of the day, allowing a more direct and pointed castigation of the absolute monarchy which was abhorrent to all. Unfortunately, this timeliness* was sometimes taken one-sidedly. The latest facts gained attention, not those that were typical, faithful to the spirit of the times. In "The Past" Lu Hsün interprets timeliness more broadly. He transposes the action to the 1890s, has his characters recall the fifties and sixties, and alludes to the revolution that has just passed. Thus, a broad view of history and a closer approximation to the mysteries of the typical laid the groundwork for realism in Chinese literature.

The laconic form of "The Past" is further evidence of the young writer's departure from traditional fiction of the last few centuries, the basic genre of which was the novel. The "multi-chapter novel" was based on convention, included an enormous number of characters who had little connection with one another, and sometimes even bored the reader. All this apparently did not appeal to Lu Hsün. "The Spartan Spirit," *Short Stories from Abroad*, and "The Past" comprise a whole series of challenges which he hurled at the multi-chapter novel. A short work is more accessible to the reader, gives the author an opportunity to develop a few characters more fully, and forces him to be more economical in his use of literary techniques. Without rejecting the multi-chapter novel itself, it would have been difficult in China during the first two decades of the twentieth-century to break away from traditional approaches to characterization and to focus interest on the individual.

In an attempt to convey the psychology of a child in all its uniqueness, Lu Hsün narrates the story in the first person. Several other novelists of the early twentieth century resorted to this relatively new device in Chinese literature (Wu Wo-yao, for example, in *Strange Events of the Last Twenty Years*). But whereas other figures in their novels scarcely profit from this, all four "secondary" characters in "The Past" are no less vividly portrayed than the

---

*The term *zlobodnevnost'*—"actuality, actualness; on the issues of the day [hence, timely, tendentious], topical" (Smirnitsky) is elusive. It seems to me that what Semanov calls "facts" are nothing more than rumors or just plain gossip. But on the whole he regards this as a *positive* feature of the works in question.—C.J.A.

main hero. In the outward appearance of the teacher Yang Sheng, for example, the writer emphasizes two basic traits, near-sightedness and baldness; but he does not forget about them, and twice he uses them to good advantage. In long Chinese novels such motifs, having been mentioned once, often vanish from the reader's memory.

Description of actions and situations also acquires great concreteness and picturesqueness in "The Past." Recall, for example, the following incident: the teacher Yang Sheng, having found out that there are no rebels whatsoever in the vicinity, sets off for home a calm man. In all likelihood the early twentieth-century satirist Li Pao-chia would have been content merely to establish this fact. But Lu Hsün points out that only a few people remained under the *wu-t'ung* tree where the teacher sat, shows how long it takes for the man to make preparations, how he takes along his anthology of examination essays, how he peers at the boy before leaving, what he says (direct speech), how the boy meanwhile becomes gloomy and tosses a glance at the servant Wang, what Wang does at that time, and so forth. Although a bit protracted, an actual picture of everyday life emerges.

In the tradition of the best Chinese novelists of the early twentieth-century (Liu O, for example), Lu Hsün attaches great importance to scenery. There are not many depictions of scenery in "The Past," but they are highly original:*

> The rain began to fall harder. Raindrops gently struck the broad leaves of the plantain growing in front of the window, and they sounded like crabs crawling along sand. Laying my head on the pillow, I listened to these sounds for a long time and, at length, they disappeared . . . .[104]

The first critic of "The Past," Yün Shu-chüeh, admired the simile of the rain dripping like crawling crabs and, in my view, with good reason. "The last few words aptly convey the idea that the child has fallen asleep."[105]

"The Past" is written in *wen-yen*, which Lu Hsün is able to use so freely that Yün Shu-chüeh showers compliments on the story's lively—and this is the classical language—unconstrained dia-

---

*This is true of most of Lu Hsün's short stories. The volume of scenery is usually small (less than in Liu O's novel) but the description itself is fraught with meaning. The pathetic fallacy is a common "fault" of Liu O and Lu Hsün both, and perhaps of Chinese literature in general.—C.J.A.

logue.[106] Moreover, in the journal *Fiction Monthly* (*Hsiao-shuo yüeh-pao*), where the story was printed, it became the first publication with European punctuation marks. Lu Hsün follows present-day conventions for citing direct speech. In a number of instances, with remarks almost completely eliminated, the dialogue moves along without any necessity for the verb "said" or the name of the speaker. The old Chinese word order (the verb "to say" followed by the speech itself) is completely discarded. Nevertheless, Lu Hsün still does not break the dialogue down into segments, discrete syntactical units.

"The Past" did not begin a new era of Chinese literature; it only hailed the approach of one. Nevertheless, this story has rightly attracted more attention from contemporaries[107] than any of the writer's earlier works.

* * *

During the Hsin-hai revolution Lu Hsün established firm ties with Chinese writers within the country. Soon after the Republic established authority over Shaohsing, he became one of the publishers of the student newspaper *The Bell of Yüeh* (*Yüeh-to jih pao*) and opened its first issue with one of his own articles. A month later the "Travel Notes" and the "Preface to Neglected Ancient Tales" mentioned earlier were published in the *Yüeh Society Miscellany*; and on August 21 one of Lu Hsün's well-known poems, "Mourning for Mr. Fan," appeared in another Shaohsing student newspaper, *Rebirth of the People* (*Min-hsin jih-pao*).

"The inhabitants of Yüeh, who have since ancient times regarded themselves as the first under the Heavens, have been brought to destitution by predatory barbarians (the Manchus—V.S.)," writes Lu Hsün in the article "Introducing *The Bell of Yüeh*." "Now the time has come to liberate the people, to restore justice, and to continue the work of our great philosophers who fought for enlightened government. But, alas, too long has absolutism ruled the country, and it will not be easy to uproot it. Moreover, people have once again begun to strive for fame and profit; none cast a glance at the high hills behind them. Their hearts are filled with endless grief; and that is why we have decided to publish *The Bell of Yüeh*."[108]

Here, as before, despite the victories of the revolution, a harsh criticism of Chinese society can be detected; and this is quite natural. Almost immediately after the Wu-ch'ang uprising, and especially after Sun Yat-sen resigned his presidential post to the militarist Yüan Shih-k'ai (February 14, 1912), power in the country fell into the hands of the reactionaries. The rejuvenated revolutionary Wang Chin-fa became goverer of Chekiang province. Those collaborating on the newspaper *The Bell of Yüeh*, among them the well-known revolutionary poet and member of the Southern and Yüeh societies, Ch'en Ch'ü-ping, sought to expose the militaristic government,[109] though not very skillfully to be sure. Ch'en Ch'ü-ping, for example, had no qualms about attacking the governor's concubines. In the end, the editors of the newspaper, believing they had gained a victory over the new regime, accepted money from Wang Chin-fa to publish the paper, when in fact they were making themselves dependent on the authorities. All of this forced Lu Hsün to withdraw from the editorial staff of *The Bell of Yüeh*, although he did maintain his ties with the Shaohsing press later on, even after moving to Nanking and later to Peking.[110] On January 13, 1913, Lu Hsün wrote in his diary:

> Received the fifth issue of *The Bell of Yüeh*. The photo of Sun Te-ch'ing appears in a conspicuous place, right beside rather unique shots of Hsü Hsi-lin and T'ao Ch'eng-chang. How absurd! Anyhow, the stupidity of people today is already frightening.[111]

Sun Te-ch'ing (a wealthy man from Shaohsing and one of the publishers of *The Bell of Yüeh*) was wounded by the secret police of the Shaohsing regional administration in a raid on the editorial office of the newspaper on August 5, 1912.[112] Naturally, Lu Hsün could not put him in the same category as the fallen heroes of the revolution.

And so, the writer "detested the old, but at the same time was dissatisfied with the primitiveness of the new."[113] This same statement applies to Lu Hsün's attitude toward the whole of contemporary Chinese literature. In 1912, for example, he went to the theater three times because he was interested in the new "colloquial" drama, but the Peking dramatic troupes, more conservative than, for example, the Shanghai ones, could not satisfy his demands. "Only one play was running—'Flood North of the Yangtze,'" writes Lu Hsün on July 11. "One can rejoice at its boldness, but knowledge of life and craftsmanship are lacking. All the rest of the plays were old."[114] As for prerevolutionary literature, at the time

Lu Hsün was primarily attracted by the works of Li Tz'u-ming,[115] a well-known scholar of the late nineteenth century whose diaries were considered a model of the memoir. Having studied the technique of Li Tz'u-ming, Lu Hsün created his own diary style. But as a whole, the writer regarded the literature of the nineteenth and early twentieth centuries as being oriented toward the past.

During the time of the revolution Lu Hsün continues to familiarize himself with foreign literature (Turgenev, Dostoevsky, Greek poetry, etc.),[116] though not as systematically as in Japan. He tries to increase the readership of *Short Stories from Abroad* by freely giving away copies to his acquaintances. But most of all Lu Hsün devotes his energies to the study of representational art and aesthetics, to which his new duties (supervisor of museums and libraries in the Republican Ministry of Education) are conducive. Lu Hsün's interest in aesthetic problems was already evident in his articles of the Japan period, but now this interest is intensified, owing to the possibility that it might in some way influence the development of culture. The young writer familiarizes himself with Chinese and Western books on aesthetics, translates the Japanese Ueno Yoichi's articles on aesthetic education,[117] reads lectures on the same theme for the Ministry of Education's summer lecture series and, finally, publishes his own "Proposal for Dissemination of the Arts" (February 1913) in the *Editorial Section Monthly* of the Ministry.

Although we do not know how this proposal was received by his contemporaries, it should be considered an important step in the development of Lu Hsün's views and in the formation of the new Chinese aesthetics. "A work of art is a natural object (*t'ien-wu*) that has undergone beautification (*mei-hua*) through a process of intellectual analysis (*szu-li*),"[118] writes Lu Hsün, asserting, in this possibly oversimplified formula, a materialistic view of art not very widespread in China during the early twentieth century. Chinese philosophes (including Lu Hsün himself from 1903 to 1906) were primarily concerned with the influence of art on society, and they hardly even gave a thought to its source.

In 1907-08 Lu Hsün had taken a stand against the pragmatic view of art, and his idealistic conception of the relationship between fiction and life even went to extremes,[119] making social progress dependent on the number of men of genius. Now he affirms the primacy of reality over art and at the same time speaks of the active, creative role of the artist:

> It is well known that there are two capabilities inherent in man—perception and creation. When the morning sun rises over the sea or delicate grasses bloom magnificently, only a madman would fail to be moved by such sights. But among those who perceive an object there are only one or two talented people who can re-create (*tsai-hsien*) it, instill new life into it. This is called creativity. Thus, the artist proceeds from a definite idea; without an idea there is no art. Nevertheless, the natural phenomena which he observes are not always perfect. For example, the leaves may be withered and faded, the forest overgrown and decayed. At the moment of re-creation one must restore them, pick out their favorable qualities. This is called beautification. When there is no beautification, art disappears.[120]

In other words, the creativity of the artist is manifested in "intellectual analysis" and "beautification" (as Lu Hsün interprets it, this concept is somewhat similar to typification).

The first of these categories is related to aesthetic views, the second to the theories of the philosophes. Thus, immediately after mentioning "intellectual analysis" Lu Hsün writes:

> A leaf chiseled from jade and lacquer imitating gilt may resemble the real thing, but they cannot be considered art; plates of ivory on which have been written thousands of characters and peach pits containing a row of summer houses might be masterfully carved, but they cannot be regarded as art.[121]

What Lu Hsün rejects in this passage is the senseless bric-a-brac made in feudal China, though he scarcely denies the value of applied art.

The writer allots even greater space to rebutting the views of the philosophes.

> Almost all aesthetic theories proclaim that the basic goal of art is to give man enjoyment. Conflicts arise only over the question of what this enjoyment should be. Champions of beauty think that art exists only for itself and has nothing to do with other things. Frankly speaking, this is the correct view. But the adherents of utilitarianism suggest that art is obliged to help the world, otherwise it has no right to exist.
>
> I think that art should first of all be sincere, and gladden people by the glorification of true beauty. Direct use is only a secondary fruit. To view art solely in terms of its usefulness seems to me extremely one-sided.*[122]

---

*It seems to me, after what has been said above, that Lu Hsün's attitude is not a jot more "materialistic." He continues to emphasize individual genius and still insists on the "uselessness" of art.—C.J.A.

Here the theory of the independent value of art set forth in the 1907-08 articles seems to have been developed and made more precise.

Lu Hsün flatly rejects the nihilistic approach to cultural tradition[123] and at the same time dreams of a special platform for modern art where new plays and musical works would not be confused with the old.[124] He attaches special importance to promulgating literature.

> It is necessary to convene meetings of writers and scholars to discuss national literature, award prizes to the best works, and assist in their popularization. In these meetings it would be determined which famous foreign works ought to be translated into Chinese.... It is necessary to establish a society for the study of the national literature, to collect from all over songs, proverbs, legends, tales, and so forth, clarify their meaning and explain their idiosyncrasies, since, being highly developed, they can contribute to public enlightenment.[125]

This passage, and the "Proposal" as a whole, show that while criticizing contemporary views on art and advancing his own theories, Lu Hsün still believed in the good intentions of the Republican authorities and for a time even tried to speak on their behalf. But reality shattered his dreams. An entry in Lu Hsün's diary dated June 21, 1912, mentions that his lectures in the Ministry of Education's summer lecture series "were attended by a grand total of thirty people, five or six of whom left in the middle." On July 5 he writes: "All of the lecturers have asked for leave, not one of the participants has remained either; (I too) had to return (home)." And finally on July 12: "Found out that in the final analysis it was the Providional Committee on Education that abolished aesthetic education.... Damned swine, dogs!"[126] As we see, the writer's diary, with all its laconicism, sometimes conveys quite clearly not only the surrounding circumstances but the author's feelings as well.

The "years of silence" (1914—early 1918)

These are the four years in Lu Hsün's life that have been studied least. Some facts are yet to be discovered, but as a whole this period probably can be called the "years of silence," as suggested by Wang Shih-ching and L. D. Pozdneeva.[127] After the defeat of the 1911-13 revolution many progressive Chinese writers continued to work on the staff of the Republic (Hsia Tseng-yu, Tseng P'u) or, leaving the political scene, plunged into deep pessimism (Su Man-shu). Lu Hsün stayed in the Ministry of Education, though he too became disheartened and everywhere resisted the "new" order. After the revolution Lu Hsün apparently did nothing for the Republican Party, which he had joined in 1912. To protest openly was unthinkable. The spies of Yüan Shih-k'ai kept a close watch on all dissenters. So Lu Hsün made use of his involuntary seclusion to collect imprints from ancient monuments and Buddhist books and to study ancient Chinese literature and popular tales seriously.

Lu Hsün also maintained a definite interest in foreign literature and aesthetics. He ordered and received from Japan (in Japanese, English, and German) the works of Dostoevsky, Chekhov, Kuprin, Gorky, Sienkiewicz; stories by Polish writers; the books *Ideological Currents and the Literature of Contemporary Russia, An Introduction to the Study of European and American Literature, On Literary Trends*, and so forth.[128] He also became acquainted with the Chinese translations of Sienkiewicz, Wells, and other European writers.[129] Some of these translations he helped to publish, and later, if they were successful, he assisted in their popularization.[130] From 1914 to 1916 Lu Hsün again tried to publish A. K. Tolstoy's novel *Prince Serebryany*, but he was unsuccessful, apparently because this novel had already been translated by Lin Shu. First the new translation, furnished with Lu Hsün's preface and a cover letter, was declined by the publisher "Chung-hua shu-chü," and later it was lost in the editorial office of some newspaper.[131]

The revolutionary romanticists, about whom Lu Hsün was so enthusiastic in the article "On the Power of Demoniacal Poetry," he "neglected . . . after the proclamation of the Republic,"[132] partly because he had shifted to a realistic position and partly because in those years he was in general extremely depressed. Of course "Notes on Literature" (*Wen-i tsa-hua*), published in 1914, is devoted to one of the greatest romantics, Heinrich Heine; but in the first place, Lu Hsün uses his old translations; secondly, he only discusses Heine's love poems; and thirdly, he focuses primarily on their form. "The German poet Heine knew how to express profound thoughts in simple language, achieving clarity and sonority in his choice of words, and beauty and naturalness in sentence constructions. None of his imitators could compare with him. Once I translated several of his verses and now I am including two of them."[133] Considering the censorship, it would have been difficult for Lu Hsün at this time to turn his attention to Heine's satirical and insurgent poetry.

On June 3, 1914, Lu Hsün wrote an article "On Foreign Literature" (*I yü wen t'an*) and the following day he sent it to the journal *Common Talk* (*Yung-yen*),[134] but nothing further is known about this article. Possibly it was too pointed for the journal, whose chief editor was Liang Ch'i-ch'ao; or perhaps *Common Talk*, like many other periodicals during those years of reaction, was promptly shut down.[135] In the summer of 1917 a three-volume series of *European and American Short Stories*, compiled by a well-known early twentieth-century translator and member of the Southern Society, Chou Shou-chüan, was sent to the Ministry of Education for examination, and Lu Hsün was assigned the job of reviewing it. This was almost the first time the writer had a book to evaluate, rather than some "incoming" or "outgoing" trivia, and although Lu Hsün could not agree with many of the translator's theories, he gave the work a very high evaluation, which is to say, he made use of the Ministry's seal to encourage the popularization of progressive foreign literature. Lu Hsün approved of including in the collection "other writers" besides Western European and American authors, and he expressed the hope that the translator would continue his work.[136] "Other writers" apparently meant the writers of Eastern Europe, toward whom Lu Hsün was, as before, sympathetic.

Lu Hsün hardly mentions contemporary Chinese literature at all in this period. True, in 1916 he did rejoice over the news that the *Works of Chang Ping-lin*[137] were to be published. And from September 15, 1915, to February 4, 1917, he took part in the work of the Society for the Promotion of National Learning (Kuo-hsüeh chen-ch'i she), including its prose section.[138] Nevertheless, other than obscure references, the diary devotes only a few words to this, and the same is true for entries apropos of lectures on aesthetic education.

The diary remains as Lu Hsün's one constant "interlocutor" in the years 1914 to 1917. Of course it cannot be included among his creative works without some reservations, but it did to some extent anticipate Lu Hsün's later publicism and unquestionably played a role in strengthening the writer's views on realism. Typical entries for the years 1912 and 1913 still include quite a few straightforward comments, a characteristic of the literature of enlightenment, although in the years 1914 to 1917 this technique is supplanted by more subtle devices—understatement, and a wealth of synonyms. Although the magnificent landscape descriptions of the years 1912 and 1913[139] disappear in the years 1914 to 1917, the stylistic richness of the classical Chinese language is, nevertheless, sustained.

The extremely laconic style of the diary could be interpreted as one more manifestation of Lu Hsün's polemic with nineteenth- and early twentieth-century writers. "Chinese authors invariably value brevity and simplicity in diaries," writes Hu Ping. "This has always been the case, beginning with Huang T'ing-chien's[140] *Family Chronicle from the Region of I-chou* and ending with T'an Hsien's[141] *Diary from the Hall of Rebirth*. As for the *Diary from the Hall of the Extraordinary* by Li Tz'u-ming, who wanted to transform the diary into a literary composition and exerted every effort to make it flourish, that is in essence an entirely different diary form."[142] Lu Hsün accepted the traditional method for composing a diary developed by T'an Hsien, and rejected that advanced by Li Tz'u-ming in the nineteenth century. The laconic, restrained form of the diary was apparently a reaction against the blatantly verbose style of the philosophes and was in accord with Lu Hsün's psychological state in the years 1914 to 1917. The chief characteristic of the diary at this time is not angry exposure but a caustic irony often hidden behind an exterior imperturbability. The entry for January 5, 1941, may serve as an example: "At nine in the morning a meeting with tea and conversation was arranged at the Ministry. There was tea, but no conversation, and the biscuits were as hard as stone. We sat down awhile and then dispersed."[143]

If Lu Hsün sharply attacked the militaristic government in 1912 and 1913, then General Chang Hsün's attempt to restore the monarchy in July of 1917 is recorded in the diary almost without comment. In 1913 Lu Hsün actively resented his depressed mood, but in 1917 he is simply bitter over his loneliness and loss of the sense of time: "According to the old calendar today is New Year's Eve. In the evening I sat alone and copied inscriptions from monuments. There was absolutely no sensation that the year had passed."[144] The blackest year for Lu Hsün, however, was 1916, when President Yüan Shih-k'ai finally trampled on Republican freedoms and proclaimed himself emperor. As far as Chang Hsün's restoration is concerned, it did help, to a certain extent, to reawaken the writer. Progressive social circles were outraged and many realized that it was no longer possible to go on like this. No sooner had Lu Hsün heard the news of the restoration than he took his first energetic step after the "years of silence." He handed in his resignation and only returned to the Ministry after the putsch of Chang Hsün was put down.

In late 1916, following the anti-Yüan Shih-k'ai movement, sometimes called the "third revolution," attempts were being made to revitalize the national literature. The journal *New Youth* (*Hsin ch'ing-nien*) led the struggle for "literary reform" and, soon thereafter, for "literary revolution." This journal started to come out in September 1915 and was from the very beginning antagonistic to the government. Before May 1918, when Lu Hsün first joined the journal, *New Youth* carried a number of lampoons against K'ang Yu-wei, who suggested making Confucianism the State religion; an article on the February revolution in Russia; one of the first Chinese works on European materialistic philosophy; and so forth.[145] By 1917 works of a more traditional nature (Su Man-shu's short story "Tale of the Broken Hairpin," the poetry of Hsieh Wu-liang) began to be replaced by newer ones written in the colloquial language (the poems of Hu Shih, Shen Yin-mo, Liu Fu, and Ch'en Tu-hsiu). In addition, *New Youth* actively promulgated foreign literature. From September 1915 to May 1918 the magazine published the tales of Turgenev, the plays of Wilde, the short stories of Maupassant and Kuprin, the poems of Tagore, articles on contemporary European literature, patriotic poetry from Ireland, Byron, Tolstoy, Dostoevsky, and many others. Apparently Lu Hsün did read some of these articles. He knew, for example, that one of his works, *Short Stories from Abroad*, was being exploited by supporters of the 'literary revolution." The critic Ch'ien Hsüan-t'ung, aware of the progressive nature of the collection, listed it among several older Chinese translations that ought to be read,[146] but the poet Liu Fu regarded it as an extremely archaic work, proof of the acute need for a transition to the colloquial.[147]

The theoretical basis for "literary revolution" was laid down by Hu Shih and Ch'en Tu-hsiu, people of very diverse fortunes who met equally infamous fates. Even at the stage when they approached a number of problems from a progressive point of view, they were still quite contradictory. Their appeals for a rejuvenation of literature[148] remained, to a large extent, appeals. It is not surprising, therefore, that for some time Lu Hsün stood on the sidelines in the debate over "literary revolution." Only when *New Youth* implemented an additional phase of its program, shifting to the colloquial language in articles as well as in poetry (January 1918), did Lu Hsün become interested in the journal. From then on the writer regularly distributed *New Youth* among his friends.[149]

Lu Hsün's interest in the journal was encouraged by Ch'ien Hsüan-t'ung, who once attended Chang Ping-lin's lectures with him, and who now became, if not the most influential, at least the most radical adherent of "literary revolution." It was Ch'ien Hsüan-t'ung who began to correspond for *New Youth* in the colloquial language and who ardently appealed that others do likewise.[150] At the time Ch'en Tu-hsiu was convinced that it was still too early for a complete transition to the colloquial,[151] but after several months he too bowed to the progressive trend.

Ch'ien Hsüan-t'ung exercised a benign influence on the journal, though he was not always just in his opinions. Like other radicals, he was at times inclined to extremes.[152] But even so, Ch'ien Hsüan-t'ung ought to be regarded as the most progressive activist in the literary "revolution" prior to 1919. For us, his friendship with Lu Hsün is especially interesting, as well as his conception of the development of Chinese literature, comparable to the view Lu Hsün later held. Curiously, in his early works on this theme Ch'ien Hsüan-t'ung's views on contemporary Chinese literature (Lin Shu, Liang Ch'i-ch'ao, Li Pao-chia, Wu Wo-yao, and others) were very mild, though in the course of his debate with Hu Shih and Ch'en Tu-hsiu, who tended to exaggerate the importance of their predecessors, his attitude toward nineteenth- and early twentieth-century writers became noticeably more critical,[153] something similar to what happened to Lu Hsün later on.

Ch'ien Hsüan-t'ung's influence on Lu Hsün is beyond question, and Lu Hsün's influence on Ch'ien Hsüan-t'ung is equally undebatable. Since Lu Hsün and Ch'ien Hsüan-t'ung often met and had long conversations together, it is not impossible that one or the other idea published by Ch'ien Hsüan-t'ung in the pages of *New Youth* did, in fact belong to Lu Hsün.[154] "Sometimes my old friend Chin Hsin-yi[155] came over to shoot the breeze," recalls the writer of Ch'ien Hsüan-t'ung:

> Placing his large briefcase on the broken table and removing his robe, he

would sit down opposite me....

"What's the use of copying this?"[156] he inquired one evening, paging through my manuscript.

"No use."

"Then, what's the sense of it?"

"No sense."

"Why don't you write something..."

I knew what he meant. At the time he and his friends were publishing the journal *New Youth*, but the society had met neither with approval nor disapproval. In truth, they were suffering from loneliness.

"Let us imagine," I observed, "that in an iron cell without doors and windows, a cell that is impossible to break down, many people are sound asleep. Death awaits them; but they will depart from this life in oblivion, without any death pangs. Would your conscience allow you to let out a cry and awaken the more sensitive ones so that these unfortunates would have to face the anguish of an inevitable end?"

"But if some are already awake, you can't maintain that breaking down the cell is an impossibility."

"Yes, that's true," I thought. "Regardless of my convictions, I cannot renounce my hopes. They belong to the future...." Finally I agreed to write, and that's how my "Diary of a Madman" made its appearance.[157]

That provocative short story in the vernacular, which shattered traditional ethics and was written under the influence of Gogol (who wrote a story with the same title), ushered in a new era of modern Chinese literature. Needless to say, Lu Hsün was more prepared for such a step than might appear from this modest account of his conversation with Ch'ien Hsüan-t'ung.

On close inspection Lu Hsün's "years of silence" shrink from six[158] to four (late 1914 to early 1918), but one must not forget that these years played an important role in the writer's development. As Ou-yang Fan-hai rightly observes, "Lu Hsün himself did not realize that his silence had a positive side. Gradually the writer learned to look at the world with detachment [literally, 'with cold eyes'—C.J.A.]. As he grew more demanding and began to understand more deeply what was happening around him, this inculcated in him the habit of seeing the truth behind every act, no matter how noble it might seem."[159] It is precisely this pointed criticism coupled with gentleness and humanity that we now value in Lu Hsün.

CHAPTER II

A Caustic Sense of Values (1918-36)

This chapter will analyze Lu Hsün's statements regarding various genres of nineteenth- and early twentieth-century Chinese literature; the problem of tradition versus innovation—the concrete relationship between his art and this literature—will be examined in the final chapter. In the twenties and thirties Lu Hsün continues to treat his predecessors very sternly, although now this sternness is more for the sake of argument and is more often coupled with objective comments.

Essays and poetry

I have combined such diverse types of literature because the majority of Chinese publicists were poets, and also because after the May Fourth Movement essays and poems in the classical style were usually contrasted with fiction and drama in the colloquial. Within the category of *wen-yen* literature there were various schools, and Lu Hsün, naturally, reacted differently toward each of them. Though the writer was familiar with the orthodox literature of the nineteenth and early twentieth centuries (the essays of the T'ung-ch'eng School, "Sung-style" poetry, etc.), he hardly ever mentioned it. He simply refused to consider such things as literature. In one of his 1925 articles, for example, he quotes the poetry of a certain Ho Shih (1816-72) and observes that, by his standards, the man was no poet at all.[1] Elsewhere Lu Hsün scornfully relates how the Japanese aggressors tried to foist off on China an "outstanding writer" like Jao Han-hsien, who in the early years of the Republic wrote telegrams to President Li Yüan-hung in "parallel prose."[2] Only in one instance, it seems, did a line from the work of an orthodox nineteenth-century essayist prove useful to Lu Hsün, although in its original context the phrase was in *praise* of antiquity. Lu Hsün changed Tseng Kuo-fan's saying "It was but yesterday that the ancients died" into the absurd aphorism "It seems like only yesterday that rich minds died," alluding to the degeneration of the Kuomintang.[3]

Welcoming the female students' rejection of the barbarous custom of breast binding* (1927), Lu Hsün ridiculed the poet Fan Tseng-hsiang [1833-1916] who, following the example of a certain emperor [Ming Huang—C.J.A.], enthusiastically compared a concubine's breast to a euryale seed. Once this is known, the caustic nature of Lu Hsün's remarks becomes apparent.

> Some people regret that there was no Fan Tseng-hsiang to draw up this regulation. In public documents one does not see expressions like "the flesh of the euryale," but without them it is extremely difficult to satisfy the appetites of scholars and literati.[4]

A single satirical blow demolishes an absurd ideal of beauty, the poet who extolls this ideal, and the reactionary literati of the twenties, who were not too different from Fan Tseng-hsiang.

Lu Hsün mentions Fan Tseng-hsiang a second time in 1932 when he exposes those conservatives who connive for a reputation as liberals yet fight for what is outmoded. "After the revolution everyone began to wear foreign clothes because they looked forward to change.... One such person reproached old man Fan Tseng-hsiang (should be Wang K'ai-yun—V.S.) for wearing a Manchu gown. 'And what kind of a suit are you wearing?' inquired Fan Tseng-hsiang. 'A foreign one,' answered the youth. 'So am I!' replied Fan."[5]

Of all the works of traditional nineteenth- and early twentieth-century Chinese literature, Lu Hsün, as in his younger days, paid most attention to the diary of Li Tz'u-ming [1830-94]. In one 1926 article Lu Hsün says that the author of the *Diary from the Hall of the Extraordinary* (*Yüeh-man-t'ang jih-chi*) included everything from the edicts of the gentry to the squabbles between scholars. "Although it does not resemble orthodox diaries," ob-

---

*Even here Lu Hsün has some reservations. He goes on to say that merely to oppose breast binding is useless. "First we must change popular ideas and have less inhibitions about breasts!" See *Selected Works* (English), II, 334-336.—C.J.A.

serves Lu Hsün, "it would do no harm to learn a lesson from it if ... you wanted to say something about someone but were afraid of doing so."[6] A year later the writer was even more caustic in his remarks,[7] but he did not lose interest in Li Tz'u-ming, and just prior to his death he requested that someone buy him the *Supplement to the Diary of the Hall of the Extraordinary*.[8]

Wang Kuo-wei [1877-1927], one of the first to turn to the study of Western aesthetics and the genres of the "common" folk, i.e., drama and *tz'u* poetry, stands midway between orthodox and reformed literature of the early twentieth century. His historical works are of unquestionable value, and Lu Hsün extolled some of them[9] in an attempt to distinguish Wang Kuo-wei from orthodox writers. "Wang Kuo-wei was a simple man who invested himself and his faith in the emperor.... Nevertheless, because of his naïveté, he often had to play the role of the ham in the now widely advertised *sandwiches*."[10] It is possible that Wang Kuo-wei's works on aesthetics had an influence on Lu Hsün, but Kuo Mo-jo's comparison of these two writers seems unconvincing. One cannot compare incomparably great figures, even though in reality individual facts in the biographies of Lu Hsün and Wang Kuo-wei (a difficult childhood, study in Japan, a rapid transition from natural science to literature, many years of working in the field of education, etc.) are similar. And is it worth the effort to reach the obvious conclusion that "Lu Hsün moved forward with his era, whereas Wang Kuo-wei stopped halfway and fell prey to it"?[11]

Lu Hsün made a number of important comments about the works of the reformers. In a conversation with T'ang T'ao, for example, he praised the "seven-word poetry" of the first poet-patriot of the nineteenth century, Kung Tzu-chen [1792-1841],[12] who by his radical and innovative articles exerted some influence on Lu Hsün's own essays.[13] The writer was well aware that the Reform Movement was a progressive step in China's development. "At first you were accused of belonging to K'ang Yu-wei's party and later of belonging to a revolutionary one,"[14] he says, doing justice to K'ang Yu-wei [1858-1927], who "headed the group that memorialized the throne and became the chief figure in the Hundred Days' Reform of 1898."[15] At the same time, however, the writer points out the limitedness of K'ang Yu-wei's programs, practically equating them to his "Manchu bureaucracy," which "also intended to carry out reforms."[16] Though skillful in ridiculing vain attempts to imitate the West, here Lu Hsün does not show a great deal of historical objectivity:

> At the end of the Manchu dynasty when "reforms" were contemplated, "cadres" had to be sent abroad to study the local customs. Reading the memoirs of these cadres, we discover just what it was that struck them most—a chess match in some hotel or other between wax figurines and human beings. But best of all are those by the sage from the district of Nanhai, K'ang Yu-wei. After traveling through eleven countries and landing in the Balkans, he finally realized the reason for the frequent "murders" of sovereigns abroad—the walls of the palaces there were too low.[17]

In assessing the career and creativity of Liang Ch'i-ch'ao [1873-1929], another leader of the reformers, Lu Hsün is just as impulsive (at one moment following strict logic and at another giving way to emotion). He mentions Liang Ch'i-ch'ao's book *A Method of Reading Japanese Texts in Chinese* as a definite landmark in the development of the Chinese language and draws upon Liang Ch'i-ch'ao's experience to support the principle of precise translation.

> To cure an illness one must patiently swallow bitter pills. To think in the words of a foreign tongue—ancient, modern, far or near—is to gradually make them one's own. This is no utopia. Take the Japanese for example. In their language European expressions are a common phenomenon. When Liang Ch'i-ch'ao started to pronounce Japanese words in Chinese, he encountered completely unexpected difficulties.[18]

But more often than not the name of Liang Ch'i-ch'ao appears in an entirely different context. "Ever since a European doctor cut out Liang Ch'i-ch'ao's kidney, the cries of reproach against Western medicine have turned into a storm,"[19] sneers the writer at the vacillation of the reformers' ideals. Ridiculing Liang Ch'i-ch'ao's adherence to Confucianism and questioning the very fact of Confucius' existence,* Lu Hsün recalls that he has only seen the portrait of Confucius three times, once "on the title page of the journal *Public Opinion* which Liang Ch'i-ch'ao published in Yokohama when he was an emigrant in Japan."[20]

This harsh assessment of many of the statements and actions of the reformers was dictated by the conservative role which K'ang Yu-wei and Liang Ch'i-ch'ao played, not at the turn of the century,

---

*It would have been patently absurd for Lu Hsün to "deny" the existence of Confucius. For the context see the article "Confucius in Modern China," *Selected Works* (English), IV, 175.—C.J.A.

but during the period of the May Fourth Movement. Proof of this can be found in a number of the writer's articles.[21] Later, when the heat of controversy subsided, Lu Hsün had second thoughts about the work of the reformers and some revolutionaries in the period following the 1911-13 revolution. "K'ang Yu-wei will be known forever as the saint of the restoration of the monarchy. Yüan Shih-k'ai wanted Yen Fu to support his ascension to the throne. And Marshal Sun Ch'uan-fang asked Chang Ping-lin to revive the ancient ceremony of pitching arrows."[22] In other words, while condemning K'ang Yu-wei, Yen Fu, and Chang Ping-lin, the writer did not overlook the efforts of reactionaries, who managed to entice to their side some of those who had been progressives in the past.

Lu Hsün does not mention the poetry of K'ang Yu-wei and Liang Ch'i-chao or even that of Huang Tsun-hsien [1848-1905], the most prominent Chinese poet of the nineteenth and early twentieth centuries. As for Hsia Tseng-yu [1865-1924], who promoted a "revolution" in the field of poetry at the end of the nineteenth century, to Lu Hsün he was no more than a colleague in the Ministry of Education and the author of an accusatory *Primer of Chinese History*.[23] Soon after Hsia Tseng-yu forced the employees in his department to offer sacrifices to Confucius (1912), Lu Hsün severed personal relations with him. Then Hsia Tseng-yu, discouraged by the half-heartedness of the revolution, degenerated; and it seems quite likely that it was he who served as the prototype for Mr. N, the hero in Lu Hsün's "Story of Hair" (1920) who loses faith in people and in progress.[24]

Lu Hsün mentions only one composition by a poet-reformer, a powerful poem, and the last but one by T'an Ssu-t'ung [1865-98], whom he ranks, and rightly so, alongside the revolutionary poetess Ch'iu Chin [1875-1907].[25] Nevertheless, Lu Hsün is less interested in the resemblance between the ideologies and fates of the two authors (both were executed by the Manchus) than he is in the archaic form of their verse. While stressing the innovativeness of T'an Ssu-t'ung and Ch'iu Chin (whose works were "not polished enough" to go into official anthologies), Lu Hsün makes it clear that "in modern times" one could write more simply.

During this period [post 1918] Lu Hsün was far more interested in the essays of the revolutionaries than in those of the reformers. For example, he devotes two articles, one speech, and a number of statements to Sun Yat-sen. The writer sympathetically quotes Sun's last will and testament lamenting the fact that revolutionaries have forgotten their leader.[26] And right up until the end of his life Lu Hsün mentions with respect the names of those writers who had fallen in battle against the Manchu yoke—for example Tsou Jung [1885-1905], author of the publicistic work *The Revolutionary Army*. "Poetry and prose (*wen*), which exude pathos and austerity, survive only on paper," writes Lu Hsün, laying it on a bit thick. 'For its role in the subsequent Wu-ch'ang Uprising nothing could rival the brief and direct *Revolutionary Army*, written by its soldier Tsou Jung."[27] Then too, Lu Hsün contributed much to the analysis of the works of his teacher Chang Ping-lin [1868-1936]. The literary critic Sung Yün-pin justly remarks that the short articles "A Few Matters Connected with Chang T'ai-yen" and "Some Recollections of Chang T'ai-yen,"[28] which Lu Hsün wrote just before his own death, are of no less value than any of the "critical biographies" of Chang Pin-lin.[29]

Lu Hsün rated Chang Ping-lin's work prior to the 1911-13 revolution very highly. In a letter to Hsü Shou-shang on September 25, 1936, he recalls how deep an impression the poems which Chang Ping-lin wrote in prison[30] had left on him three decades before, and adds: "Now all of Mr. Ping-lin's poems and his words 'Better death!' (*su szu*) are priceless documents. We should take advantage of the fact that the majority of them are in Peking, collect and publish them as an example to the world, and preserve them for posterity."[31] On the other hand, Lu Hsün did not ignore the weaknesses of Chang Ping-lin, particularly his utopian attempts "to save China through the aid of Buddhism"[32] and the nationalistic ideas which drove him into the arms of reactionaries. It would be unjust, however, to think that in the years between 1910 and 1930 Chang Ping-lin surrendered completely to the reactionaries. The words 'Better death!" which Lu Hsün considered "invaluable," were written by Chang on the wall of his prison cell as early as 1915 in sign of protest against Yüan Shih-k'ai's accession to the throne. In 1926 Chang Ping-lin actually refused[33] to "pitch arrows in a jug with commander Sun Ch'uan-fang." Lu Hsün, however, neglected to mention this, even though it constituted an appreciable shift in Chang Ping-lin's views. Only the general trend was important to him. Even so, Lu Hsün's critical attitude toward his teacher did not prevent him, even in his maturer years, from appropriating several of Chang's ideas, as for example, in the article "It's Hard to be Stupid" (1933).[34]

According to the literary critic Wang Yao, the "Diary of a Madman" was Lu Hsün's "hymn to his predecessors," i.e., Sun Yat-sen and Chang Ping-lin, who were called madmen in the early twentieth century;[35] and this hypothesis is partly borne out by the writer's own reminiscences. In addition, he acknowledged that it was Chang Ping-lin who helped him create the story "Beyond the Frontier."[36]

Of the poets in the Southern Society Lu Hsün had direct contact with only one, Liu Ya-tzu [1887-1958]. They met in the late twenties and early thirties and even exchanged messages in verse.[37] The value of Su Man-shu's [1884-1918] poetry and prose, in Lu Hsün's mind, was confined to the early years of the twentieth century.[38] But this appraisal is unjustified. His reflections on why the first revolutionary poets were unable to sustain their progressive views are much more accurate.

> There have been instances in China too when writers dreamt of revolution, then sank into silence the minute it arrived. Take the Southern Society, a literary organization that extolled revolution even before the end of the Ch'ing dynasty. The members of this organization grieved over the sufferings of the Chinese and were indignant over the cruelty of the Manchus. They hoped to "resurrect the past," and yet after the formation of the Republic they suddenly fell silent. This happened, I think because what they really had in mind was resurrecting formidable Chinese officials with high hats and wide belts, and life far from justified their hopes. Then they lost interest in everything and discarded their pens.[39]

The writer comments not only on the impracticality of the Southern Society's ideals (China was incapable of a complete renaissance because feudalism and imperialism had sunk their roots too deeply into the country) but on their limitedness (to the Southern Society the dream of a Chinese renaissance meant the rebirth of national feudalism, not a social revolution) as well. Lu Hsün could have made similar remarks about his own career in the years from 1907 to 1917; and yet, unlike the majority of the members of the Southern Society, he was able to continue along the path of revolution.

Translations

During the twenties and thirties Lu Hsün quite often cited the lessons learned by earlier translators to reassert the principle of precise translation and to promulgate Russian and Soviet literature. "Once we read of the marvelous 'Adventures of Sherlock Holmes' in *Current Affairs*, a periodical published by Liang Ch'i-ch'ao," recalls the writer. "And later, thanks to the magazine *New Fiction*, we were entertained by many unusual things in science-fiction novels like Jules Verne's *Twenty Thousand Leagues Under the Sea*.[40] Lin Shu translated many works by H. Rider Haggard, and it was from him that we learned of the fragility of London's young ladies and the strange habits of African savages."[41] Lu Hsün mentions these things with a touch of irony, but only because he looks at the problem from an already achieved vantage point. We must not forget how much of an educational role the works of Chinese translators played in the late nineteenth and early twentieth centuries.

Even in his main work, "The True Story of Ah Q," Lu Hsün indulges in irony at the expense of Lin Shu [1881-1924]. "In short, this is more of a genealogy," he writes, "but owing to its content and the coarseness of my style, which is like *the language of carters and street vendors* (italics mine—V.S.), I dare not bestow on it such a title."[42] It was for these words, in opposition to a literary language intelligible to all, that Lin Shu, sadly, became famous during the May Fourth Movement of 1919. Lu Hsün also mentions with contempt the fantastic tales of "Ching-sheng the Giant" and "The Nightmare," in which Lin Shu predicted the failure of the "literary revolution."[43] Nevertheless, already in the 1928 and 1933 articles we observe a more relaxed attitude toward this, the first prolific translator of foreign literature. Lu Hsün believes that the time has come to evaluate both the merits and the mistakes of Lin Shu objectively.[44] "At present," says Lu Hsün, "we have only one version of *Don Quixote*—the first half of the novel, translated by Lin Shu into the classical language and entitled *The Tale of a Mad Knight*; but even that is abridged."[45] There is a note of dissatisfaction in these words, but the fact remains that Lin Shu's translation, with all of its inadequacies, went unreplaced in China for over two decades.

Despising the dime novel, Lu Hsün feels the necessity of distinguishing it from certain translations, particularly those of Lin Shu:

> After all, the literature of the talented scholar and the delicate beauty produced *A Short Biography of Joan* (H. Rider Haggard's *Joan Haste*, a translation from the English), a work that upset an entire generation. Yet

only the first part was published.⁴⁶ The translator claimed that he saw the book in a secondhand bookstore and became very interested in it, but unfortunately he could not find the ending.

As one might expect, the book not only melted the "delicate hearts" of talented youths and beautiful maidens but gained a very wide circulation. Finally it touched Mr. Lin Shu, and he translated it in its entirety, entitling it, as before, *A Short Biography of Joan.*⁴⁷

All of a sudden vile abuse was heaped on Lin Shu. The first translator declared that Lin Shu should not have translated the novel in its entirety, because in so doing he had denigrated the image of Joan and upset the readers. As a result, everyone found out that the reason the first edition only consisted of one volume was not because the original was incomplete, but because in the second half Joan gave birth to an illegitimate child.⁴⁸

Given a choice between bigotry and sentimentality, Lu Hsün sides with Lin Shu; but on the whole he was rather cool toward him, not at all as warm as toward another well-known translator of that time, Yen Fu [1853-1921]. Part of the reason for this is that Yen Fu was the first to actually acquaint China with foreign scientific accomplishments, and Lu Hsün, as we know, had a lifelong interest in the natural sciences and sociology. Moreover, Yen Fu did not promote literature for entertainment, and this won favor in Lu Hsün's eyes by comparison with Lin Shu.

The writer's sympathies toward Yen Fu become apparent from the following, seemingly insignificant remarks:

Once I came across a curious story in one of Yen Fu's works. The title of the work and the original text have already escaped my memory, but it went something like this: "On the streets of Peking you can see youngsters who run between carriage wheels and horses' hooves. I am always afraid that they will be maimed, and I am terrified for their future..."

I too share Yen Fu's anxiety and respect the fact that it was he who gave us Huxley's *Evolution and Ethics.* He was one of the most perspicacious men of late nineteenth-century China.⁴⁹

Yen Fu attracted the writer simply as a human being, by his humaneness. But the main reason for Lu Hsün's interest in Yen Fu was, of course, the definite similarity in their literary theories. Whereas Lin Shu translated orally, line by line, and very freely at that, Yen Fu was thoroughly familiar with the English language and strove for accuracy. When the critic Ch'ü Ch'iu-po took an oversimplified view of Yen Fu's work ("the broad masses and the youth of China only chuckle at him"),⁵⁰ Lu Hsün stood behind the translator and defended his archaic style on the basis of the situation that prevailed in China during the late nineteenth and early twentieth centuries.[51] Nevertheless, the writer does not absolve the translator himself of responsibility and is aware of the unacceptability of the majority of his findings for ensuing generations. Such was the case, for example, with Yen Fu's attempt to translate scientific terms by the descriptive method, so that they were intelligible but inaccurate. On the other hand, sometimes Yen Fu transliterated foreign concepts, and this pleased Lu Hsün, even though he selected characters that were too obscure.[52]

In summarizing his observations on early translations, Lu Hsün maintains that the efforts of twentieth-century Chinese literati produced very insignificant results. The Chinese reader still was not familiar with the foreign classics, even Shakespeare. "Yen Fu mentions 'Ti-ssu-p'ei-erh' and leaves it at that. Liang Ch'i-ch'ao starts talking about 'Sha-shih-pi-ya'[53] and no one pays any attention either."[54] Nevertheless, although Lu Hsün justifiably condemns both the timidity of the translators and the passivity of society, Lin Shu, who translated Charles Lamb's versions of Shakespeare's plays, did achieve some success in popularizing the playwright's works. Yen Fu, on the other hand, did not take the most progressive stand on questions of translation. Some contemporaries placed greater emphasis on the "faithfulness" of the translation than did Yen Fu, who sometimes substituted "elegance."[55] In the translation of scientific terminology, Liang Ch'i-ch'ao, who advocated the use of ready-made Japanese terms, turned out to be considerably more far-sighted.[56]

Attempting to widen this opposition between Yen Fu and Lin Shu initiated by Lu Hsün, the authors of *A Brief History of Chinese Translations* call one a "reformer" and the other a "reactionary,"[57] though the biographies of the translators provide no basis for such a crude demarcation (though earlier both Yen Fu and Lin Shu were allied with the reformers, later both became alienated from them). Lu Hsün's comparison should be understood in a different light, namely, that Lin Shu's translations had a greater impact on literature, Lu Hsün's own works included, than did the translations of Yen Fu.

Drama

In his mature years Lu Hsün adopted a new, and even somewhat unexpected, approach to nineteenth- and twentieth-century Chinese drama. While recognizing the merits of popular performances, he rejected almost completely the "drama of the capital" [Peking opera—C.J.A.], which to this very day remains the primary form of classical theater. Generally speaking, however, Chinese researchers omit Lu Hsün's most pointed comments on the national theater.[58] They ridicule the bourgeois writers Hu Shih and Chou Tso-jen for their negative attitude toward Peking opera[59] while neglecting to mention that on the question at issue Lu Hsün adopted a similar view. Ou-yang Fan-hai, on the other hand, approaches the problem from a different perspective. He characterizes the writer's reaction to Peking opera as strange, original, and uncompromising —the last being a trait which he considers typical of Lu Hsün in general.[60]

"Looking back over the past twenty years," writes Lu Hsün in 1922, "it appears that there were only two occasions on which I saw a Chinese theatrical performance.[61] During the first ten years I didn't go to them in general because they didn't hold any interest for me; and besides, there was no opportunity. Both times that I did see a Chinese play it was during the second decade, but each time I went away without discovering anything extraordinary."[62] In the short story "The Village Opera," from which this passage is quoted, Lu Hsün creates a brilliant satire on the traditional theater, aimed primarily at the professional theater of the early twentieth century, or to be more precise, Peking opera (as indicated by the spectacles depicted in the story). The writer ridicules the monotony and lifelessness of the performance, the hackneyed themes, the unintelligible language, the primitive music, and other weaknesses of the traditional drama. Lu Hsün's antagonism toward this art form is so great that he displays indifference* toward Kung Yün-fu, an outstanding actor of the late nineteenth and early twentieth centuries, and he leaves without waiting for another outstanding actor of the time, T'an Hsin-p'ei.

At first, a similar problem arose in Lu Hsün's relationship with world-famous master of Peking opera Mei Lan-fang [1894-1961]. In 1926, for example, he reports: "A few days ago I unexpectedly heard the voice of the 'actor' Mei Lan-fang—on a phonograph, of course; and my eardrum became so painful that it seemed as if

---

*Generally speaking, Semanov equates Lu Hsün with the first-person narrator in his stories.—C.J.A.

someone were trying to perforate it with a thick, blunt needle."[63] From a 1934 article it is clear that Lu Hsün regarded Mei Lan-fang as a spokesman for aristocratic art, or more likely, a popular favorite exploited by the upper crust.[64] The writer had a similar view of Peking opera as a whole. In this same year, however, he began to investigate the historical background and the details of Chinese theatrical make up; and even though his labors were in response to an article devoted to Mei Lan-fang's tours in the U.S.S.R.,[65] he did not have a single word of reproach for the actor. Evidently the warm reception of Soviet audiences to the Peking opera had something to do with this.

Read "The Village Opera" and you will be convinced that the author of this story will never again go to the professional theater. But Lu Hsün behaved otherwise; and two years later he even donated a sizable sum for staging classical plays.[66] Lu Hsün was very lively and contradictory by nature. His mistakes sometimes turned out to be not so much mistakes, but rather the seeds of new, productive ideas. The basic problem was how to develop these ideas—whether to attempt to perfect Peking opera, or to cram it full of ultramodern ideas, thereby destroying the genre itself.

The author of "The Village Opera" contrasts the officially recognized theater with a popular pageant, "a marvelous spectacle" he saw in "the remote past."[67] Once again, it does no harm to mention that in this story hyperbole is not at all an impossibility, and that when Lu Hsün saw the two types of opera, it was in different years and in different states of mind. In the first instance we have a boy, ecstatic over the fact that they have allowed him to attend the village festival. The performance itself is hardly more important than the journey on the boat or the "hunt" in the bean field. The spectator of the Peking opera, however, is already a man, one who has come to despise the pseudo-art of the feudal era. He is tormented by the thought of executions, and even innocent rows of theater seats seem like racks of torture. Lu Hsün [i.e., the narrator—C.J.A] is annoyed by various trivialities connected with the Peking opera: the price of the tickets is too high; a noted actor is deliberately late; the crowd, yearning to gape at the spectacle, throngs around the entrance. "It is clear," comments the critic Yen Chia-yen, "that the writer's disgust was aroused not by the opera itself, but by the sickening vulgar social atmosphere surrounding it. Likewise, the lyrical mood of the country performance, which the author saw in childhood, is not brought about by any special merit of the country theater (even at the time the author was not very enthusiastic about the old man with the 'iron head' who could turn eighty-four somersaults in a row), but primarily by the simplicity and amicability of the peasants."[68]

Nevertheless, I believe that the main reason for Lu Hsün's attitude lies in the very nature of local and Peking opera itself, and one of his 1933 articles testifies to this. "At the beginning of the reign of Kuang Hsü in the Ch'ing dynasty [1874]," recalls Lu Hsün, "there was an opera company in my hometown which called itself the Jade Company but did not live up to its name, for it gave such poor performances that no one wanted to see them. The countryfolk, who are no whit inferior to great men of letters, made up a song about it:

>Above, the actors staged a play;
>Below, the audience ran away;
>They bolted doors to make them stay,
>But then the people climbed the wall,
>Till not a soul was left at all,
>Just poles the pedlars had let fall."[69]

"Local theater" (*ti-fang hsi*) was actually more progressive than "Peking" opera. It was more natural in its style of performance and more often imbued with social and domestic themes. The arias of the local theater were written in the respective dialects and were comparatively easy to comprehend.

Lu Hsün could make many important observations about the popular Chinese theater (and particularly about the theater of the Shaohsing region where he was born) precisely because he endeavored to look at Peking opera through the eyes of simple folk. The writer even prefers popular mystery plays over Peking opera, and he emphasizes (though not without irony) their liveliness, ingenuousness, and humanity.[70] Often these mystery plays had a democratic flavor. For example, one of the plays, which Lu Hsün describes, depicts with great sympathy a young girl who, though yet a child, is given as a "bride" to a strange family. The mother-in-law sells her to a house of prostitution, and there she hangs herself in grief. Another hero of the popular mystery plays, Wu Ch'ang, "snatched souls from among the living."[71] A more somber figure would probably be difficult to imagine. "And yet, why did Wu Ch'ang inspire the people and bring them joy?" inquires the writer, at the same time answering his own question: "Many years of experience have taught them (simple folk—V.S.) that in the world of the living, society alone maintains justice. But this society is so remote that all of their hopes are invested in the world beyond the grave."[72]

References to nineteenth- and early twentieth-century Chinese theater sometimes crop up in Lu Hsün's creative works. For example, the phrase Ah Q sings ("In my hand I am holding a steel mace, and I am going to smite you!") is adapted from the play "The Tiger's Battle with the Dragon," included in the repertoires of both the Peking and the Shaohsing opera companies.[73] In the play these words are spoken by a youth who takes revenge against a cruel monarch for killing his father. Here Lu Hsün makes them sound satiric rather than pathetic, but at times the writer borrows his satire directly from the Shaohsing opera.[74]

Occasionally Lu Hsün singles out folk motifs in popular plays and comments ironically on their sense of light-hearted amusement. "Since the performance is staged in the village, you won't, thank Heaven, find plays like 'The Emperor Ch'ien Lung Goes South' (a blatantly orthodox production about a Manchu ruler—V.S.). Usually they stage 'The Princess Pursues the Barbarians' or 'Hsüeh Jen-kuei Finds Himself a Bride' (i.e., historic or adventuristic plays—V.S.) in which the heroines are called 'generals.' Two long feathers from a pheasant's tail stick out of their heads and in their hands are two swords or a double-edged lance. When the 'generals' come out on stage, the spectators begin to watch even more intently. Knowing full well that all this is for the sake of frivolous comedy, they still strain their attention."[75] Essentially, therefore, the author *does* take a critical view of local drama in "The Village Opera" (in the depiction of the popular play here there are several additional things like deafening gongs and drums), and yet researchers, as a rule, fail to mention how the humorous description of the local opera pales before the devastating portrayal of the Peking opera.

Lu Hsün hardly mentions the "colloquial drama" of the early twentieth century. Only in one 1933 article, speaking of the degeneration of humor into idle slapstick, does he remark in passing that "... this is precisely how the 'new' plays, having once 'seen the light,' were turned into 'civilized' drama."[76] The first Europeanized plays in the colloquial language were called "new plays" (*hsin-*

hsi or *hsin-chü*). They were also called "civilized drama' (*wen-ming hsi*); but with the extension of the term "colloquial drama" (*hua-chü*) the concept of "civilized drama" was narrowed and came to apply solely to the entertainment in the Shanghai theaters "The Great World," "The New World," and others. It is in this last sense that Lu Hsün employs the term "civilized drama," without disclaiming the value of earlier colloquial drama.

It is common knowledge that after 1919 radicals in China "took a very harsh view of traditional theater," considering it feudal and contradictory to science, while the new drama was hailed as "democratic, scientific art."[77] Lu Hsün was never so apologetic toward Europeanized theater and, by the same token, avoided complete nihilism in his attitude toward traditional drama, partly because he divided it (albeit with too much oversimplification) into two genres, popular and orthodox.

Fiction

The writer is more detailed in his analysis of nineteenth- and early twentieth-century Chinese prose fiction. In the twenties and thirties Lu Hsün himself was beginning to earn a reputation as a writer, and clarifying his own views of the national heritage certainly did not hamper his progress. Moreover, the lectures he delivered in 1923 and 1924 at the universities of Peking and Sian provided an opportune occasion for such an analysis. Yet not only did these lectures influence the careers of young Chinese prose artists, they also served as an example of the methodology of modern literary criticism.

In his lectures Lu Hsün supports "popular" fiction, but by no means does he place it on an equal footing with "colloquial" literature, arbitrarily singled out from tradition by Hu Shih. He concentrates on those works that are most democratic in nature, which explains not only why he prefers local opera to Peking opera but the earlier novel (from the fourteenth to the eighteenth century) to the later (the nineteenth and early twentieth centuries). Of course, sometimes contradictions, a nihilistic bias, or a lack of important data become apparent, and A Ying is correct in taking exception, for example, to Lu Hsün's jaundiced view of Taiping literature and the novel of exposure, as well as to his other idealistic conclusions.[78]

Of the twenty-eight chapters in *A Brief History of Chinese Fic-*

tion (the lectures in Peking), seven are devoted to the literature of the Manchu era, but the chapters on the satiric novel (*feng-tz'u*) and the novel of manners (*jen-ch'ing*) do not mention a single work of the nineteenth and early twentieth centuries. The analysis of these works is confined to the chapters on imitative prose, "novels used to display the author's erudition," erotic novels [really novels about prostitution, *hsia-hsieh hsiao-shuo*—C.J.A.], novels of adventure and detection, and novels of exposure. Toward the end of *The Historical Development of Chinese Fiction* (the lectures in Sian) the author adopts a fresh approach to the study of the Ch'ing novel. He classifies it into four schools: the imitative novel (*ni-ku*), the satirical novel (*feng-tz'u*), the novel of manners (*jen-ch'ing*), and the adventure novel (*hsia-i*).[79] The erotic novel falls into the category of the novel of manners, the novel of exposure into the category of the satiric novel; novels of adventure and detection are grouped together; and novels of erudition disappear altogether. Such a classification could theoretically have been used to point out the similarity between the novel of manners and the erotic novel, the satiric novel and the novel of exposure, but Lu Hsün uses it mainly to censure nineteenth- and early twentieth-century literature. In the analysis of the writer's views which follows, therefore, I have found it expedient to use the more detailed and exact headings of the *Brief History of Chinese Fiction*.

Lu Hsün begins his analysis of fiction in the period that concerns us with the chapter entitled "Imitations of Tsin and T'ang Tales in the Ch'ing Era and Their Variety" (XXII). Such a chapter is, *per se*, justified, because there are sufficient numbers of imitative works in *every* literature. Moreover, the analysis of previous works provided Lu Hsün with a more natural transition to his lectures on the Manchu era. Yet one can hardly consider the celebrated tales of P'u Sung-ling (seventeenth century) as mere "imitations of Tsin and T'ang novellas,"[80] and it is a stern criticism indeed which characterizes T'u Shen's (1744-1801) *Miscellany Within and Without the Universe* as "quite superficial."[81] From among subsequent novels Lu Hsün selects Chi Yün's (1724-1805) *Notes of Yüeh-wei Hermitage* a work he had known since childhood. The writer is attracted by Chi Yün's rich language and the author's ability to observe not only the details of everyday life but those things that usually go unnoticed.[82]

Lu Hsün is especially fond of the satire in these novels of fantasy. "It required uncommon courage during the Ch'ien Lung

[1736-95] era, when laws were so severe, to direct one's literary efforts against unjust social mores and inane customs. . . . Chi Yün's imitators were unable to master his critical spirit, and they could only understand the more mystical and moralistic side of his art. As a result, almost all representatives of this school slip into didacticism."[83] Lu Hsün, for example, considers the late nineteenth-century writers Wang T'ao and Hsüan Ting as "imitators" of Chi Yün and ironically observes that the number of foxes and spirits in their novels had already decreased in favor of beautiful women.[84] This must imply that the frivolous and fantastic were giving way to the purely erotic. But in reality the Chinese novel followed a more complex line of development. Moreover, it was quite natural that "foxes and spirits" should disappear from the novels of Wang T'ao [1828-90] in particular, since he was a European-educated journalist and a collaborator of the Taipings. Opposition to mysticism has been a characteristic of many enlightened men [*prosvetiteli*], and the Chinese are no exception.

"Novels of Erudition in the Ch'ing Dynasty" (XXV) contains an equal number of pointed critical comments. The very title itself reveals Lu Hsün's central thesis; and this thesis, on the whole, is justified, so long as the discussion revolves around works like Hsia Ching-ch'ü's (second half of the eighteenth century) *A Rustic's Idle Talk* (*Yeh-sou p'u-yen*) or T'u Shen's (late eighteenth to early nineteenth century) *The Book Worm* (*T'an-shih*). But to include Li Ju-chen's (1763-1830) *Flowers in the Mirror* in the same chapter is debatable. Having calculated that discussions of philosophy and literature occupy seven-tenths of the work, Lu Hsün describes *Flowers in the Mirror* as something between a novel and an encyclopedia.[85] Though such a criticism may be more or less natural for the twenties, in more recent works[86] it stands out as an obvious anachronism. Nevertheless, it should be pointed out that Lu Hsün is not only aware of the satirical nature of the novel,[87] he even cites various episodes from it in his own essays. In the article "Murderers of the Present" (1919), for example, he utilizes *Flowers in the Mirror* to ridicule proponents of the archaic classical language who are themselves guilty of distorting it.

> The sad thing is that those gentlemen cannot measure up to the waiter from the Land of Gentility (*chün-tzu kuo*) in *Flowers in the Mirror*, who continually demonstrated his culture by utilizing the classical language to describe two pots of wine or a plate of sweetmeats: "One vessel of wine?

Two vessels? One entrée? Two entrées?" (*Chiu yao i-hu hu, liang-hu hu, ts'ai yao yi-tieh hu, liang-tieh hu*).⁸⁸

In the chapter entitled "Erotic Novels of the Ch'ing Era" (XXVI) Lu Hsün's attitude toward his research remains ultracritical. Novels about love (as a rule completely platonic) and everyday life in the nineteenth century he calls "erotic," and the transition from the fantastic to the depiction of everyday life is interpreted from a purely negative standpoint. Thus, the appearance of fox fairies at first, then singsong girls and actresses, and finally boy actors (*hsiang-ku*)⁸⁹ is attributed solely to the cowardice and corruption of scholars.* Lu Hsün cites Ch'en Sen's** *A Mirror of Theatrical Life* (*P'in-hua pao-chien*, mid-nineteenth century) as an example of this type of fiction and maintains that the idealized heroes Mei Tzu-yü and Tu Ch'in-yen were fabricated by the author, i.e., that the relationship between the scholar and the boy actor, which the author attempts to describe in lyrical tones, is not at all true to life. Supposedly Mei Tzu-yü and Tu Ch'in-yen resemble all the other "talented scholars and delicate beauties" of traditional feudal literature. "The only difference is that the 'beauties' are not women, something that had not yet been described in other works,"⁹⁰ comments Lu Hsün ironically. At the same time, however, Lu Hsün does strive to be objective, and he takes note that structurally ("the close connection between the plot and the central characters"⁹¹) *A Mirror of Theatrical Life* carried on the best tradition of the Chinese novel, Ts'ao Hsüeh-ch'in's *Dream of the Red Chamber*. Some scholars claim that Lu Hsün underemphasized the ideological value of *A Mirror of Theatrical Life*. The literary critic Ch'en Tse-kuang, for example, contends that Ch'en Sen's novel, with all of its inadequacies, "exposes and criticizes" the dissoluteness of the urban aristocracy.⁹²

From *A Mirror of Theatrical Life* the author of the *Brief History* passes on to Wei Hsiu-jen's (1819-74) *The Flower and the Moon* (*Hua yüeh hen*), which uses a double plot line. The young friends

---
*This comment undoubtedly refers to *Brief History* (Yang), p. 337: "There were quarters of ill fame in the Ming dynasty, but scholars were forbidden to frequent them or to hire singsong girls, although they could hire actors. In order, therefore, to keep within the law, officials and scholars often invited actors to their feasts, enjoying their singing, dancing and conversations."—C.J.A.

**In the Yangs' translation the name is rendered Ch'en Sen-shu, incorrectly romanized Chen Shen-shu—C.J.A.

Wei Ch'ih-chu and Han Ho-sheng fall in love with the singsong girls Ch'iu-hen and Ts'ai-ch'iu. Han Ho-sheng's fate turns out happy. He is rewarded with a lofty title for military victories and makes Ts'ai-ch'iu a "concubine [literally, "lady"—C.J.A.] of the first rank." Lu Hsün describes all of this with obvious contempt, and the same can be said of the three-day feast in honor of the occasion. The fate of the other hero, Wei Ch'ih-chu, turns out less fortunate, for he already has a wife and cannot claim Ch'iu-hen as his own. According to Lu Hsün's rather pointed conclusion, the author has, so to speak, a split personality: the fate of Wei Ch'ih-chu reflects the gloomy side of his life, while his dreams of a career are embodied in the more traditional, stilted figure of Han Ho-sheng.[93]

"*The Flower and the Moon* is hardly a precious gem, but if someone wants to reprint the novel ... let him,"[94] remarks Lu Hsün in the article "No Need for 'Corrections'" (1924). Here he reveals an excellent knowledge of the text of *The Flower and the Moon*, and he exposes apologists of traditional culture (in this instance Wang Yüan-fang) in their inept attempts to doctor certain works by adding melodramatic touches to them.

> Ch'iu-hen was tying a silk kerchief on her head ... when suddenly she saw Ch'ih-chu, and suppressing a laugh said, "Just as I thought, you couldn't wait for ten days. But why torment yourself?" "We'll talk about that some other time," laughed Ch'ih-chu.
> Although both of them were depraved, neither as yet felt any great sense of remorse, and so they laughed. But in the corrected edition the smiles in both instances have been replaced by tears. It is hardly appropriate to let the heroes cry the very instant they meet, which is why the tears are, for the most part, worthless and, to be sure, the expression "with quiet tears said" is nonsense.[95]

Lu Hsün, as it were, defends the novel from its interpreters and in so doing acknowledges that the plot and language of the original have ample vitality.

The writer considers Han Pang-ch'ing's (1856-94) novel *Lives of Shanghai Singsong Girls* (*Hai-shang-hua lieh-chuan*) as the highest achievement of nineteenth-century Chinese erotic literature. "Here, also, the gay quarters are described, but not so idealized as in *The Dream of the Green Chamber*.[96] The author more closely approximates reality, showing both the good and bad qualities of the singsong girls."[97] The most notable part of the novel is the tragedy of the brother and sister Chao P'u-chai and Chao Erh-pao, who have come to Shanghai in search of happiness. The former becomes a rickshaw driver,[98] the latter a singsong girl. The novel comes to an abrupt halt with Erh-pao's nightmare, instead of a "grand conclusion" with the traditional happy ending, as in other nineteenth-century novels of manners; and as a result, the novel truly reveals "a slice of life." Lu Hsün is not particularly interested in the exalted love of Erh-pao for young master Shih, because it resembles the traditional affair between a "talented scholar" and a "delicate beauty," but he is moved by the young girl's suffering. "The author shows how the singsong girls have no deep feelings whatsoever for their 'guests,' and although the situation that he depicts is imaginary, it seems real. There is very little exaggeration."[99] *

It is understandable that Lu Hsün does not share the majority of the opinions of his predecessors regarding *Lives of Shanghai Singsong Girls*. One of the Ch'ing critics, for example, maintained that this novel "could only be read by natives of Chekiang province and that people from other provinces would not understand it fully."[100] Lu Hsün believed that dialects enrich the national language, and hence it was worth enduring a few hardships to understand them.

> I judge by my own personal experience. My dialect differs greatly from that of Soochow, but the novel *Lives of Shanghai Singsong Girls* allowed me to understand the so-called Soochow accent without going out of my house. At first I read with difficulty; but then I began to ponder the facts more deeply and to compare phrases in the dialogue, and I understood everything.[101]

In the Sian lectures Lu Hsün attempts to account for the development of later romantic fiction:

> In the early twentieth century[102] novels like *The Nine-Tailed Tortoise*[103] were written. These are different again, since all the prostitutes are bad characters (different already from *Lives of Shanghai Singsong Girls)* and

---

*The first part of this passage is basically correct, the word "guest" being added to clarify the meaning. In fact, it is better than the Yang's "heartlessness" (p. 350), which is too strong. The phrase "and although the situation is imaginary" is a misinterpretation of *"yü fei-suo."* A literal translation, for which I thank Professor Liu Wu-chi, would read: "He upbraids the singsong girls for their lack of deep feelings, and although he admonishes them to virtues *they are not expected to have* [italics mine—C.J.A.], his descriptions are, nevertheless, realistic with little exaggeration." Unfortunately, this quotation does not support the finding that Lu Hsün was "moved" by the young girl's suffering.—C.J.A.

> all of their patrons are rogues. Thus, there have been three approaches to prostitutes: first there was undue praise, then a more realistic attitude was adopted, and finally the writers became hypercritical, using deliberate exaggeration and abuse, which sometimes amounted to slander and blackmail. It really is amazing how this type of novel evolved.[104]

Here Lu Hsün wants to show the degeneration of Chinese fiction, so he confines his remarks on erotic works to the end of the selection on the novel of manners and sees a connection between *Lives of Shanghai Singsong Girls* and the early twentieth-century romantic novel. Nevertheless, sinologists should take into account another, more important line of development, that is, from the *Lives of Shanghai Singsong Girls* to the early twentieth-century novel of exposure.

Naturally, the writer condenses his analysis of "Novels of Adventure and Detection in the Ch'ing Dynasty" into a single chapter (XXVII) of the *Brief History of Chinese Fiction*, because, despite the difference in terms by which these genres are traditionally designated (*hsia-i hsiao-shuo* and *kung-an*), they had much in common. One similarity results, for example, from the fact that both of these genres originated from popular legends and, having preserved their popular form, are more easily understood than others. Lu Hsün rightly notes that although classical Chinese fiction reached its zenith in the mid-eighteenth century (with the psychological novel *Dream of the Red Chamber*), the sympathies of the common folk were still on the side of the heroes of *The Three Kingdoms* and *The Water Margin*.[105] Toward the beginning of the nineteenth century, however, the heroic novel, in Lu Hsün's opinion, lost its popularity.

> Men's tastes change with the times, and as readers grew tired of old books, new trends developed. These new adventure stories, it is true, had their origin in the early novels, but the spirit of these later books is completely different: they praise heroic deeds and acts of rough justice only if these accord with the feudal concepts of loyalty and right. When the literati lost interest in the *Dream of the Red Chamber*, a new type of novel appeared, represented by *The Gallant Maiden*; and when people could no longer understand the spirit of the *Water Margin*,[106] books like *Three Heroes and Five Gallants* won favor.[107]

The Gallant Maiden (*Erh-nü ying-hsiung chuan*) is a novel by the Manchurian Wen K'ang which depicts a young lady knight named Ho Yü-feng, who married the youth An Chi. The fathers of both heroes have suffered at the hands of cruel officials, and the daughter takes revenge on the villains. Thus, the novel also acquires an accusatory character; but Lu Hsün ignores this and regards Ho Yü-feng as a completely imaginary, idealized heroine.[108] Be that as it may, Lu Hsün's critical view of *The Gallant Maiden* differs from that of bourgeois writers of his time, particularly Hu Shih, who wholeheartedly agreed with the persuasive, though not wholly justifiable, formula of Wen K'ang:

> Embellishment is already an assertion of some sort of principles. If everything filthy and evil is consciously concealed, pushed away in contempt, and shoved into the background, is this not a cry from the heart for what is good, kind, and happy?[109]

Imagining that they are adopting Lu Hsün's line, contemporary critics, as a rule, attack *The Gallant Maiden*, calling it a reactionary work directed against the *Dream of the Red Chamber*.[110] But this is a vulgarization of the writer's views. He points out several similarities between Wen K'ang and Ts'ao Hsüeh-ch'in, biographical as well as artistic. Wen K'ang, for example, restricted the role of fantasy and looked at reality, so to speak, from various angles, etc.[111]

Though *The Gallant Maiden* could be considered a typical chivalrous novel, Lu Hsün regards Shih Yü-k'un's *Three Heroes and Five Gallants* (*San-hsia wu-i*, 1879) as the most characteristic of nineteenth-century detection novels. This is a work devoted to the heroic feats of nine gallants who destroy evildoers, unmask the Prince of Hsiang-yang's plot, and accomplish a number of other feats. The warriors are led by the just Prefect Pao, which is enough to convince Lu Hsün of the novel's orthodox character, even though Prefect Pao had long ago figured in popular Chinese legends. Lu Hsün judges *Three Heroes and Five Gallants* harshly from an artistic point of view, yet he also honors it with praise, something quite valuable from the lips of so carping a critic. "Though some of the incidents are rather naive, the gallant outlaws are vividly presented, and the descriptions of town life and jests interspersed throughout the book add to the interest."[112]

Ten years after the appearance of *Three Heroes and Five Gallants*, published in 1889, the number of "heroes" was increased, and the work began to be called the *Seven Heroes and Five Gallants*. This established a precedent for endless sequels to Shih Yü-k'un's novel. In 1890 the *Five Younger Gallants* appeared, in October of the same year *A Sequel to Five Younger Gallants*, and so on. Lu Hsün's reaction to all of these works is extremely negative. Nevertheless, it is instructive to observe how, from exactly the same comments of Ch'ing critics regarding this series of "brave and gallant" heroes, he and Hu Shih come to completely different conclusions. Both cite the preface to *A Sequel to Five Younger Gallants*, although Lu Hsün also mentions that the "main plot of the book is the Prince of Hsiang-yang's conspiracy and the struggle of the heroes to unmask him."[113] In other words, he shows how this loyalist episode becomes the main theme. Hu Shih, on the other hand, is preoccupied with establishing whether it was Shih Yü-k'un or someone else who wrote *Five Younger Gallants* and the *Sequel to Five Younger Gallants*. The one critical remark that he does inject relates to form.[114]

The expression "one of the seven heroes and five gallants" later became an ironic term in Lu Hsün's essays for an outwardly invincible man who is, in fact, utterly shallow.[115] The writer shows how this synthesis of the feudal and bourgeois became a typical feature of early twentieth-century art, and he traces the sources of Chinese literature for entertainment.[116] This material can be supplemented with the very interesting article "The Evolution of Roughs" (1929-30) where Lu Hsün explains the degeneration of chivalric fiction.

> When the Manchus came in and China was gradually subdued, even those with a "sense of gallantry" dared not think of being brigands, upbraiding evil ministers, or serving the emperor directly. Instead, they attached themselves as bodyguards to some good official or high commissioner and caught robbers for him. This is clearly stated in *The Cases of Lord Shih*, and up to the present there have been endless examples like those in *The Cases of Lord P'eng* or *Seven Heroes and Five Gallants*. These men have a blameless past and have never committed a crime. Though they are under the high commissioner, they are at least over the people; so while they have to take orders from their master, they can lord it over all the others. With a greater degree of security, they are correspondingly more servile.[117]

It would appear that Lu Hsün had a completely negative attitude toward nineteenth- and early twentieth-century novels of adventure and detection. But the critics who include *Three Heroes and Five Gallants* among works of reactionary literature[118] have, nevertheless, been misled. Lu Hsün distinguishes Shih Yü-k'un's novel, which "expresses the views of ordinary townsfolk,"[119] from those that imitate it, and even more so from novels dealing with Manchu officials. "The chivalric fiction of the Ch'ing era is a direct continuation of the tales of the Sung," he states in reference to *Three Heroes and Five Gallants*. "Thus, popular literature was once again revived after almost seven hundred years."[120]

In the chapters from the *Brief History of Chinese Fiction* examined above Lu Hsün hardly ever sketches a picture of the social background, because novels of erudition, romance, adventure, etc., provided a rather dim reflection of changes in the social and political life of China. In his analysis of "the late Ch'ing novel of exposure" (XXVIII), however, the situation is different.

> Though the common people, who were in darkness and ignorance, still listened to romantic stories about the suppression of rebels while sipping tea, intelligent men realized that changes were necessary and started agitating for political reforms and patriotic action, emphasizing the need to make the country "rich and strong." Two years after the failure of the 1898 Reform came the Boxer Rebellion, a result of the people's complete loss of faith in the government.[121]

Here Lu Hsün provides a rather clear explanation of the ideological basis underlying literature of exposure—the movement among the masses and the reform movement. In addition, he expresses one other important view—that progressive ideas alone are not enough to create a true work of art. Without a highly artistic form literature degenerates into didacticism.

> Fiction revealed its (the government's—V.S.) true nature and exposed its corruption. It greatly intensified the attacks against the existing regime and, gradually broadening the scope of its exposure, touched even on social conventions. But although outwardly its function was to aid society, somewhat like the satirical novel (*feng-tz'u hsiao-shuo*), the words floated on the surface, and the writer's pen had no hidden sting. Moreover, the authors of these novels expressed themselves in a very high-flown manner, adapting their styles to suit the tastes of their contemporaries. As a result, the craftsmanship* of their works was also far below that of the satirical novel. This is why I have given them another name, the novel of exposure (*ch'ien-tse hsiao-shuo*).[122]

Lu Hsün judges the achievements of authors of the novels of ex-

---

*The Chinese original refers not only to the "craftsmanship" (*chi-shu*) of the novel of censure but to the author's point of view, his lack of "judgment" (*tu-liang*), as implied in the Yang version (p. 372): "the spirit of these works is intolerant."—C.J.A.

posure more rigorously than those of authors from other schools. Though there were quite a few writers in the early twentieth century worthy of attention, he only selects the works of four major prose writers of that time (Li Pao-chia, Wu Wo-yao, Liu O, and Tseng P'u) to illustrate the characteristics of the novel of exposure; and he only analyzes in detail one work by each author. Nor can the peculiar distribution of space in the *Brief History of Chinese Fiction* be ignored. Lu Hsün allots just as many pages (15) to "novels of erudition" as he does to the novel of exposure, even though the latter deserves more.

From among Li Pao-chia's (1867-1906) works Lu Hsün selects *Exposure of the Official World*, and he quotes extensively from the author's preface. In evident sympathy he cites Li Pao-chia's statement to the effect that officials "did not possess any talents except taking bribes and boasting,"* and he quotes the passage in the preface where the author exposes the system of collecting taxes. "Thus," recapitulates Lu Hsün, "the hordes of officials fleece the impoverished commonfolk. The people dare not say a word, and so the officials become even more impudent."[123] Here Lu Hsün stresses an idea that Li Pao-chia himself did not make very clear, *viz.*, that the people were suffering. Still, in the *Brief History* it is rather rare that one encounters a favorable clarification of the ideas in the novel of exposure. In the majority of instances Lu Hsün maintains a skeptical attitude toward the genre and does not have faith in its capabilities.

> There are many different episodes and characters, and each anecdote usually deals with a different individual. Thus, the book as a whole consists of a number of loosely connected stories like Wu Ching-tzu's *The Scholars*. But many scenes are completely imaginary, not at all true to life, and there is far less "innuendo" (*han-hsü yün-niang*) than the author claims; hence the novel is not up to the standard of *The Scholars*. Moreover, the tales collected were current "stories" (*hua-ping*) about official circles strung together into a novel, but without much variety. It was only the general interest in the subject at the time that made this novel famous overnight. It was followed by many imitations like the *Exposure of the Merchant's World*, *Exposure of the Teaching World*, and *Exposure of the Women's World*.[124]

---

*There is no footnote in the Russian text, but see the *Brief History* (Yang), p. 374: "I have seen officials whose sole work is to welcome visitors and see them off, whose *sole ability is polite talk*" (italics mine—C.J.A.).

Here more profound and just conclusions are intermingled with conclusions that do not correspond to the facts. Lu Hsün correctly points out the similarities and dissimilarities between *Exposure of the Official World* and *The Scholars*, but he exaggerates the disparity between these two novels.[125] Li Pao-chia's fantasy, to which Lu Hsün objected,[126] served but one purpose—to reinforce the central theme through the creation of grotesque, revealing situations.

Even the passage from the twenty-sixth chapter of *Exposure of the Official World* (hardly the best in the novel), which is quoted in the *Brief History*,[127] disproves many of Lu Hsün's harsh judgments.

> When it was nearly time to go to court, Chia rehearsed the ceremony in the ministry and all went according to the rules; but enough of this. On the appointed day he rose at midnight and drove into the city.... He waited till eight, when some officer ushered him into the palace. When he and the others reached a certain court, the officer flapped his sleeve and they all fell to their knees at the steps, about twenty feet from the throne. It dawned on him that the man sitting there was the emperor!... Since he was a recommended scholar, he was ordered to wait for a summons the following day....
>
> Though Chia came from an official family, this was his first audience with the emperor, and despite the fact that he had asked advice on every side he still felt unsure of himself. So his first act on his return was to call on Minister Hua, who had accepted ten thousand taels' worth of curios from him, and naturally the minister talked with him cordially and showed friendly concern.
>
> Chia said: "Tomorrow at court, in view of the fact that my father is Minister of Justice, should I kowtow to his Majesty or not?"
>
> The minister was not listening carefully and caught only the word "kowtow." He promptly replied: "Kowtow a lot and say little: that is the way to be promoted."
>
> Chia made haste to explain: "If the emperor asks after my father, of course I shall kowtow; but if he doesn't, should I kowtow or not?"
>
> Minister Hua said: "If the emperor doesn't ask you anything, don't speak out of turn. But when it is right to kowtow, be sure to do so. Even kowtowing when it isn't strictly necessary will do no harm."
>
> This advice left Chia more confused than ever. But before he could ask further questions, the minister rose to see him off and he had to leave. He decided not to trouble Minister Hua any more but to call on War Minister Huang... who might be able to enlighten him.
>
> But when Chia had explained the purpose of his call, Minister Huang

asked. "Have you seen Minister Hua? What did he say?"

Chia told him.

The war minister said: "Minister Hua is experienced. If he told you to kowtow many times and say little, this is the advice of an experienced man, absolutely correct...."

Still at a loss, Chia called on Minister Hsü. This minister, who was elderly and rather deaf, sometimes pretended to be deafer than he was. He believed in peace at any price, and his mottos were: "Take it easy!" and 'Don't worry!"... All his colleagues had seen through him and called him "The Crystal Egg."... So today, when they had greeted each other and Chia brought up this problem, Minister Hsü said: "Of course to kowtow a lot is best, however, it is not absolutely necessary. After all, you should kowtow when kowtowing is called for, not otherwise."

When Chia told him what the others had said, Minister Hsü rejoined: They are both right: you had better take their advice." He talked at length without committing himself to any thing definite, till Chia had to take his leave. Later he found a minor official in the Ministry of War who happened to be a good friend of his father, and only then did he get a clear explanation of the ceremony. The next day, when he was summoned by the emperor, all went smoothly....

This scene, as we see, relies on the grotesque and the gradual accumulation of absurd facts. By and large, all three important officials in Li Pao-chia's description talk the same nonsense; and the character of each is only outlined—the first has experience, the second no personal opinion, and the third is consciously evasive. In this passage, it would seem, distortion plays a purely positive role, because it enables the author to expose the obsequious, slavish morals of officials through the creation of a caricature. To expect a picture of the bureaucratic world that is authentic to the last detail is to make demands on the novel of exposure that do not accord with its unique nature. The artistic weakness here lies, in my opinion, not in "exaggeration," but elsewhere, and one early twentieth-century Chinese critic identified it more accurately than Lu Hsün: "... the book suffers from a surplus of words and a scarcity of ideas; moreover, it is not very interesting."[128] This statement really pinpoints a weakness of many novels of exposure, *viz.*, their prolixity (an almost exclusive reliance on repetition to reproduce fact), which results in a kind of structural amorphousness.

In sketching the biography of Wu Wo-yao (1866-1910) Lu Hsün traces the author's career as a writer, stresses his experience in life, and discusses his ties with bourgeois circles. In analyzing Wu's novel *Strange Events of the Last Twenty Years*, however, he indulges in the same kind of exaggeration evident in the analysis of *Exposure of the Official World*. "Wu is said to have been proud and honest, unwilling to submit to authority; so he remained poor all of his life and was a cynic," writes Lu Hsün and, basing his claims on the testimony of the Ch'ing writer Chou Kuei-sheng, now launches into an attack, "But since he wrote hastily, often exaggerated, and cared little for realism, his works fail to make a strong appeal, merely providing some gossip (*hua-ping*) for idle talk."[129]

Lu Hsün cites a passage from chapter seventy-four of *Strange Events of the Last Twenty Years*, where the author, having exposed the degeneration of the old morality, becomes horrified* at the all too plausible cruelty of Minister Fu Mi-hsien, who starves and then nearly kills his own grandfather. Of course, for Lu Hsün in the 1920s, himself an author of marvelous short stories and prose poems, Wu Wo-yao's exposés already seemed like the product of a bygone era; but they were hardly written for idlers. Lu Hsün looks at the novelist from the vantage point of his own era, and this is part of the reason for his hostile attitude toward the novel of exposure in general. But one must not forget that Lu Hsün also had to contend with epigonic prose writers of his own generation, the bourgeois writers of the twenties and thirties, and that he took a decisive stand against their superficial, tearful attitude toward social conflicts. Perhaps this is why the thesis that novels of exposure "distort" reality turns up so persistently in the *Brief History*, despite the fact that sentimentality, attention to the details of an individual's private life, might just as well have been regarded as progressive features of early twentieth-century fiction.

Nevertheless, one should recognize that Lu Hsün had definite grounds for reproaching authors of the novel of exposure with alienation from reality. Novelists of the early twentieth century, Wu Wo-yao included, often strove for the unusual and the sensational, and this is reflected in the very titles of their works. "Truth is the soul of satire," wrote Lu Hsün. "It is not necessary that the facts described be real, but it *is* necessary that such things could have occurred. Only then can satire be prevented from turning into fabrication, slander, exposure of secret intrigues, or 'amazing

---

*Wu Wo-yao wrote in the first person.—C.J.A.

rumors' (*ch'i-wen*) and 'strange events' (*kuai hsien-chuang*) the main purpose of which is to terrify the reader."[130] Here the terms "fabrication, slander, and exposure of secret intrigues" are directed against feudal-bourgeois literature, and the last two phrases, which Lu Hsün places in quotation marks, are reminiscent of the titles of Wu Wo-yao's tale *The Amazing Rumors of a Blind Man's Lies* and his novel *Strange Events of the Last Twenty Years*. Lu Hsün by no means denies the necessity of criticizing the social evils that troubled Wu Wo-yao and Li Pao-chia, but his harsh criticism of the techniques they utilized did lay the groundwork for a distorted interpretation of "abuse" (*man-ma*), that quality which, in Lu Hsün's opinion, typified novels of exposure. Thus, Cheng Chen-to is led to the conclusion that the distinctive feature of early twentieth-century prose writers was their "cold laugh" (*leng hsiao*)—indifference toward the things they described and the fate of their own people.[131] Such a notion, however, already belies the views of Lu Hsün who, while judging his predecessors harshly, did not accuse them of vulgarization.

The third novel of exposure which Lu Hsün analyzed in detail in his *Brief History* was *The Travels of Lao Ts'an* by Liu O (1857-1909), and here the difference between the revolutionary-democratic and the bourgeois approach (during the twenties and thirties) to the novel of exposure becomes particularly apparent. Let us compare, for example, some of Lu Hsün's ideas with those of Hu Shih.

> His novel describes the travels, views, and adventures of T'ieh-ying or Mr. Derelict. The descriptions of scenery and incidents are often well written. The author expresses his own views too and in many places attacks bureaucracy. One episode concerns an official, Kang Pi, who believes that a man named Wei and his daughter are responsible for the death of thirteen people. Wei's servant tries to save them by offering Kang Pi a bribe, but the latter considers this a proof of their guilt. This story aims to show that a strict official [or "honest" official, *ch'ing-kuan*—C.J.A.] could be worse than a corrupt one.[132]

Lu Hsün later quotes Liu O, who prided himself on exposing officials who, though free from vice, were cruel and ignorant despots, and he cites a passage from the sixteenth chapter of the *Travels* where Kang Pi subjects an innocent old man and his daughter to torture. Unlike several later critics, Lu Hsün accurately pinpoints the main theme of *The Travels of Lao Ts'an*.[133] He does not touch upon Liu O's antipathy toward "northern rebels and southern revolutionaries," because apparently he does not consider this essential to the novel. Hu Shih does examine this question, but only to justify the author in the end.[134] For Lu Hsün, the main element in *The Travels of Lao Ts'an* is the specific nature of the accusations (the examples of cruel officials), and he hardly even mentions the landscape. Hu Shih, on the other hand, reduces the merits of the novel purely to its literary aspects. "The greatest contribution *The Travels of Lao Ts'an* made to Chinese literature was not its ideas, but the techniques utilized in the depiction of nature and the creation of characters."[135] It seems to me, however, that the deciding feature, the litmus paper, so to speak, that brings out the distinction between the revolutionary-democratic and the bourgeois approach, is that Lu Hsün is very biting in his criticism of the novel of exposure when taken as a whole. This was necessary to strengthen modern Chinese literature. But Hu Shih's attitude toward the novel of exposure is apologetic. He sees it as the embryo of bourgeois fiction and comments only on its most petty, superficial inadequacies. Yet this is rather typical of Hu Shih. His interest is drawn to those nineteenth- and twentieth-century works that are most limited in their philosophy, yet he considers them the most progressive.

Lu Hsün devoted the final pages of the *Brief History of Chinese Fiction* to the forerunner of revolutionary fiction, Tseng P'u (1871-1935), and his novel *A Flower in an Ocean of Sin*; but, it should be noted, he did not adequately stress the uniqueness of this work.

> The first chapter is reminiscent of a prologue in which the entire contents of the novel, intended for sixty chapters, are catalogued. The author describes in all their complexity the multitude of events that took place over the last thirty years of the Ch'ing Dynasty. Eventually he intended to portray the victory of the revolution, but halfway through the work was abruptly terminated.[136]

Since nothing further is mentioned about the revolution, the reader might assume that Tseng P'u failed to mention Sun Yat-sen's followers or the Russian populists. Yet all this occupied an important place in the novel and is quite evident in the works of critics with whom Lu Hsün was familiar.[137] He does not even point out that the action in *A Flower in an Ocean of Sin* takes place abroad, in Germany and Russia, for example, as well as in China. Not only was this a completely new feature of Chinese fiction, but it was also mentioned by Ch'ing critics whose works were at Lu Hsün's disposal.[138] It is no coincidence, therefore, that the writer omits those references from previous critics in which *A Flower in an Ocean of Sin* is praised as "the most outstanding of recent works" and where it is ranked, by virtue of its harmonious plot and the profundity of its satire, above Li Pao-chia's *Modern Times*, Liu O's *The Travels of Lao Ts'an*, and Wu Wo-yao's *A Sea of Woe*.[139] Incidentally, the veiled controversy between Lu Hsün and Hu Shih, who in general denied Tseng P'u's role as an innovator, is examined by the literary critic Ch'en Tse-kuang.[140]

The main heroes of *A Flower in an Ocean of Sin* are the scholar laureate and his concubine, characters that enable the author to expose the examination system and the corruptness of society, to which Lu Hsün also calls attention. "Chin Wen-ch'ing and Fu Ts'ai-yün are subjected to particularly harsh ridicule, and the conduct of celebrated scholars of the time, who were striving for careers as officials, is also vividly portrayed. But at times the work reflects a common inadequacy of the novel of exposure—the tendency to exaggerate. Only its skillful plot and refined language are worthy of mention."[141] Lu Hsün correctly senses the flaw in the work, but in my opinion he does not describe it very accurately. The problem lies not so much in hyperbole, which plays basically a satirical role, as in the element of adventure, which Lu Hsün does not mention. Whereas Chin Wen-ch'ing, the representative of a dying class of scholars, is in fact "subjected to . . . ridicule" (albeit not "particularly harsh"), the author often waxes poetical over the adventures of Fu Ts'ai-yün, and the so-called "refined" language (in reality, archaic and grandiose) plays no small role in this regard.

In attempting to recapitulate what has been said in this chapter, we see that the writer's stern attitude toward nineteenth- and early twentieth-century fiction, including its greatest accomplishment, the novel of exposure, was brought about by a number of objective and subjective causes. What seemed inadequate to Lu Hsün was that the novel of exposure was directed not against society as a whole, but merely against its vices. The didacticism (blatant exposure or allegation with little artistic form), the mixture of styles (a synthesis between a subdued, objective tone and grandiloquence), and the attempt by authors to portray the extraordinary at the expense of more important, commonplace phenomena were repugnant to him. The writer could not have failed to see that in its thematic diversity and pungency of criticism the novel of exposure outstripped *The Scholars* and *The Dream of the Red Chamber*. Nevertheless, a century and a half had elapsed, and it was reasonable for him to place higher demands on the novel of exposure than on *The Scholars*.

The novel of censure was one of the last noteworthy achievements of traditional Chinese prose fiction to precede the mature art of Lu Hsün, and it was out of the controversy surrounding these novels that the new literature grew. But the novel of censure displayed bourgeois as well as feudal characteristics, and both of these were odious to Lu Hsün. Moreover, during the twenties and thirties, when imitators of this type of fiction made their debut in the literary arena, the writer, so to speak, witnessed the demise of the novel of censure; and this, of course, could not help but influence his assessment. He scoffed at attempts to revive the traditional novel. "As for the multi-chapter novel, whose authors still try to imitate it (i.e., the popular story-telling tradition—V.S.), it is a useless appendage, like an appendix in the intestines."[142] In this respect the writer's views coincided with those of other progressive literary critics.

The polemical nature of the chapters discussed above throws a great deal of light on the conclusions and evaluations contained in a *Brief History of Chinese Fiction*. As a result, we not only have a more adequate notion of the writer's attitude toward nineteenth- and early twentieth-century fiction but can detect many of the real weaknesses in the novel of that era, whereas in the majority of treatises on modern Chinese literature Lu Hsün's statements are either dogmatically accepted or passed over with an embarrassed silence.

There are important contradictions in Lu Hsün's criticism of nineteenth- and early twentieth-century fiction. The writer felt that the Chinese novel was limited and outmoded, but what precisely its flaws were he could not articulate. While mentioning, and rightly so, the wordiness and pretentiousness of early twentieth-century fiction, Lu Hsün in the same breath praises Tseng P'u's *A Flower in an Ocean of Sin* for its "beautiful and refined language." And although he admires the stylistic beauty of orthodox novels (*The Bookworm* and others), he hardly prefers them to the novel of exposure. Sometimes a protest against pompous language or blatant exposure leads to outright rejection of the grotesque [in the sense of distortion of reality—C.J.A.], and the author unexpectedly finds himself a prisoner of traditional views regarding verisimilitude in the representation of reality, even though he made excellent use of the grotesque in some of his own works and recognized its importance in others ("On Satire" and "What is Satire?" for example). "When a writer uses concise or even exaggerated language—of course this must be done artistically—to tell the truth about a certain aspect of a certain group of people, those writing about call the work a 'satire.'"[143] After this statement it becomes apparent that what displeased Lu Hsün most about the novel of exposure was not the use of the grotesque, but simply its limited artistic form.[144] In overcoming the weaknesses of nineteenth- and early twentieth-century fiction, Lu Hsün automatically overcame his prejudice toward this literature.[145] Despite a generally negative attitude toward it, his own creative works were basically a continuation of this tradition as well as the classics of Chinese literature.

CHAPTER III

The Innovator

To gain a full appreciation of Lu Hsün's role as an innovator it is necessary to compare his works with those of many other writers in the world, for he was armed not only with the riches of Chinese literature, but the riches of other literatures as well. It is toward this goal that the efforts of all literary critics who have written about Lu Hsün are directed. I will endeavor to explain just what Lu Hsün contributed that was new in comparison with his immediate literary predecessors.

Genres

When one compares modern Chinese literature to the works of Lu Hsün, the richness and variety of his art becomes particularly apparent. It was typical for the majority of nineteenth- and early twentieth-century writers to have a genre "speciality." The novelist Li Pao-chia, for example, seldom even wrote short stories, and Huang Tsun-hsien's fame in the field of *belles lettres* was based solely on his poetry. Of course, even in this period there were comprehensive, well-rounded individuals who, so to speak, tried to accomplish the work of several lifetimes. Liang Ch'i-ch'ao was a publicist, poet, playwright, and novelist, Su Man-shu a poet, prose writer, and translator; but even they must yield to Lu Hsün, who not only achieved outstanding success in prose, rhyme prose (*Wild Grass*), the memoir, and translation work, but also created a new genre in the field of Chinese publicism, *viz.*, "random notes" (*tsa-wen*) or "random thoughts" (*tsa-kan*). In the early twentieth century the writer had yet to discover as pointed a weapon as these "random thoughts," and he wrote ordinary articles (*lun-wen*),[1] not much different in form from those written by other publicists. But later, when he combined traditional "refined" prose (*ku-wen, p'ien-wen*) with the European "essay," he strengthened Chinese publicism philosophically as well as artistically. It was in the year 1922 (with "Pu Chou Mountain") that Lu Hsün first made use of historical allegory to describe the present, an approach to the classics that was comparatively unknown to nineteenth- and early twentieth-century Chinese writers, or in this case, writers of prose fiction. The fantastic nature and remoteness of the era described (Lu Hsün turns primarily to traditional mythology for material) allowed the author greater freedom to manipulate the facts and to show the grotesque nature of the contemporary world. Though historical novels *were* written in the early twentieth century, they seldom went beyond the limits of actual historical fact (Wu Woyao's *The History of Pain*, etc.).

The short story had become Lu Hsün's basic literary genre, and this was a result of various circumstances, but one reason no doubt was Lu Hsün's private polemic with traditional prose fiction from the fourteenth to the early twentieth century. After the five-century reign of the novel, Lu Hsün once again revived, though in a new form, the more laconic short story.

To recapture the decisive moment of this breach with traditional literature one need only contrast the novel of exposure, the most remarkable of early twentieth-century literary accomplishments, with *Outcry* (1918-22), Lu Hsün's first collection of short stories and an important landmark in the history of modern Chinese literature. The eminent writer and literary critic Shen Yen-ping [Mao Tun] believed that "each of the ten or so stories in the collection *Outcry* was an attempt to create a new form of modern Chinese literature."[2] Another critic construed this to mean that "Diary of a Madman," "Medicine," and "The True Story of Ah Q" were similar in spirit to classical Chinese prose. "'My Old Home,'" he says, "is a lyrical poem; 'The Rabbits and the Cat,' 'The Duck's Comedy,' 'The Village Opera,' and 'A Small Incident' are like short essays; and 'The Story of Hair' is written in the form of a dialogue, etc."[3] As a matter of fact, Lu Hsün's creative works were so bold and so unusual for Chinese readers that some critics even refused to acknowledge that the majority of his creations were short stories.[4]

Almost all critics, however, pointed out the uniqueness of the writer's technique and his genuine ingenuity. Let me cite here, for example, Chang Ting-huang's comparison of *Outcry* with the short stories of Su Man-shu, one of the most talented prose writers prior to Lu Hsün.

> I have no intention of equating "A Tale of Twin Chessboards" (*Shuang-p'ing chi*)* with "Diary of a Madman," though I do have definite reasons for contrasting them. In the first place, I feel that "A Tale of Twin Chessboards" is rather unique and true to life. And secondly, this makes it easier to understand the significance of *Outcry*. "A Tale of Twin Chessboards" was published in the first volume of *The Tiger* (*Chia-yin*, The Year 1914), and *New Youth* published "Diary of a Madman" in 1918. Between them there were only four years, but what a difference! Two languages, two sensations, two different worlds! "A Tale of Twin Chessboards," "A Tale of Crimson Silk," and "A Tale on the Burning of the Sword" are the last stories in the classical language that carry the vanishing aroma of the old style, shades of the talented scholar and delicate beauty, dying gusts of romanticism, and remnants of the traditional world view! When we set these aside and turn to "Diary of a Madman," it is like leaving some dark, ancient temple where a single lamp flickers and suddenly coming into the clear sunlight. We have stepped from the middle ages into the modern world.[5]

One can concur with this statement if the term "medieval" is not taken in a purely negative sense and merely implies that Su Man-shu's [1884-1918] fiction, which followed the defeat of the 1911-13 revolution, was more "medieval" in spirit than the novel of exposure.

Outcry contained the seeds of many an idea which germinated in the course of Lu Hsün's life. "The Rabbits and the Cat," "The Duck's Comedy" and other stories are thematically linked to the collection *Wild Grass* (1924-26). "The Village Opera" and "The Story of Hair" are linked to the collection *Hesitation* (1924-25); and "Pu Chou Mountain" (later entitled "Mending Heaven") is linked to the collection *Old Tales Retold* (1927-35). And yet, *Outcry* has its own permanent value, or it would not have remained, even till now, the most popular of Lu Hsün's literary collections. All of these facts make it clear that any comparison of *Outcry* with the novel of exposure will decide the question of tradition versus innovation in favor of Lu Hsün.

*This short story was not written by Su Man-shu himself, but by Chang Shih-chao who was Su Man-shu's friend. Su Man-shu wrote a preface to the work. See Liu Wu-chi's *Su Man-shu* (New York: Twayne, 1972), p. 111.—C.J.A.

Themes, heroes, ideas, and moods

The portrayal of intense social conflicts was the main objective of early twentieth-century novelists, but Lu Hsün improved on their work by freeing literature from the preoccupation with adventure. His stories are very interesting to read, not because they excel in gripping intrigue like some novels of exposure (for example, Wu Wo-yao's *A Crime Involving Nine Lives*, where the plot hinges on a detective's investigation; Tseng P'u's *A Flower in an Ocean of Sin*, liberally salted with the amorous adventures of Fu Ts'ai-yün; or *The Travels of Lao Ts'an*, where in the end the hero himself becomes a detective), but because of their natural, even masterful construction, the typical nature of the incidents selected, and the depth of their psychology.

In 1933 Lu Hsün wrote: "Ten or so years ago my views were those of a philosophe, i.e., one who believed that it was necessary to write "for humanity" and for the improvement of human life. I detested those who considered fiction an 'idle pastime' and regarded the slogan 'art for art's sake' as merely the latest excuse for 'literature of entertainment.'"[6] Here the continuity of tradition is undeniable, for it was the reformers themselves (Liang Ch'i-ch'ao and others) who launched a sharp attack on literature for entertainment's sake—that literature which was so abhorrent to Lu Hsün. They too professed enlightened views and believed that a writer should become actively involved in life (see, for example, Liang's essay "On the Relationship Between Fiction and Popular Sovereignty"). The difference was that Lu Hsün and his cohorts understood life itself more deeply than early twentieth-century writers, and for him enlightenment was no longer reduced to raw didacticism, as it was for many of his immediate predecessors. Moreover, Lu Hsün was more consistent in putting his "enlightened" views into practice. The authors of the novel of exposure often fell prey to the very literature they were attempting to oppose, whereas Lu Hsün attacked "pure art" unmercifully and to the bitter end. In other words, even though "enlightenment" in the concrete historical sense was no longer Lu Hsün's philosophy after 1907, he proved to be more of a champion of enlightenment than those who had brought the age into the history of Chinese literature.

Like traditional fiction writers of the early twentieth century,

Lu Hsün attempted to discover heroes in everyday life and to create real-life situations in his short stories. In this respect his realism has much in common with the literature of enlightenment, and it is no accident that critics search for and find the living prototypes for characters in Lu Hsün's works and the novel of exposure. This also accounts, in my opinion, for several similarities in plot construction used by Lu Hsün and authors of the novel of exposure, e.g., the discovery of a manuscript to strengthen the illusion of verisimilitude in the narrative. Many Chinese novelists of the early twentieth century inform the reader that they found the manuscript accidentally (Wu Wo-yao in *Strange Events* and Tseng P'u in *A Flower in An Ocean of Sin*), and Lu Hsün does the very same thing in his short story "Diary of a Madman."*

Authors of the novel of exposure often placed emphasis on realistic subject matter. Thus, Li Pao-chia creates grotesque caricatures of officials and reformers; Tseng P'u takes on the satirical traits of the scholar Hung Chün (Chin Wen-ch'ing in the novel[7]), and so forth. Nevertheless, these writers must bow to Lu Hsün, who made use of literally every detail of everyday life to intensify his social criticism and did so masterfully. (One only need cite, for example, "The True Story of Ah Q.") Early twentieth-century novelists depicted scenes of unheard of cruelty and abuse, and sometimes they even drew harsh conclusions from the facts they cited (e.g., Li Pao-chia's statement that "all officials seem to have been taught by one and the same teacher" and Liu O's comment on "incorruptible" officials); and yet, not one of them succeeded in passing a death sentence on the old morality, as did Lu Hsün, by branding it as "cannibalism" in his "Diary of a Madman."

Like Li Pao-chia, Wu Wo-yao and others, Lu Hsün attempted to describe either his own times or those of the comparatively recent past. In many of the stories of *Outcry* the action takes place after the 1911-13 revolution ("A Small Incident," "My Old Home," etc.), and in several others, after the May Fourth Movement of 1919 ("The Dragon Boat Festival"). At the same time, however, Lu Hsün explores the period prior to the revolution of 1911-13 ("Medicine," "K'ung I-chi," "The White Light," "The Rabbits and

---

*This is a traditional gimmick and can be found much earlier than the novel of exposure. The *Dream of the Red Chamber* is the most famous example. As far as I know, very few of Lu Hsün's works (perhaps only the *Diary*) use this technique.—C.J.A.

the Cat"*), or links the old and the new together ("The True Story of Ah Q," "The Village Opera"), so that in many ways he seems to complement his predecessors. Several of his stories ("Tomorrow," "Diary of a Madman") are not strictly determined in time, and it would be equally effective to place them either in the past or in the present. This new feature, almost unknown in the novel of exposure, reached its peak of development in Lu Hsün's collection *Wild Grass*.

The writer understood reality in all its fullness. Not only the painful present, but the even more painful past of the Chinese people came to life, so to speak, before his very eyes. This is why several themes of traditional Chinese fiction of the last few centuries reappear in his short stories, particularly the theme of officialdom. "Lu Hsün masterfully forges a link between *The Scholars* and the new literature, which appeared after the May Fourth Movement, revealing to us the difficult path traversed by the Chinese intelligentsia over the course of the last few centuries,"[8] writes Chu T'ung of the stories "K'ung I-chi" and "The White Light." Unfortunately, this overlooks the real triumphs of the novel of exposure in depicting the intelligentsia and officialdom. It was basically Wu Ching-tzu, author of *The Scholars*, who exposed Confucian scholasticism and the official examination system. The early twentieth-century novelists not only continued this theme (Li Pao-chia's *Exposure of the Official World* and Tseng P'u's *A Flower in an Ocean of Sin*) but developed it more fully by providing broad evidence of the bribery which corrupted the bureaucracy (*Exposure of the Official World*) and unleashing an attack on so-called "incorruptible" officials who succeeded in their careers by dint of demagogy and cruelty (*The Travels of Lao Ts'an*).

Lu Hsün goes one step further than *The Scholars* or the novel of exposure. He allows for the fact that from previous works his readers are already well aware of the hardships experienced by the unsuccessful scholar. Perhaps that is why K'ung I-chi (from the story with the same title) seems like such a ready-made product of the bureaucratic system. Not content, however, simply with revealing the psychology of debased intellectuals or portraying their conflict with society, Lu Hsün devotes two additional short stories

---

*I suspect that Semanov has dated these last two on the basis of theme and content rather than on any internal evidence of time.—C.J.A.

("K'ung I-chi" and "The White Light") to the theme of the scholars. The writer shifts focus from the exposure of corruption in general, which will not allow a talented man to obtain a degree, to the problem of the "pernicious power of feudal ideology over the little man."[9] Not only does he show disgust for those who prevent "the little guy" from struggling or even crawling up the social ladder, he brands the slaves themselves for naively believing that they will secure freedom from the hands of their masters. In addition, a new character appears in *Outcry*, one that is unique in Chinese literature, the intellectual-official who belongs to the period following the revolution of 1911 and the May Fourth Movement (Fang Hsüan-ch'o of "The Dragon Boat Festival"). His plight is somewhat different—they will not pay his salary; yet he does have a way of overcoming his suffering, one that is also quite new—an appropriately "higher" level of intellectual development. Fang Hsüanch'o fabricates a convenient philosophy for himself and adapts to life with the theory that "it's all the same." Soon afterwards Lu Hsün depicted still more types of modern intellectuals in the collection *Hesitation*.

But let us return to the "old" problems, which had hardly vanished from Chinese life and, therefore, demanded Lu Hsün's attention. In the stories "Diary of a Madman," "Medicine," "Tomorrow" and others he debunks quackery, as did the early twentieth-century novelists Wu Wo-yao (*Strange Tales of Electricity*) and Tseng P'u (*A Flower in an Ocean of Sin*). He also devotes quite a bit of energy to another favorite theme of these novelists, the struggle against superstition. Many of the episodes from his short stories, the blood-stained bread in "Medicine" or the censer and candlestick in "My Old Home,"[10] for example, bear witness to the ignorance of simple folk and appeal for the elimination of ignorance. A short episode or a seemingly insignificant detail in the great writer's short stories can sometimes force one to ponder the harm caused by superstition more deeply than an entire novel by the early twentieth-century satirists (Li Pao-chia's *The Fate Which Awakens the World*, Wu Wo-yao's *A Blind Man's Lies*, and others). This attention to the past, to the seamier side of life, made Lu Hsün a "feudal splinter"[11] in the eyes of "left-wing" critics, who demanded that all writers immediately shift to "proletarian" literature. But Lu Hsün understood fully the importance of his works on the "old" themes. More than any other of his short stories he loved "K'ung I-chi," and he even translated this story into Japanese.[12] One of the writer's plans that did not materialize was a novel dealing with "four generations" of Chinese intellectuals (beginning with that of Chang Ping-lin[13]), i.e., another retreat to the turn of the century.

In stories devoted to the revolution of 1911-13 Lu Hsün usually describes the countryside, whereas in those dealing more with the May Fourth Movement, the intelligentsia gains the center of attention.[14] In my view, this is because the May Fourth Movement produced greater changes in the lives of the intelligentsia than it did in the fortunes of the broad masses. Of course there was a certain stagnancy even among the intelligentsia ("K'ung I-chi," "The White Light") and at times serious changes did occur in the lives of the peasants and workers ("My Old Home," "A Small Incident"). In each instance, however, the writer's choice of the time of the action is closely related to his choice of heroes. This was still not much of a problem for early twentieth-century novelists, because their heroes did not as yet possess such historical and social concreteness. The heroes of the novel of censure (*Exposure of the Official World, Modern Times, Living Hell, Strange Events, After the Disaster, The Travels of Lao Ts'an,* and *A Flower in an Ocean of Sin*) were mostly representatives of the upper classes—officials, scholars, landowners, and rich peasants. Lu Hsün's works present a different picture. The main characters in the short stories "K'ung I-chi" and "The White Light" are degraded, impoverished scholars; in "Medicine" the proprietor of a small teahouse, his dying son, and a young revolutionary who is executed; in the story "Tomorrow" a poor weaver; and in "A Small Incident," a rickshaw puller, and so on. This difference in the heroes chosen by early twentieth-century novelists and by Lu Hsün is best explained by his great sense of democratism, though a different conception of how to remold society also played a major role. More traditional writers generally depicted representatives of the upper classes whom they hoped to reeducate (see the ending of Li Pao-chia's *Exposure of the Official World* and also *The Travels of Lao Ts'an*), whereas Lu Hsün depicted the lower classes in an effort to reawaken the people.[15] The first dream was groundless, the second very real. The authors of the novel of exposure sympathized with the people but did not recognize their real strengths. Lu Hsün, on the other hand, believed in the simple man and attempted to fathom the very laws of his evolution.

Of the officials, intellectuals, and other representatives of the "upper" classes who belonged to the old society, Lu Hsün was most intrigued by those who had been alienated from their own class (K'ung I-chi, Ch'en Shih-ch'eng). From the author's point of view they deserved to be pitied, and to reveal their suffering was to lay bare their spiritual world. (As for the landowners and officials—the Honorable Chao, the Successful Provincial Candidate, or the Imitation Foreign Devil in "The True Story of Ah Q"—Lu Hsün regarded them with undisguised contempt.) The writer included these dispossessed intellectuals (especially those who refused to fawn on the rich and powerful) among the people, though he did not fail to show what set them apart from the workers and peasants. K'ung I-chi, for example, is brought to utter destitution, yet he still wears the robe of a scholar and disdains the paupers around him. In the story "My Old Home" we encounter still another kind of alienation between peasant and intellectual, but of a quite different nature. The narrator (an entirely different person from K'ung I-chi) believes that someday people themselves will destroy this alienation. "Actually, there are no roads upon the earth, but when many men pass, a road is paved."[16]

Researchers often maintain that Lu Hsün "introduced the simple man into literature"[17] and that "the struggle and suffering of the peasantry, as a rule, lay outside the field of vision"[18] of early twentieth-century fiction writers. Meanwhile, in Li Pao-chia's *Exposure of the Offical World* and *Living Hell*, in Liu O's *Travels of Lao Ts'an* and other novels considerable space is devoted to the suffering peasantry. It matters little that early twentieth-century novelists interpreted the term "people" in a much broader sense than "simple folk" (as opposed to officials and scholars) and included the wealthy, something we no longer find in Lu Hsün's works. Authors of the novel of exposure, in imitation of the chivalric novel of the fourteenth to the eighteenth century, depict mass scenes. (This is especially evident, for example, in Li Pao-chia's *Exposure of the Official World*, when the military leader Hu Hua-jo, official Fu, and others mock the people.) Occasionally the early twentieth-century novelists even give names to the commoners in their works and describe their suffering in detail (Li Pao-chia's *Living Hell*, Liu O's *The Travels of Lao Ts'an*), although these characters never really attain independent stature. (Something comparable can be observed in the first story of the collection *Outcry*,

"Diary of a Madman," although subsequently Lu Hsün changed his approach and created a whole array of unforgettable popular heroes.) Lu Hsün, therefore, did not "introduce the simple man into literature," but he did take the next important step—he made the common people the main heroes of literature. Having transcended his predecessors, the writer (in *Wild Grass, Hesitation,* and *Old Tales Retold*), so to speak, rejoins them, displaying an equal interest in all levels of society. But already this reconciliation has a new basis. In his mature years, Lu Hsün portrays each of the social classes—but for the sake of the people as a whole. And though writing for their benefit, he does not view reality solely through their eyes. As a writer his vision is broader and more far-reaching than the people whom he portrays. One might say that in his short stories Lu Hsün combines sympathy for the "little man" and criticism of his weaknesses with a hymn to his greatness.

Although early twentieth-century Chinese novelists devoted thousands of pages to the portrayal of human suffering, they did not portray the conflict between the "haves" and the "have nots" as clearly as did Lu Hsün. Much that demanded an enormous effort from his predecessors Lu Hsün achieved with apparent ease by virtue of his talent and revolutionary world outlook. Each of his suffering heroes is, so to speak, one of those who has been "put in stocks by the local magistrate, struck in the face by a landlord, whose wife has been abducted by the local constable, or whose parents have perished from the wrath of moneylenders."[19] In the tradition of his predecessors, Lu Hsün describes the tragic fate of concrete people: Hsia Yü is beheaded; Ah Q is shot; K'ung I-chi has his legs broken; Hua Ta-ma and Fourth Shan's wife are deprived of their children, and so forth. Why does all this seem more harsh than in the novel of exposure? Part of the reason is that Lu Hsün's heroes, as in real life, are aware only of the dreadful *effects* of suffering, *viz.*, their own torments; they do not understand what *causes* them. K'ung I-chi suffers because his legs are broken, and yet he does not even attempt to complain. Hua Ta-ma and Fourth Shan's wife are overwhelmed by the death of their children, but they are not even aware that it is inept medical treatment which has destroyed them. As for Ah Q, he is almost glad when they lead him to his execution.

In the novel of exposure the enemy is right at hand—a certain official, a certain robber, a certain foreigner, etc.—whereas Lu

Hsün forces the reader to ponder and to ferret out the deeper causes of the suffering he describes. For the authors of the novel of exposure it was enough to remove the villain (Kang Pi, the myopic magistrate in Liu O's *The Travels of Lao Ts'an*, or the foreign thieves in Wu Wo-yao's *After the Disaster*) and the conflict was resolved. For Lu Hsün this is impossible, because the causes of suffering are deep-seated and diverse, rooted not only in the cruelty of oppressors, but in the ignorance and passiveness of the very victims themselves. And so, in truth, there are very few happy endings to his stories. Lu Hsün deliberately makes the incident that brings about the destruction of the hero insignificant and absurd—K'ung I-chi has stolen something ridiculous, and Ah Q is accused of a theft which never even crossed his mind. But the punishment for such a "crime" leaves a horrifying, not a ridiculous impression! Then too, the fate of Lu Hsün's little people is all the more tragic because, other than the author and the reader, almost no one sympathizes with them. The early twentieth-century novelists (Li Pao-chia, Wu Wo-yao) also stressed the loneliness of man, but in several of their works (in Liu O's *The Travels of Lao Ts'an*, for example) the suffering person is attended by a specific individual who sheds tears along with him. Lu Hsün, on the other hand, mercilessly alienates secondary characters from the main hero. No one sympathizes with the hero of "The Diary of a Madman," K'ung I-chi, Ah Q, Fourth Shan's wife, or Hsia Yü. The customers in the tavern laugh at K'ung I-chi, and the proprietor is only interested in the coppers K'ung I-chi owes him. True, the children are more kind to the unsuccessful scholar, but even the young lad, who is the narrator of the story, considers it shameful to discuss anything with K'ung I-chi or to learn new characters from him.

This sensation of inconsolability in Lu Hsün's works is further intensified by the fact that the hero is surrounded neither by sadists nor scoundrels, but by ordinary people.[20] In the majority of the works in *Outcry* (in "Medicine," "K'ung I-chi," and "The True Story of Ah Q," for example) the action occurs, so to speak, on three different levels—the suffering hero, his chief tormentors, and the stupidly cackling crowd. The reader realizes that if tomorrow someone from this crowd were himself to fall into misfortune like K'ung I-chi or Ah Q, all the others would cackle at him with the very same zeal. Here already we see the first signs of a critical attitude toward the national psychology, a volte-face similar to that which the revolutionary democrats and Chekhov brought about in Russian literature. This complex, contradictory approach toward the hero, sometimes defined by the classical dictum "to sympathize with the unfortunate man and be indignant at his meakness,"[21] is not unprecedented in Chinese literature, but it is to Lu Hsün's credit that he carried on the tradition and used it in the service of the common people. The necessity for criticizing the national psychology came about because the old morality had managed to infect the very broadest strata of society. This is evident both from "The Diary of a Madman"[22] and "The True Story of Ah Q," where a little man, corrupted by feudal morals, even emerges as the main hero. Comparable characters in the novel of exposure (see Li Pao-chia), people who collected bribes for the officials, for example, blend into the background.

Ah Q, a poor and disenfranchised individual who is constantly used as a scapegoat by his fellow villagers, is particularly interesting. Incapable of gaining a real victory over his enemies, he attempts to soothe his conscience with "moral victories." Many have suggested, and rightly so, that this tendency toward so-called "moral victories" relates primarily to the ruling classes, particularly the politicians of the Ch'ing government in their relationship with foreigners (after 1840).[23] This cowardly, servile, and at the same time self-complacent way of practicing politics was clearly described by early twentieth-century Chinese novelists like Li Pao-chia (*Modern Times*) and Tseng P'u (*A Flower in an Ocean of Sin*). But only Lu Hsün observed it in other areas of life and crystallized it artistically. More than simply "revealing the tendency of the ruling classes and the intelligentsia to gain 'moral victories,'" Lu Hsün "discovers a similar trait even among uneducated people, among whom traditions of slavery had been fostered from generation to generation."[24] This gives the character of Ah Q unusual breadth, and makes him typical, so that he embodies the negative qualities in the national character as a whole.

The contrast between Lu Hsün's first collection of short stories and the novel of exposure is striking. His early works are almost completely devoid of overt anti-imperialist themes. P'ing Hsin explains this noble self-criticism as Lu Hsün's attempt to discover the causes of misfortune *within* the country,[25] but the writer's expectation that "really honest" foreigners would "curse us for the present conditions in China"[26] also played a definite role here. Later, after realizing the true nature of imperialism, Lu Hsün shifted toward sharp exposure of foreign aggressors, once again drawing closer (though on a new basis, of course) to his predecessors. Nor did the writer's attitude toward the people remain unchanged. Lu Hsün's criticism of the ignorance and passivity of the masses stemmed from a desire to cleanse the souls of common people and to eradicate the feudal contagion among them (even though, as is well known, at certain stages in his career he could not escape the influence of Nietzsche and his theory of "the crowd"). Thus, in the collections that follow *Outcry* there are far fewer satirical images of the common people.* Now the writer's anger is unleashed primarily against the exploiters, and this likewise is somewhat of a return to the tradition of the novel of exposure.

Lu Hsün, of course, did not simply criticize his compatriots. He emphasized the brighter, more poetic traits of the people—the best features in the national character. The alluring people in Lu Hsün's stories are the peasant children, to whom fear and greed are unknown ("My Old Home," "The Village Opera"). Then too, the narrator, and in turn the reader, is moved by the noble deed of the rickshaw puller ("A Small Incident"). All this goes hand in hand with a search for strong heroes who are capable of transforming life, and is, therefore, almost uncharacteristic of the accusatory novel. Only in *Exposure of the Official World* and *The Travels of Lao Ts'an* is there anything similar. The theme of the nobility of the common man, one who becomes the hero of a "small" incident, is totally alien to the novel of exposure. And yet love for the people only intensifies the social criticism in Lu Hsün's short stories. If, for example, the young Jun-t'u ("My Old Home") were not portrayed so attractively, the reader might be less sympathetic toward his more recent hardships. This technique of contrasting the nobility of the people with the humiliations that have become their lot is also used in the novel of exposure (in Li Pao-chia's *Living Hell* and Wu Wo-yao's *Strange Events*, for example) but not so profoundly and universally as in the works of Lu Hsün. Thus, with all their defects, Ah Q and K'ung I-chi still possess attractive traits.

*This is simply not true. There is ample evidence of Lu Hsün's contempt for the "crowd" both in his essays and in *Wild Grass*. Even in *Hesitation*, the very next collection of short stories, there are two poignant tales ("An Example," "The Eternal Lamp") that develop this theme. See my introduction for a more thorough discussion of this issue.—C.J.A.

The novelists of the early twentieth century portrayed not only popular suffering but popular protest as well. In *Exposure of the Official World* and *Modern Times* Li Pao-chia depicts revolts against local officials, and another novel by the same author, *Ballad of the Great Incident in 1900*, is entirely devoted to the Boxer Rebellion. Thus, even in this respect Lu Hsün follows in the footsteps of the authors of the novel of exposure. But what is the function of given episodes, and what is the author's attitude toward them? This is an entirely different question. In the works of Li Pao-chia there is a definite consistency. If a popular uprising is of a local nature, he portrays it sympathetically, as a natural rebuff against self-seeking and cruel officials (*Exposure of the Official World*), but the minute an uprising poses a threat to the entire empire, the writer takes a negative attitude toward it (*Ballad of the Great Incident of 1900*).[27] Lu Hsün, on the other hand, consistently evaluates a popular movement from the viewpoint of a revolutionary.* In this respect the writer even goes beyond Tseng P'u, who in the novel *A Flower in an Ocean of Sin* portrays the followers of Sun Yat-sen and the Russian populists with complete sympathy. Lu Hsün describes the execution of the revolutionary (in "Medicine") with enormous pain, but without the sentimentality which, to a certain extent, was typical of Tseng P'u. In scenes where revolutionaries appear Tseng P'u's novel sometimes seems outmoded and naive,[28] while in Lu Hsün's works high-flown romanticism gives way to a serious and realistic approach in no way devoid of elegance.[29] Lu Hsün, so to speak, steers Chinese fiction away from the broad, abstract portrayal of revolution to a psychologically profound illustration. Sometimes Tseng P'u's novel reads like a popular textbook on history—there are so many editorial digressions, allusions to the exploits of ever more recent heroes, and excursions into the past. Lu Hsün, on the other hand, depicts a single revolutionary ("Medicine"), shows only the final, most dramatic segment of his life, and without even introducing Hsia Yü onto the scene, pieces his character together from the dialogue of others. Nevertheless, Hsia Yü leaves no less an impression on the reader than the nihilistic Sara, whose fate Tseng P'u describes from the very moment of her birth.

---

*On this point see my introduction, p. xvii.—C.J.A.

Lu Hsün proves closest of all to his predecessors in the portrayal of the enemies of the revolution. The executioner,* "clad entirely in black, with eyes 'glittering like two daggers,' enormous hands, and a hoarse voice"[30] seems literally to leap out of the pages of the novel of exposure. Both in his internal makeup and external appearance this character is very similar, for example, to the gendarme Nikolaev in *A Flower in an Ocean of Sin*. It is true that while the words and deeds of Hsia Yü are in essence noble, others react to them with bewilderment or malice. But more often Lu Hsün takes a different tack and devotes his energy to the exposure of pseudo-revolutionaries, as he does in "The True Story of Ah Q," and in this respect he is more akin to his predecessors. Had either Lu Hsün or Li Pao-chia depicted such dynamic events as the revolution of 1911-13, the Boxer Rebellion, or even more so, the Reform Movement, apologetically, their works would hardly have survived their time. It is precisely this keen, artistic "skepticism" which enables them to focus attention on the truly weak aspects of the revolution of 1911-13, the Boxer Rebellion, and the Reform Movement. Still, authors of the novel of exposure did not possess Lu Hsün's keenness of vision. The great writer, whose whole soul was dedicated to the revolution, knew how to pinpoint its negative aspects more accurately than his predecessors, who at times had ulterior motives for uncovering the deficiencies in progressive movements.

There is one story in the collection *Outcry* where the revolution is described by a method completely unknown to the authors of the novel of exposure. Here I have in mind "The Story of Hair." Its basic theme is one of sorrow over the defeat of the revolution of 1911-13. The anniversary of the revolution (October 10, 1911) is not celebrated, and the lives of the people, apart from cutting off the queue, have not at all changed. Almost all the events Mr. N describes happened to Lu Hsün himself, but the final page introduces a very important nuance into the work. Mr. N, crushed by the difficulties he has encountered, advocates refusal to struggle, whereas Lu Hsün himself, even though his experience is the same as Mr. N's, does not surrender and holds a completely different

---

*Semanov, like other Soviet scholars, equates the executioner with the character Uncle K'ang. I have deleted the name, because the equation is invalid.
—C.J.A.

point of view. It is no accident that the author keeps his distance from the storyteller.*

Only a writer of the 1920s could have depicted the Chinese revolution from the viewpoint of a man who is disgruntled with it. Lu Hsün, writing after two revolutions have taken place, is confronted not only with the problem of the revolution, but with the problem of reaction, one that seldom arises for early twentieth-century novelists. The story "Storm in a Teacup" (1920) illustrates, for example, the different reactions of villagers in the countryside to the news of Chang Hsün's restoration.[31] The rich stick their noses in the air, and the ignorant, downtrodden peasants tremble. And only when the restoration—which is something remote and unrelated to them—fails, does life in the village fall gradually back into the old rut. Curiously, the restoration, which is used here as a backdrop by the artist, serves the same function (*viz.*, to expose passivity and submission to fate) as the revolution in "The True Story of Ah Q." Lu Hsün links Ah Q's fate with the revolution, and the two are tightly interwoven. The revolution of 1911-13 suffered defeat because people like Ah Q had not yet awakened. And in turn, the defeat of the revolution brought new misfortunes to the people, Ah Q included. It is no coincidence, therefore, that the hero, enthralled by the execution of revolutionaries, is himself sacrificed to reactionary forces. Lu Hsün does, however, show Ah Q's hankering for revolution, a fact which is sometimes underplayed in works of literary criticism.[32] Lu Hsün takes a different attitude toward the Wei-chuang gentry than he does toward Ah Q, even though both attempt to "join" the revolution. The writer simply reviles the former, ridiculing them maliciously, whereas he both ridicules and pities Ah Q. He is bitter because the efforts of the high and mighty are forever crowned with success, while a poor hired hand, who has more right to join the revolution, is alienated and crushed. No wonder Wang Shih-yen believes that "The True Story of Ah Q" is as much concerned with the future (the hero's attempt to join the revolution is unsuccessful) as is "Medicine" (the wreath on the grave of the revolutionary).[33]

---

*The story is one long antirevolutionary tirade in response to which the first-person narrator (Lu Hsün) says nothing. For a translation see *Ah Q and Others: Selected Stories of Lusin*, trans. Wang Chi-chen (first reprint) (Westport, Conn.: Greenwood Press, 1971), pp. 59-64.—C.J.A.

One other similarity between early twentieth-century novelists and Lu Hsün, during the period when he wrote *Outcry*, arises from the fact that family problems are always pushed into the background to make room for problems that deal with the interrelationships between men and their government or between various social classes. These authors did not as yet show a real interest in the family—the society in minature.[34] In the novels of Tseng P'u (*A Flower in an Ocean of Sin*) and Wu Wo-yao (*Strange Events*), to say nothing of others, relatively little space is devoted to portraying the family; and the same can be said of Lu Hsün. Though he "tries to expose the family system and the harm of feudal morality"[35] in "Diary of a Madman," family relationships actually do not play a major role in the story, and it is no surprise that V. F. Sorokin[36] is forced to extract this theme from a morass of details dealing with entirely different problems and events.

At this point, it is possible to draw yet another parallel between early twentieth-century prose writers and Lu Hsün. While devoting significant attention to the difficult position of women, both attributed that position to social rather than domestic conditions. Lu Hsün portrays ignorant, suffering women who are maimed by life (Fourth Shan's wife, the two mothers in "Medicine," and Yang Erh-sao), and in so doing he follows the tradition of the novel of exposure. At the same time, however, the writer deviates from tradition by refusing to portray any episode that is fraught with eroticism. There are almost no love conflicts in the collection *Outcry*, and the writer's contemporaries reproached him for this.[37] In my opinion, however, such an approach was inevitable at this stage in the development of Chinese fiction, and the uniqueness of Lu Hsün's art bears this out in each instance. By taking a stand against the old morality, the writer, whether consciously or unconsciously, repudiates two other beliefs held by his predecessors. He not only ridicules the view that women are basically seductive creatures (Ah Q and Amah Wu), he debunks paragons of Confucian virtue. Recall, for example, the wife of the "foreign devil," the woman who jumps into the well three times because her husband cut off his queue, or the servant Amah Wu who wants to hang herself because of a single "proposition" from Ah Q. Incidentally, this relative deemphasis on family problems did not hamper Lu Hsün from becoming the first in the history of Chinese literature to portray children realistically. This is one of the most important humanistic features of his works. Lu Hsün admires children as lively, unspoiled creatures among whom there is a genuine feeling of comradeship and humanity ("The Village Opera," "My Old Home"). The author places special hopes in his young heroes. Recall, for example, the appeal in "Diary of a Madman": "Save them, save the children!"

Here already we begin to touch on problems that were unknown in Chinese literature of the nineteenth and early twentieth centuries. In the stories "The Rabbits and the Cat" and "The Duck's Comedy"* Lu Hsün celebrates the *joie de vivre* of even tinier creatures, those in whom the zest for life has hardly begun to glimmer. With a tender smile he recalls "the blind Russian poet Eroshenko," a man also noted for his sensitivity toward living things, and he notes the attraction of children and animals toward this kind man. Nevertheless, even these stories do not completely break with tradition, because they are accusatory in spirit. Lu Hsün shows how often the life of one creature depends on another. Not only do the strong and evil devour the weak, just as the cat devours the rabbits, but even the sympathetic ducklings eat the no less sympathetic tadpoles. The indifference of the majority of people toward the fortunes of others saddens the writer. "Here two living creatures perished," he writes, "and no one—neither human nor devil—knows when it happened."[38] Or again, "People walked by indifferently, without realizing that here a life had perished."[39] Lu Hsün mentions rabbits, larks, a small dog, and so forth, but the reader is not cognizant of any obvious allegory, especially since the author himself hints at the possibility of generalizations. It is surprising** that in critical analyses of the collection *Outcry* these marvelous stories have almost always been neglected.[40] In my opinion, they are perhaps the richest and most original examples of Lu Hsün's art by comparison with previous works of Chinese literature.

* * *

*For a translation of "The Duck's Comedy" see *Journal of Oriental Literature* (Honolulu: Oriental Literature Society of the University of Hawaii), vol. I (1947), pp. 7-10.—C.J.A.

**Actually, it is not so surprising since, according to Lu Hsün, Eroshenko was an *anarchist* (XII, 514; 1938 ed.; cited in Petrov, *Lu Sin'*, p. 143). These two stories did not appear in the English language *Selected Works* (Yang) either. —C.J.A.

Sometimes Chinese fiction of the early twentieth century is difficult to read. And while Lu Hsün's short stories may also pose definite problems, they are of an entirely different nature. The main difficulties with the novel of exposure are those of language[41] (no longer a problem in Lu Hsün's post-1918 works) and structure[42] (difficulty in tracing the development of the plot and keeping track of the multitude of protagonists), while in Lu Hsün's works one encounters a complex conception of reality coupled with diametrically opposed conclusions, the same type of difficulty one might experience in talking with an intelligent conversationalist. Some of Lu Hsün's short stories, therefore, are open to various interpretations, whereas in an analysis of the novel of exposure such a problem hardly ever arises, and the ideas of the authors are, as a rule, fairly similar. For the most part, early twentieth-century novels are devoid of any philosophical foundation, i.e., excluding the author's particular political bias, be it that of a reformer or a revolutionary. Of course, in the novel *The Travels of Lao Ts'an* Liu O does develop his own philosophy, but it is merely a synthesis of Confucian, Taoist, and Buddhist ideas.[43] By 1907-08 Lu Hsün, by contrast, had already become acquainted with many of the trends in European thought, and from then on he continued to perfect his knowledge. This enabled him to depict human life in the process of its development, to penetrate the inner world of man, and to become a true psychologist.

Despite the complexity of Lu Hsün's ideas and moods, his stories are, on the whole, optimistic. In "My Old Home," "The Village Opera," and "A Small Incident" there are very clear major chords, and even "The True Story of Ah Q" convinces the reader that all is not lost for China's toilers. "Though in the eyes of the reformer the past and present have, at least for the time being, come to naught, the national character can be changed,"[44] commented Lu Hsün in 1926, as if deciphering the main theme of the tale. During the late 1910s and early 1920s China presented Lu Hsün with a rather unattractive picture. The writer attempted to describe it without any adornments, though occasionally, when following "the general's"[45] orders and wishing to fortify the readers' hopes, he did, nevertheless, make his stories more optimistic. "Just as I made a wreath appear from nowhere at the son's grave in 'Medicine,' so in 'Tomorrow' I did not say that Fourth Shan's wife would never dream* of her little boy."[46] Lu Hsün's brand of optimism, however, bears no resemblance to the hopeless utopia of Liang Ch'i-ch'ao, who envisioned a mighty bourgeois China (see "The Future of the New China"), or even the more justified notion of "humanitarian government" in Liu O's novel *The Travels of Lao Ts'an*.

Lu Hsün was very cautious in his use of "embellishment," and this explains why the stories "Medicine" and "Tomorrow" admit of various interpretations. Compare, for example, the following critiques on the story "Tomorrow" made by two sinologists. First, Hsü Ch'in-wen: "Lu Hsün concludes the story with comments that convey the impression that the author is full of hope for the future: 'Only the dark night fled through this silence, making way for the oncoming day.' Even the title 'Tomorrow' emphasizes that a bright new society will soon arrive."[47] Second, B. Krebsová: "From now on there is nothing left for the woman to do but wait for her own death in order to escape this never-ending 'Tomorrow,' as anguishing as the one which followed the death of her child."[48] Which of the two critics is correct? In my view both, and yet neither, because in each instance only one aspect of Lu Hsün's art has been emphasized. The fate of the woman, who has lost her one and only son, is infinitely tragic; but the writer, as it were, challenges the people not to become engulfed in this tragedy.

Allegory—a characteristic of classical Chinese literature, though practically lost in the novel of exposure—is one of the basic features of Lu Hsün's works. This is already apparent when one compares his "Diary of a Madman" with that of Gogol.[49] It seems to me, therefore, that a symbolic interpretation of some details in Lu Hsün's stories is justified, especially if the interpretation is based on the author's own allusions and does not lead to vulgarization of his ideas or concentrate merely on an "advantageous," revolutionary aspect, as is the case in several articles dealing with the crow on Hsia Yü's grave.[50] The main purpose of the crow, in my opinion, is to intensify the melancholy tone of the final scene "in the spirit of L. Andreev,"[51] although there is undoubtedly an optimistic strain in "Medicine," as reflected in the very title of the work itself. The story, so to speak, operates on two levels: the

---

*In other words, Lu Hsün leaves open the possibility that the widow may once again "see" her son, in a dream.—C.J.A.

thin, outer surface (steamed bread soaked in the blood of the revolutionary, which does not save the consumptive), and a second, underlying theme which is incomparably more broad. Lu Hsün believes that the blood spilled by the revolutionaries is not shed in vain. This is the whole idea behind the wreath which Lu Hsün "added" to Hsia Yü's grave. Sooner or later the "medicine" *will* cure the nation, and that is why, in my opinion, the title of the story should not be translated "Drug."[52]

Along with these optimistic sentiments, which were later developed in Lu Hsün's essays, certain prose poems of *Wild Grass*, and the satiric-heroic tales of *Old Tales Retold*, there is also a melancholy, pessimistic note sounded in *Outcry*. The majority of the writer's early critics have overemphasized[53] the importance of this, while the majority of present-day critics have underemphasized[54] it. Nevertheless, Lu Hsün is so complex and important a writer that any attempt to "straighten him out" or "smooth his wrinkles" will only lessen his literary worth. The writer himself was well aware that some of his stories would leave the reader depressed. Not only did he take a firm stand against letting children read his "Diary of a Madman," but in 1924 he even delayed the republication of the collection *Outcry*.[55] "My works are too somber, because the only 'reality' that seems to exist for me is 'darkness and emptiness,'" he wrote in 1925.[56]

Such feelings of melancholia, which impart particular psychological depth to Lu Hsün's works and which are most apparent in the collections *Hesitation* and *Wild Grass*, were primarily the result of tragic circumstances. Undoubtedly the influence of modern literature (Nietzsche, Artsybashev, L. Andreev, et al.[57]) was partly responsible, as also the writer's harsh attitude toward traditional art. "The Chinese have never dared to look life straight in the face," wrote Lu Hsün. "They only know how to lie and deceive. Hence the false literature which plunged them even more deeply into deceipt."[58] Part of the blame for the flourishing of such literature clearly belongs to early twentieth-century novelists; although, of course, they approached social problems more seriously than did many other Chinese writers. In Lu Hsün's works, however, the superficial optimism of the majority of his predecessors is replaced by a deep insight into the workings of the old society and a caustic criticism in which one can sense the pain he feels for his own people. Life around him was gloomy, and yet Lu Hsün discovered new facets of it that strengthened his hope.

In general Lu Hsün's short stories are characterized by complexity and a changing of moods, as opposed to a certain monotony found in the novel of exposure (with the exception, perhaps, of Liu O's *The Travels of Lao Ts'an*). The mood of the author and the heroes changes, not just from story to story, but within the confines of a single work. In "My Old Home," for example, the narrator returns home with melancholy feelings. Before him stands the ruined countryside. Then he dreams of meeting Jun-t'u and speaking to him like an old friend, and once more disappointment, even more profound than at first, overtakes him. Nevertheless, a new hope is expressed at the end of the story. The hero [i.e., the narrator—C.J.A.] believes that people will break down the barriers along the way to happiness with their own hands. Such complexity, a complexity characteristic of life itself, is extraordinarily alluring in Lu Hsün's works.

Principles of characterization

It is primarily through his characters that Lu Hsün's humanistic ideas are conveyed to the reader. The concrete, living person plays a role in his short stories that he never played in traditional Chinese literature. But let me begin with what, at first glance, may appear to be a biased interpretation of how Lu Hsün and the early twentieth-century novelists chose the names or the nicknames of their heroes. In so doing, Li Pao-chia stressed the most prominent features of his characters, such as a particular physical peculiarity (Fat Mama Huang, Blockhead Fu, Moneybags Ho the Third). Occasionally Lu Hsün also makes use of this device (e.g., Red-eyed Ah-yi in "Medicine"); but sometimes he chooses the character's name in a completely different way, and this very technique, it seems to me, reflects the modern character of his art.

Lu Hsün devotes six pages of the introduction to "The True Story of Ah Q" to a caustic "explanation" of his hero's real name and whether or not in general it is really possible to write about such people as Ah Q. Artfully parodying traditional researchers, the author demonstrates step by step how the old rules for describing a man like Ah Q do not apply. Are you curious about the hero's surname? He has none. And the proof is supplied in the brilliant scene with the "Honorable" Chao. Would you like to know the hero's first name? No one even has any idea what character to use; and so, the Latin letter "Q" appears in its place! This single letter, however, has a greater satirical impact than most of the nicknames found in early twentieth-century novels. Though the letter "Q" in the name of the hero Ah Q seems to have been chosen arbitrarily, on closer inspection one discovers throughout the narrative the outline of a pitiful and ridiculous hero with a large bald head and a tiny, scanty queue.[59] Moreover, Li Pao-chia uses his nicknames to ridicule the one who bears them, be he an official, a moneylender, or a shopkeeper. In this instance the sting of Lu Hsün's satire is aimed not at Ah Q himself, but at those who have deprived him of everything, including a name.

From each and every one of Lu Hsün's short stories the reader gains a clear impression of the hero's social standing. (Ah Q, for example, is "a day laborer and a tramp, who never knows what he will do tomorrow, or where and what he will feed himself."[60]) While authors of the novel of exposure did identify the role of their characters in society, this role was almost always a stereotyped one: an official was an official, a peasant a peasant. In Lu Hsün's works, however, the relationship between the hero and his environment is complicated and involved. What the hero thinks about himself (K'ung I-chi, for example) is sometimes belied by his actual situation. Some critics, therefore, have even debated whether or not Chinese writers in general had a limited conception of the internal world of man, a problem that arose because "popular" fiction, the novel of exposure included, attempted to reveal the hero's character simply by describing his actions, without any effort to show the complex workings of the soul.[61] But this was not so much a national idiosyncrasy as a limitation of traditional prose writers, and Lu Hsün's works supply the proof.

Overcoming the inertia that had taken hold of Chinese literature (and Gogol's work gave Lu Hsün a good deal of support in this radical departure from tradition), the writer created "Diary of a Madman," a tale that hinges on the revelation of the hero's internal world. V. F. Sorokin is no doubt correct in stressing "the mastery with which Lu Hsün describes the course of the hero's illness, from the first, still vague suspicion to the full realization that *he himself* is not only a victim but an accomplice in the crime."[62] Nothing similar or even remotely similar to this can be found in the early twentieth-century Chinese novel. Generally speaking, the characters in the early twentieth-century novel of exposure were monochromatic (scoundrel, saint, dupe, etc.), but Lu Hsün, who had learned from his more perceptive predecessors (Ts'ao Hsüeh-ch'in, Wu Wo-yao, and Tseng P'u), could understand both the complexity and contrariness of human psychology. In the stories "My Old Home," "A Small Incident," "The Dragon Boat Festival," and others he even demonstrates how effective a device like interior monologue, which was new to Chinese literature, can be. Since many of the "stand-in" narrators in the collection *Outcry* reflect the views of the author, the introspection [literally "self-analysis"—C.J.A.] of these characters applies to the writer himself. This gives his style unusual strength and credibility, for no other Chinese writer had a greater right to say: "I do indeed experiment on others, but most often it is myself that I mercilessly dissect."[63]

Unlike the novelists, Lu Hsün made use of the most laconic genre in creative fiction—the short story; skillful choice of the moment of action, therefore, plays a decisive role in his works. The writer leads his hero right into the thick of the action and very seldom or very sparingly describes his past. The background of the heroine in the story "Tomorrow," we might say, is revealed in a total of two lines.[64] More details are given about Jun-t'u's past in the story "My Old Home," and even though there is still a large, thirty-year hiatus, "the peasant's entire life seems to pass before the reader's eyes."[65] Such skill was unknown among the satiric novelists. Moreover, although Wu Wo-yao (*A Crime Involving Nine Lives*) and Tseng P'u (*A Flower in an Ocean of Sin*) had already begun to explore the technique of plot inversion, Lu Hsün even more thoroughly undermined the principle of strict temporal sequence, a characteristic of traditional Chinese literature. In his works, present and past are freely interwoven. Reminiscences of the past, which are just as clear and sometimes even clearer than what is happening, intrude upon the present. "It is upon such contrasts that 'My Old Home' and 'The Village Opera' are based," writes L. D. Pozdneeva. "At first 'My Old Home' is described through the irridescent recollections of childhood, and then as it appears in the eyes of a mature man: grey, dismal, and dilapidated. The reverse process takes place in the plot of 'The Village

Opera.' The author's unpleasant impressions of a theater in Peking
... are replaced by recollections of the marvelous days of childhood and the popular theater."[66] Fortunately, this reverse parallelism has been noticed mainly by researchers and not readers, otherwise Lu Hsün might have been accused of oversimplification.*
Actually, the story "My Old Home" also begins in the present, recollections of the past are wedged in naturally, and then the author again shifts back to the present. The distribution of parts is unequal, but this creates a sensation of perfect compositional homogeneity.

In the novels of Tseng P'u (*A Flower in an Ocean of Sin*) and Wu Wo-yao (the Lucky Man in *Strange Events*) it is already possible to speak of gradual character development. Lu Hsün's intrusion into the lives of his characters is, as a rule, only momentary. In the majority of his short stories the author has neither the opportunity nor the need to show how the characters evolved, although when he does consider this necessary, he does so with great skill. Recall, for example, Jun-t'u in "My Old Home," Mr. N in "The Story of Hair," and finally, Ah Q. In the stories "My Old Home" and "The Story of Hair" there is a gradual decrescendo, a process of degeneration. In "The True Story of Ah Q" there is a temporary crescendo, and then the dénouement. But character development does not always require an extended period of time, and in Lu Hsün's short stories sometimes a single episode or even a single strong impression will suffice. And although such an approach to characterization was beyond the novel of exposure, Lu Hsün realized quite well the effectiveness of this technique, as demonstrated in "A Small Incident," the story with the deliberately understated title.

At first the passenger in "A Small Incident" is annoyed by the strained circumstances and does not believe that anything important has happened. "I saw how slowly you fell," he thought. "Now how could you have hurt yourself? You're just pretending; and that's disgusting. The rickshaw puller is poking his nose into someone else's business and causing unnecessary trouble for himself. Why don't you solve your own problems?"[67] But when the rickshaw puller takes the old woman by the hand and boldly walks to

---
*Literally "schematicism," presumably the indiscriminate use of formulas.
—C.J.A.

the police station, facing an inevitable fine, or perhaps even prison, the passenger's opinion changes abruptly. "Suddenly I had a strange feeling. His dusty, retreating figure seemed larger at that instant. Indeed, the further he walked the larger he loomed, until I had to look up at him. At the same time, he seemed gradually to be exerting a pressure on me that threatened to overpower the small self under my fur-lined gown."[68] Of course the writer has chosen a hero who is already somewhat prone to change, but this only testifies to Lu Hsün's keen sense of artistry. (The noblest of Ah Q's deeds could no more have moved the "Honorable" Chao than Hsia Yü's words could have made the jailkeeper or the executioner see the light of reason.) It is, after all, no coincidence that Lu Hsün wrote the story "A Small Incident" [1920] in the first person, for there is no doubt about the spiritual communion between the author and the narrator.

In order to give his characters greater depth Lu Hsün exploited fully the relationships between them, a technique known as indirect description. A similar technique was employed in the works of early twentieth-century novelists, e.g., the exposure of one villainous character in the dialogue of another. Thus, in Li Pao-chia's novel *Modern Times* the author uses a Christian missionary to sneer at the venality of those with whom he comes into contact. The very same technique is used in Lu Hsün's tale "The True Story of Ah Q." "Ah Q considers Ch'ien a 'secret agent for foreigners'; and in essence he is correct."[69] In Chinese literary criticism this device is called *"hung yün t'o yüeh"* (literally "to set off the moon with the clouds," i.e., to color the clouds and leave the moon white). Although it was used both in the classics[70] and in the novel of exposure, Lu Hsün developed it to perfection. The link between characters in early twentieth-century novels is still relatively weak, but Lu Hsün makes use of all secondary characters to amplify the personality of the main hero; and in turn, secondary characters are judged by their attitude toward the main hero.

Descriptions of the hero's external appearance did not, as a rule, occupy a great deal of space in traditional Chinese fiction, and they had scant relevance to internal character development. The novel of exposure contributed little to this process, and sometimes writers even flatly refused to satirize characters because of their impressive looks. Lu Hsün, like a true Chinese artist, also uses this "method of black and white description" (*pai-miao shuo-fa*), which was familiar to the native reader. In so doing he tries to isolate the most prominent features in the external appearance of his heroes.

> Someone, I don't remember who, aptly remarked that the best way to convey a man's character with a minimum of strokes is to draw his eyes. If you draw all the hairs on his head, no matter how accurately, it will not be very much use. I keep trying to learn this method, but unfortunately I have not yet mastered it.[71]

This does not mean, of course, that for every character Lu Hsün described the eyes in detail. In several instances—the portrait of K'ung I-chi, for example—the writer remains faithful to the traditions of the Chinese novel.

> He was a big man, strangely pallid, and scars often showed among the wrinkles on his face. He had a large, unkempt beard streaked with white. Although he wore a long gown, it was dirty and tattered, and it looked as if it had not been washed or mended for over ten years.[72]

These are the typical elements of the classical character portrait—stature, facial features, hair, and dress. The accent, however, is slightly different: the tall stature accentuates the leanness rather than the powerful physique of the hero; there is color in the face, but no shape (i.e., oval, square, etc.); and special attention is given to the wrinkles, scars, and scratches—signs of adversity. Relatively little space is allotted to dress, and the cataloguing of finery or other decorative items is supplanted by intentional emphasis on filth and slovenliness. The same is true, for example, in the portrait of Jun-t'u from "My Old Home." The individual features of Lu Hsün's heroes are, in all probability, nowhere as diverse as their misfortunes; nevertheless, these individual features do exist, and Lu Hsün selects them with great resourcefulness.

Unlike traditional novelists, who usually described the hero's physical appearance immediately after his entrance onto the scene, as if to dispense with an unpleasant duty as quickly as possible, Lu Hsün usually introduces elements of the character portrait gradually, sprinkling them throughout the narrative.

> For example, at first we know nothing about the general physical appearance of Ah Q. Only in the course of his conversation with others is it explained that he loves to glare. He "deigns" to get angry. Each time Ah Q wins a "moral victory" his ringworm scars turn scarlet. And when he

is punished for putting on airs, his brownish pigtail also becomes apparent. As for his thick lips,[73] we only learn of them in the scene where Ah Q competes with Whiskers Wang in catching lice.[74]

Literally every detail of Lu Hsün's portrait reveals something about the hero's psychology, the main point of interest. What is important, we might say, is not the shape of the eyes, but their expression. Recall, for example, the executioner's eyes (in "Medicine"), which glitter "like two daggers," or the "black circles" under Old Shuan's eyes—the marks of sleeplessness and anxiety. There were some similes of this nature in the novel of exposure, but for the most part this was entirely new, and that is why Lu Hsün's heroes seem so alive to us, whereas the heroes of early twentieth-century Chinese literature, with few exceptions, are difficult to visualize.

Let me mention one other detail of considerable importance in this regard. Whereas in traditional Chinese novels the description of costume blended with the character portrait or even substituted for it, Lu Hsün, instead of becoming enamored with gorgeous attire (and the accusatory novelists were guilty of this too), uses individualistic touches, and always with a calculated effect. Recall, for example, K'ung I-chi's long robe, a "privilege" of the scholarly class that the impoverished and humiliated man cannot part with, and Ah Q's shirt and trousers, which also become grist for Lu Hsün's satirical mill. The hero's shirt is taken by the "Honorable" Chao, and he only manages to keep the pants because he "absolutely could not take them off."

It is in this relationship between the concrete and the general, in my opinion, that the most important difference between Lu Hsün's technique and that of early twentieth-century novelists lies. Individual episodes in the novel of exposure are too cursory and commonplace, without any claim to far-reaching conclusions, and in order to supply proof for one or the other generalization (the corruption of the bureaucracy, for example) the writer had to introduce more and more new episodes. Having read about a clerk who takes bribes, we are convinced that he really is a bribe-taker, but already with the very next official (the ringleader, for example) the author feels obliged to prove this to us again. Novels of exposure merely provide a glimpse of life in its totality, whereas in Lu Hsün's works every little incident possesses both concrete and general significance.

For the sake of brevity Lu Hsün sometimes discards some details that are either too personal or important only for a given individual. For example, the man who served as the prototype for the unsuccessful scholar in the story "The White Light" endured even more than Lu Hsün's hero. Not only did he fail to pass the government examinations and find the buried treasure, he was also fleeced by a certain woman. His death was a dreadful one: he stabbed himself several times in the throat with a pair of scissors, spilled burning hot oil from a lamp over himself, and then threw himself into the river.[75] Not one of the accusatory novelists could have resisted the temptation to describe such a tragedy (recall Li Pao-chia's *Living Hell*, the massacre of Chu in Wu Wo-yao's *After the Disaster*, or the dreadful torture in Liu O's *The Travels of Lao Ts'an*), but Lu Hsün cool-headedly refuses to do so. Moreover, the man who served as the prototype for Ch'en Shih-ch'eng was quite amusing. He constantly made ludicrous mistakes in pronunciation, wrote characters incorrectly, and composed absurd verse, etc.[76] Such details, of which the novel of exposure took advantage, were also discarded by Lu Hsün. He was more interested in describing incomparably complex feelings than he was in debunking "ignorant intellectuals."

Often Lu Hsün combines the character traits of many people into one hero,[77] but rather than creating an abstraction (like the Yellow Dragon in *The Travels of Lao Ts'an*), as some early twentieth-century prose writers did, the character begins to lead a life of its own. The writer's predecessors were unable to make such an aggressive, dynamic synthesis; and, perhaps because they were afraid of straying too far from reality, seldom combined several prototypes into one character. Nevertheless, Lu Hsün himself pointed out that composite images were a tradition in the field of Chinese art. "An artist who paints people observes them quietly for a long time, mulls over the image in his mind, and then, with a single stroke of the brush, sketches the portrait, always without the aid of a model."[78] Once again we see how the writer, far ahead of early twentieth-century novelists and even authors of Chinese fiction in general, pursues the most productive of aesthetic traditions.

Landscape and the hero's environment

In traditional Chinese novels, scenes of nature and the common, everyday surroundings of the people were, like character portraits, very colorful, but they were not always relevant to the actions and experiences of the characters. Often lines from traditional poetry were used to create a certain atmosphere or to arouse an appropriate response from the reader, a technique also used in the majority of the novels of exposure. This shows a tendency on the part of the traditional Chinese novel to synthesize the achievements of classical prose and poetry. Not until Lu Hsün did the author's own prose descriptions finally replace poetic reminiscences. Nevertheless, it should be mentioned that in some respects the novel of exposure did not follow this classical tradition. Some writers (Li Pao-chia, for example) kept explanations of the environment to a minimum, considering them embellishments that diverted the reader's attention from the main conflict. These writers were guided by earlier Chinese classics (the novella and drama), which were extremely laconic in their descriptions of setting, and this same tendency can be observed in the works of Lu Hsün.

> In the pages of Chinese drama there are no set descriptions, and the colored pictures sold for children during the New Year focus on the hero. (Only the contemporary ones have a background.) I am convinced that my own works do not require any background either, so I do not describe nature, and I do not create long dialogues.[79]

Other writers (Liu O, Su Man-shu), by contrast, used more elaborate and complex pictorial settings in a deliberate attempt to enlighten and expose, and Lu Hsün's art reveals this tendency also. In my view, the writer managed, when describing the hero's milieu, to draw on the achievements of classical prose and poetry as well as this quasi-conflicting feature of early twentieth-century Chinese literature. The laconicism of his stories did not lead to a complete dearth of pictorial settings, nor did their active use result in proliferation. Lu Hsün introduces landscape or environmental details with isolated, economical strokes of the brush at the same time that he develops the action and reveals the psychology of his characters.

The extreme brevity of landscape paintings in the majority of short stories in *Outcry* is fully justified, and this is borne out by the fact that the heroes portrayed could not and do not have the time to admire nature. Does Ah Q—who vents his spleen on others and hardly has time, when not working or being thrashed, to console himself with "moral victories"—really have time for nature too? Our hero does not notice the beauty of Wei-chuang village even when he has to leave it. And yet, the author does not pass over the scenery. "Most of the country outside the village consisted of paddy fields, green as far as the eye could see with tender shoots of young rice, dotted here and there with round black moving objects—peasants cultivating the fields. But blind to the delights of country life, Ah Q simply went on his way, for he knew instinctively that this was far removed from his 'search for food.'"[80] Such satirical use of scenery was unknown to the novel of exposure.

Lu Hsün describes scenery in a variety of ways, depending on the mood of the hero and the reader. The sad and touching description of the deserted village in winter in "My Old Home" is justified by the lyric atmosphere of the work as a whole, while in the tragic-comic story "Storm in a Teacup" landscape is appropriately used to parody. The writer sees such enormous possibilities for landscape to intensify expressiveness that he even concludes several of his stories ("Tomorrow," "Medicine") with it. As a matter of fact, he always paid closer attention to endings and tried to impart philosophical significance to them.[81] Thus, landscape provides its own kind of synthesis. Though concrete events may be forgotten, the individual sensation that every reader feels will never be forgotten.

In addition to the tragic description of the depopulated village in winter time, there are bright, optimistic landscapes throughout the hero's reminiscences and dreams, and these play an important role in "My Old Home."

> As I dozed, a stretch of emerald seashore spread itself before my eyes, and above, a round golden moon hung from a deep blue sky. I thought: hope cannot be said to exist, nor can it be said not to exist. It is just like roads across the earth. Actually, the earth had no roads to begin with, but when many men pass one way, a road is paved.[82]

Here the relationship between nature and the fate of the people—present and future—becomes particularly apparent. In all of the novels of exposure only one comparable example can be found. The hero of Liu O's novel *The Travels of Lao Ts'an*, while observing the ice flow on the Yellow River, ponders the disastrous fate of the Ts'ao-chou region [in reality, China in general—C.J.A.].

Lu Hsün also develops this theme in many of his short stories.

But the atmosphere Lu Hsün creates is not limited to a single type of landscape. Animals, birds, and insects appear throughout his stories. Dogs howling in the dark help the writer create the somber atmosphere in the story "Tomorrow." The fat black dog Ah Q fights in the monastery courtyard helps to set off the insignificance and weakness of the hero.* The mysterious beast or "*ch'a*," the mollusks with "multi-colored shells," and the "flying fish" enrich the character of young Jun-t'u, a brave peasant lad who has seen much. All this fills Lu Hsün's stories with the color, movement, and sound that were lacking in novels of exposure.

Common objects of everyday use, the things with which the hero comes into contact, also play an important role in the writer's works. In contrast to the pipes, tea services, and other trivia that fill the pages of one novel of exposure after another, all such things in Lu Hsün's works are concrete and relevant. The reader will never forget the cup with its eighteen rivets in the story "Storm in a Teacup," the one and only souvenir of the restoration; the peas flavored with aniseed, which the poverty-stricken scholar uses to treat the children ("K'ung I-chi"); the censer from the Hsüan Te (Illustrious Virtue) era, the booty of sham revolutionaries ("The True Story of Ah Q"); or the touching "clay figurine, two small wooden bowls, and two glass bottles," favorite toys which Fourth Shan's wife places in the grave of her son ("Tomorrow"). Very concrete objects, particularly appropriate to the given situation, acquire a significance in Lu Hsün's stories that is unusual for Chinese literature. With the aid of such details the author creates characters that stick in the memory and unobtrusively exposes the reader to the ideas he hopes to instill in him. If one were to strike out the explicit editorial comments in the novel of exposure, it would be difficult to determine the author's point of view; but if the same were done to Lu Hsün's stories, the main theme would not be lost, because it is supported by the minutest of details in the narrative.

One cannot say that there were no common, everyday objects in the novel of exposure. On the contrary, there were many, and sometimes even too many, because the majority were practically

---

*The dog and wolf (i.e., canines) are common symbols in Lu Hsün's short stories. Sometimes the dog has satirical connotations (the "pug," for instance), but mostly it is simply a carnivore, a flesh-eating mammal.—C.J.A.

useless, used purely for "illustration." Lu Hsün's works are another matter. For example, the "wind" is mentioned five times in the course of the story "A Small Incident," yet each time it is for a different purpose. The first time it creates a framework and allows the narrator to be incorporated into the action ("the north wind was raging, but I had to make a living"). The second time it explains why the carriage was moving along so swiftly ("after a while the wind subsided"). The third time it, so to speak, identifies the cause of the misfortune ("her tattered jacket, unbuttoned and fluttering in the wind, had caught on the shaft"). Fourthly, it underscores the honesty of the rickshaw puller who took it upon himself to go to the police station ("because of the high wind, there was no one outside"). And finally, in the fifth instance, the silence puts the narrator into a pensive mood ("the wind had subsided completely, but the road was still quiet").[83]

These types of details play a somewhat different role in the story "Tomorrow." "The doctor admires his long fingernails in front of Fourth Shan's widow, who has brought her last coppers to cure her only son. He spurts out unintelligible magic formulas, without even thinking of alleviating the mother's grief. The apothecary too is busy with his fingernails and does not hasten to fill the prescription."[84] Here the symbolism (the well-kept fingernails) serves not a multitude of functions like the wind in "A Small Incident," but only one—a frivolous and useless habit is juxtaposed with genuine grief. The Chinese novelists used the same technique of supercharging phenomena, but in so doing they often lost a sense of proportion. Lu Hsün, on the other hand, rarely repeats the exact same detail, even though it would not be out of place—which explains why repetition is an effective literary device in his works.

Structure

Outwardly the structure of the stories in the collection *Outcry* appears very simple, even primitive. Events are presented, as a rule, through the eyes of one man, and the fate of secondary characters is closely linked with that of the main hero. Only in the story "Medicine" are there two interdependent plot lines (the fate of Hsia Yü and the fate of Young Shuan). This is the essential difference between Lu Hsün and Chinese novelists, who attempt to introduce a multitude of plot lines into the work. Behind this seemingly simple structure of Lu Hsün's works, however, lies the great mastery of an artist. For example, having made the decision to combine such disparate events as the execution of the revolutionary Hsia Yü and the death (from consumption) of Young Shuan, the cafe owner's son, the writer must find a structural basis for his decision. And Lu Hsün chooses his connecting link with great boldness: bread stained with the blood of a revolutionary, which, according to popular Chinese belief, cures consumption. Moreover, by not introducing one of the heroes (Hsia Yü) onto the scene, he flatly breaks with the tradition of his predecessors. True, the same technique had already been used in the classic Chinese novel (Lo Kuan-chung, for example[85]), but by the time of the novel of exposure it had almost fallen into disuse, because it was too complex. It was Lu Hsün who once again revived this device, though not, of course, without the influence of foreign literature. Then, in the final episode of "Medicine," Lu Hsün brings the mothers of both victims together. The author utilizes this episode to show that no matter how much the executioners may try to separate the mothers, their grief and their interests are essentially indivisible. The scene where the two unfortunate women meet, like the wreath placed on Hsia Yü's grave, reaffirms the reader's faith in the eventual victory of the revolution.[86]

According to Chu T'ung, there are "not two, but several" plot lines in "The True Story of Ah Q" and "K'ung I-chi."[87] This is true, particularly in reference to "The True Story of Ah Q"; but the basic structural principle (maintaining one central hero throughout the work and making the majority of episodes relate to this hero) is the same here as in other stories in the collection *Outcry*. One should not, in my opinion, artificially track down secondary plot lines in Lu Hsün's works (as Chu T'ung has the tendency to do). Lu Hsün's structural innovation lies in refusing to let the plot branch off into too many directions (a trait common to all traditional Chinese novels) and in developing a "simple" composition. The story "My Old Home" seems, at first glance, to be cluttered with unnecessary reminiscences, but researchers have discovered numerous references to recurring themes in them.[88] And although such an analysis may be debatable, it does testify to the richness of Lu Hsün's art.

The structural simplicity of *Outcry* conceals a masterful effort to break loose from traditional rules. In several early twentieth-century works (Wu Wo-yao's *After the Disaster* and Liu O's *The Travels of Lao Ts'an*) we still encounter the "fortunate reunion" (*t'uan-yüan*), a technique the novel of exposure inherited from traditional literature. Usually such endings were not envisioned in the narrative, and sometimes even contradicted it, but Lu Hsün's numerous optimistic endings ("My Old Home," "A Small Incident") seem, so to speak, to reflect life's natural laws, clarified through the author's imagination. Occasionally, however, the writer clearly breaks with tradition. The critic Tan Yen-i rightly mentions, for example, that "The True Story of Ah Q" with its "grand conclusion" (*ta t'uan-yüan*), the shooting of the hero, dealt a brilliant and crushing blow "to all traditional ideas and techniques."[89]

One other specific structural feature was typical of traditional Chinese novels: the beginnings and endings were derived from the popular tale ("It is related that . . ." and "If you want to know what happened next, turn to the next chapter and everything will become clear"). For a long time these devices served a useful function, underscoring the relationship between the "multi-chapter novel" and popular art and making it more accessible to the broad masses. By the early part of this century, however, with the absorption of new themes and ideas into Chinese literature, the complex structure and other elements of the oral tale had begun to seem archaic. By the 1920s Lu Hsün and his cohorts had completely rejected them, and the traditional beginnings and endings of the novel of exposure were replaced by a variety of structural devices. Lu Hsün had dispensed with classical verses, long digressions, and typical shorthand phrases like "but we will say no more of this" (all features that were characteristic of traditional Chinese novels) even earlier—in 1904-06, following the translation of Jules Verne's novels. In his works all of the artistic elements acquire a naturalness and balance.

The author's point of view

As mentioned above, it was the authors of the novel of exposure who introduced first-person narration into the Chinese novel. This was a new device, related to the gradual awakening of individuality, and it was completely natural for Lu Hsün, therefore, to inherit the tradition of his predecessors. However, his narrator almost never becomes the central character but usually relates the adventures of more remarkable (from the author's or narrator's point of view) heroes. Obvious examples are "A Small Incident," "K'ung I-chi," "My Old Home," "The Story of Hair," "The Rabbits and the Cat," and "The Duck's Comedy," the main exception being "Diary of a Madman," the first story in *Outcry*. The speech of a lunatic often contains more truth, and sometimes even more subtlety and wit, than that of a healthy man. Lu Hsün made use of this strange fact when he put his own ideas in the mouth of the madman, and this accounts for the hero's observations about the common people (those who have been put in stocks, etc.), the information on the "history of cannibalism" in China, and so forth. The writer was able to disguise his own intelligent ideas behind the madman's gibberish.

Rare is the critic who misses the opportunity to mention that the narrator and the author of a creative work are not one and the same person. This is not always the case, and many stories by Lu Hsün, who was the first Chinese writer to reveal the inner world of the individual in all its complexity, serve as proof. The attention he paid to his own personality, in particular, helped him to accomplish this [i.e., explore the inner world of his characters— C.J.A.], for he literally took the most direct path to understanding human psychology, like the doctor who tests a new preparation on himself. Thus, some critics, without sufficient justification, have deprecated the character of the narrator in "A Small Incident,"[90] forgetting that it was he who celebrated the rickshaw puller's nobility and condemned his own essentially momentary egoism. It cannot be overemphasized that the narrator in the majority of Lu Hsün's works is either a reflection of the author himself or, in any case, a man with similar convictions. As for other characters, the situation is different. In such instances, even when the author utilizes facts from his own biography, he creates a new individual each time. That is why any attempt to equate Lu Hsün with Mr. N ("The Story of Hair"), Fang Hsuan-ch'o ("The Dragon Boat Festival"),[91] the "foreign devil" ("The Story of Hair"), the "imitation foreign devil" ("The True Story of Ah Q"),[92] or more negative characters is unjustified.

Does the narrator-author actively intrude in the narration? Most often Lu Hsün, in contrast to his immediate predecessors, refrains from explicit comments, although sometimes he is not ashamed to express his own opinion about the characters. Here, for example, is how he exposes the obsequiousness of the bourgeois Philistine in "The Dragon Boat Festival": "On this day Fang Hsüan-ch'o was seized by a new uneasiness. I say 'uneasiness,' though this 'uneasiness' went no further than idle discussion."[93] Or again, "Unaware that this was a result of his own laziness and uselessness, he regarded himself as a man who was not prone to decisive action."[94] Lu Hsün, however, cannot be accused of didacticism, because in his stories there is no disparity between the hero's deeds (in the traditional novel he would have been dispassionate and objective) and the author's evaluation of them, whereas authors of the novel of exposure were usually either irate or overzealous. Authorial comment is introduced from time to time, as part of the overall psychological analysis. The satiric novelists seldom provided such an analysis, and that is why their authorial comments seem blunt and direct. Moreover, although there are just as many explicit comments in Lu Hsün's works as in early twentieth-century fiction, they are usually distributed throughout the work and not concentrated in one place. In a number of instances Lu Hsün does use prolonged editorial digressions, in the so-called "introduction" to "The True Story of Ah Q," for example, or the first pages of "The Village Opera," but V. V. Petrov rightly regards these as "innovations in short-length Chinese fiction."[95] This device, introduced into the novel by the early twentieth-century fiction writers, was carried over into the tale and even into the short story by Lu Hsün, though in an incomparably more sophisticated form, i.e., free, unconstrained dialogue integrally linked with description. It is difficult to agree, therefore, that the "introduction" does not fit the general style of "The True Story of Ah Q."[96] It simply lends force and variety to the style.

The author of a literary work often injects satiric or humorous comments in order to express his own views of what is taking place. Of the early twentieth-century fiction writers, Li Pao-chia did this most often (*Exposure of the Official World, Modern Times*). In certain cases Wu Wo-yao (*Strange Events of the Last Twenty Years*, the episode with Kou Ts'ai, etc.) and Tseng P'u (in the portrayal of several scholars, Lu Jen-hsien for example) also used this technique, although there is nothing amusing in most accusatory novels. Comparatively speaking, Lu Hsün makes use of these devices far more often and with incomparably greater skill. In "The True Story of Ah Q," for example, three detachments of soldiers and five detectives hunt for the unarmed farmhand.⁹⁷ A similar episode takes place in Li Pao-chia's novel *Exposure of the Official World* when Hu Hua-jo, commander of a punitive expedition, chases after nonexistent bandits. Here we are shown in panoramic fashion the misfortunes of the unsuspecting victims. But Lu Hsün's comic sensitivity is much greater. Even Ah Q's neighbors in prison come in for their share of satire. "One of them, a country bumpkin, said that the successful provincial candidate was demanding payment of a debt owed by his grandfather, and the other didn't even know why he was there."⁹⁸ For Li Pao-chia (*Living Hell*) such incidents were the subject of most serious concern, whereas Lu Hsün finds the strength to laugh at them.

Be that as it may, it is easy to see why both examples of the grotesque in *Outcry* cited by V. F. Sorokin are taken from "The True Story of Ah Q." The only other story even remotely similar in this respect is "Storm in a Teacup." The others clearly show that in the years from 1918 to 1922 Lu Hsün gravitated toward exposure rather than toward satire. During that period, the author adhered to the novel of censure more closely than the satiric novel, even though personally he placed a higher value on the latter.

The phenomena the accusatory novelists and Lu Hsün described were in essence tragic. Otherwise, why would the writer have considered his tale full of "unnecessary humor" that did not suit the story as a whole?⁹⁹ However difficult it may be to agree with such a harsh self-criticism, the fact remains that Lu Hsün *did* intensify the tragic quality of the work as a whole and *did* end it with the execution of Ah Q, an event that is hardly very amusing. It seems, therefore, that the author of the collection *Outcry* was more an exposer than a satirist.

Perhaps many will disagree with this assessment; traditionally speaking, direct exposure has been regarded as inferior to satire. What is involved here, however, is not so much a difference in degree of skill as a difference in the application of tragic versus comic principles. In my judgment, the stories in *Outcry* should simply be regarded as a higher grade of accusatory literature than the novel of the early 1900s. Lu Hsün was a born satirist, and if there are relatively few comic situations in his short stories, this can be explained by the writer's fear of gravitating toward "laughter for laughter's sake."[100] "I do not like 'humor' and believe that the only gentlemen who can enjoy it are those who like to sit around the table and shoot the breeze. In China it is even difficult to find a translation for this word,"*[101] he wrote in the year 1933, criticizing the bourgeois writer Lin Yü-t'ang, the proponent of English humor. As we see, Lu Hsün drew a sharp distinction between satire and humor, but he did not see such a great difference between satire and exposure.

One other tendency that became manifested in Lu Hsün's work during this period was a gradual recognition of the effectiveness of the grotesque, for the "abuse" of which he, at first, criticized early twentieth-century writers as well as himself. "Once I thought I had written with too much 'exaggeration,' but now I no longer believe this,"[102] he remarked in the article "How 'The True Story of Ah Q' Was Written." Life in China had become so shocking and abnormal that had the writer, in his own words, thrown "a mixed brigade and eight howitzers" at the unarmed Ah Q in addition to the three squads and the machine gun, "it would not have been an exaggeration."[103] Thus, in *Outcry* one senses but the first signs of that enormous satirical talent which came to fruition (though apparently not fully) in Lu Hsün's essays and in *Old Tales Retold*.

Language

Prior to the May Fourth Movement, the classical language, unintelligible to the ear and extremely difficult to learn, held sway over Chinese literature, and only some works (primarily of fiction and drama) were written in *pai-hua*, a language close to the vernacular; then the colloquial language triumphed, and it voraciously assimilated the achievements of both classical Chinese and modern foreign literature. This movement had already begun in the latter half of the nineteenth century and had left its influuence on the novel of exposure in the form of whole dialogues written in local Chinese dialects, the introduction of vulgarisms, and words borrowed from foreign languages. Nevertheless, the final victory of the colloquial over the moribund classical did not come about immediately, and elements of both the old and the new style—mostly

---

*Curiously, this noun is foreign in Chinese (in Yale romanization, *you-mwo*). Apparently it is a recent borrowing from the English. Here Lu Hsün unquestionably associates the word with the English gentry.—C.J.A.

in a disjunct, unsynthesized form—were evident in the novels. Tseng P'u, for example, frequently used lofty and elegant classical expressions in *A Flower in an Ocean of Sin* without even stopping to realize that they were in conflict with the contents of the novel. Such incongruities are no longer apparent in Lu Hsün's creative efforts during the period from 1918 to 1936. Having chosen the colloquial as the basic language of his works, the author could even borrow various phrases from the classical without fear that it would damage the fabric of his narrative. "If a suitable word is not available in the vernacular, I prefer to borrow an expression from the classical in the hope that it can be understood."[104] One must remember, however, that Lu Hsün had studied the classical language since youth and had even composed in it. "And yet, even afterwards," remarks Lin Ch'en, "although he had shifted to *pai-hua*, he still preserved the Wei and Tsin style of *wen-yen* in his parallel constructions.*"[105]

Generally speaking, the grandiose classical language does not destroy but imparts greater expressiveness to Lu Hsün's style. Often the author employs *wen-yen* for satiric purposes. Here we need only recall the titles of the second and third chapters of "The True Story of Ah Q"—"A Brief Account of Ah Q's Victories" (*Yu-sheng chi-lüeh*) and "A Further Account of Ah Q's Victories" (*Hsü yu-sheng chi-lüeh*). Even in translation they sound ridiculous, since the hero is mercilessly thrashed, but in Chinese these phrases acquire an unusual satiric impact, because the author uses titles appropriate to an ancient historical treatise. Lu Hsün also made clever use of the pompous, self-complacent names given to teahouses, shops, etc., in China. It is no coincidence, for example, that the story "K'ung I-chi" takes place in a wineshop called the "Universal Prosperity," or that in the end the hero** crawls in there on broken legs.

Lu Hsün had a delicate sense of which classical words and ex-

---

*Parallelism is very marked in Lu Hsün's prose style, though the influence is difficult to pin down. Parallelism in general had a very long history in Chinese literature and, as Achilles Fang has noted, is "ingrained in Chinese thought." Some Japanese writers, e.g., Mori Ogai, showed a preference for parallelism. And, for that matter, so did John Kennedy. Nevertheless, the use of parallelism is widespread in Lu Hsün's works and it is not at all easy to translate.
—C.J.A.

**Actually, K'ung I-chi, like Ah Q, fits the twentieth-century notion of the "antihero."—C.J.A.

pressions would come alive in the vernacular. "The language of this story (i.e., "A Small Incident"—V.S.) has one feature worthy of mention," stresses Wu Pen-hsing. "Almost all of the dialogue is written in the colloquial language of the north, while the description, though it too mostly uses the vernacular, includes several literary terms like *tseng-o* (to hate), *ch'ou-ch'u* (to hesitate), *ch'a-i* (to be surprised), *ning-chih* (to congeal) and others. This was a peculiarity of all May Fourth Movement literature, although it stood out more prominently in Lu Hsün's works than in those of other writers."[106] Wu later mentions that all of the above-mentioned classical words were absorbed into the vernacular and subsequently became part of it (though not, we might add, without the encouragement of Lu Hsün).

The early twentieth century was the first time that Western literature [i.e., *belles lettres*—C.J.A.] really spread to China. Though the accusatory novelists were too timid to utilize foreign stylistic achievements, Lu Hsün, on the other hand, made extensive use of the vocabulary and syntactical features of European languages and still remained a profoundly Chinese writer. The satirical effects created by early twentieth-century fiction writers were almost exclusively limited to plot situations. Special linguistic effects, words that sound absurd even out of context, like Saltykov-Shchedrin's "pompadour" or Chekhov's "shilishper," were unknown to the novel of exposure. Conflict continues to be a primary factor in Lu Hsün's works also, but it is complemented by pungent and witty language. Chu T'ung,[107] for example, advises us to pay close attention to such passages in "The True Story of Ah Q" as the following: "As for the consequences of these events (i.e., the robbery of Chao's home and the execution of Ah Q—V.S.), the successful provincial candidate was the most affected: the stolen chest was never found, and his whole family broke into tears."[108] In contrasting the two situations (the execution of Ah Q and the hollow "suffering" of the successful provincial candidate's family) Lu Hsün uses a word that is intrinsically amusing—*hao-t'ao*, to wail or to weep bitterly. The translation "broke into tears" does not capture fully its satirical pungency. Likewise, the word *chua* ("to snatch"), which aptly conveys the greediness of the executioner in "Medicine," is normally used in reference to wild beasts.[109] Despite the numerous scenes of bribery in the novel of exposure, we do not find expressions that by their very nature debunk greed.

It should be mentioned, however, that words like *hao-t'ao* and *chua* were well known and were not invented by Lu Hsün himself. His basic approach is somewhat different: words that are not intrinsically absurd become absurd in context. The word *i-lao*, for example, means "one who has remained true to antiquity." Until Lu Hsün this word had a serious connotation. Confucian morals prescribed that an official or scholar remain faithful to a dynasty even after the forceful overthrow of the ruler and not give his services to the "usurper." But the creator of "The True Story of Ah Q" ironically awards this title to the successful provincial candidate and the successful county candidate, who always keep their noses in the wind and only become imbued with this spiirit of "loyalty" on the day the revolution fails.

As in the early twentieth-century novels, there are scenes in Lu Hsün's works that are fabricated mostly out of well-chosen details. But even in such instances the writer goes far beyond his predecessors, particularly in his ability to use the tone of the passage to enhance the author's "remarks" (entirely too short in the novel of exposure) and in his ability to add nuances to the verbs themselves, thereby revealing the psychological state of the hero.

> The customers continued to *tease* him ...
> "Why spoil a man's good name groundlessly?" he would ask, his eyes *bulging.**
> K'ung I-chi *flushed*, the veins on his forehead standing out as he remonstrated ...[110]

Thus, the disparity between the dialogue and the author's description, a disparity that existed in the novel of exposure, is avoided. When, on the other hand, the dialogue needs to move along more swiftly or spontaneously, the writer usually eliminates the verb "said," a word that was obligatory in traditional Chinese fiction:

> "Why spoil a man's good name groundlessly?" he would ask, his eyes like saucers.
> "Pooh, good name indeed. Day before yesterday I saw you with my own eyes being hung up and beaten for stealing books from the Ho family!"[111]

Lu Hsün uses authorial comment more aggressively and at the

---

*The phrase "his eyes wide open" (i.e., bulging) reminds me of Ah Q's "glaring," but the original language is different. Here the feeling seems more one of dismay than of anger.—C.J.A.

same time more subtly than the early twentieth-century novelists. And this does not apply solely to his remarks in the dialogue. In "The True Story of Ah Q," for example, the author frequently uses phrases like "as was his habit," "in accordance with the ancient custom," and "as usual" to give the reader a hint of the author's attitude toward events. The writer also uses indirect discourse far more freely than his predecessors. This enables him, so to speak, to shorten the speeches of his characters, to single out that which is of central importance, and to make an inconspicuous transition from the direct speech of the characters to his own personal comments. Indirect discourse provides a bridge between the words of the character and the judgments of the author. It also facilitates stylization, the inclusion of ironic (or sympathetic, as the case may be) comments. There is a blending of these elements in the scene where Ah Q returns from the city, a point when the hero's impressions (rendered through direct as well as indirect discourse) and the author's conclusions are skillfully synthesized.

The language of the early twentieth-century novel was not as rich in synonyms as that of Lu Hsün. As T'ang T'ao observes,[112] in the story "A Small Incident" the nuances alone aptly convey the changing attitude of the passenger toward the rickshaw driver: "I was aggravated..."; "I reflected..."; "I felt a strange sensation..."; "the rickshaw driver exerted some sort of power over me"; "my vitality seemed sapped"; "I was afraid to turn my thoughts to myself"; "he made me feel ashamed"; "he fortified my courage and strengthened my hope."[113] And, far more often than the accusatory novelists, Lu Hsün uses, for their satiric impact, words that have the very opposite meaning of that which he intends to convey to the reader. The author, so to speak, puts himself in the place of his ignorant heroes and voices their "ideas." In one instance, for example, he comments that "the only cause for alarm was that several bad revolutionaries began to behave outrageously, and on the following day they began cutting off queues."[114]

Lu Hsün's stories have a rich undercurrent of ideas. Every possible variety of understatement appears in the nineteenth- and early twentieth-century novel, particularly in scenes of adventure, but Lu Hsün's multi-faceted images always have rich psychological overtones and not infrequently utilize a play on words. Thus, the word "cannibalism," for example, in "Diary of a Madman" turns out to be quite pithy. It encompasses dreadful superstitions ("some people had taken out his heart and liver, fried them in oil and eaten them"), servile morality ("Yi Ya boiled his son and contributed to the feast..."), the callousness of the upper classes (the tyrants Chieh and Chou accepted Yi Ya's sacrifice), the notorious "filial" piety ("my brother told me that if a man's parents were ill he should cut off a piece of flesh and boil it for them"), and the suppression of all who protest (the savage slaying of the revolutionary Hsü Hsi-lin).[115]

Like the authors of the novel of exposure, Lu Hsün rarely uses figures of speech (metaphors and similes, for example), but when he does find it necessary to use them, he generally displays originality and artistic taste. Similes used to describe negative characters, comparing them to ants that have fallen into a hot frying pan, to dogs, or to wasps, were common in the novel of exposure and always had the same meaning. They also appear in Lu Hsün's works, not merely as direct gibes, but with a subtle touch of irony. The writer, for example, compares the numerous graves of paupers and those who have been executed (in the story "Medicine") to "steamed rolls laid out for a rich man's birthday."[116] The important feature here is not so much the apparent similarity as the implied contrast: paupers and revolutionaries die, rich men regale. As in the traditional novel, the subject of comparison [*man-t'ou*—C.J.A.] is concrete and commonplace, but the simile is very modern and original. Dry blades of grass standing "stiff and straight as copper wires"[117] are used to intensify the deathly silence at the grave of the executed Hsia Yü. The crow perches motionless, "as if moulded from iron."[118] As we see, the artist uses not one but several threads to weave his imagery into the fabric of the story, and in so doing he pays close attention to form, color, weight, and sound.

Sometimes it is asserted that each and every one of Lu Hsün's characters has his own unique language. This can hardly be true, since in the majority of the writer's wroks, no matter how much one might desire to do so, it would be impossible to discover a character whose speech has been completely individualized. Not even the pseudoclassical expressions K'ung I-chi injects into his speech are totally unique. Authors of the novel of exposure also differentiated between characters on the basis of such factors as social status and educational level. Li Pao-chia's officials, for example, use archaisms and barbarisms not found in the speech of the common people, while prostitutes use dialecticisms and vulgarisms which are practically nonexistent in the speech of officials, and so forth.

The writer's progress toward a truly unique style is already evident in "The True Story of Ah Q." L. D. Pozdneeva, for example, points out the satiric contrast in the language used by the two main characters in that tale. The laborer Ah Q expresses himself in a grandiloquent style, while the language of the "Honorable" Chao, whom one might expect to speak elegantly, is sprinkled with vile abuse.[119] In passing the critic adds that such pomposity is typical only of Ah Q's interior monologues. In the first place, he is afraid to speak to people in this manner, because they would ridicule him; and second, such an exalted style is completely unsuited to real life. It is only appropriate in dreams. Speech contrasts in the novel of exposure sometimes create a certain aura around the character, emphasizing either his servility or contemptuousness toward the people he encounters, but I have yet to discover in traditional fiction as close a connection between language and the concrete situation as one finds in "The True Story of Ah Q." Here the style of speech (the pompousness of Ah Q and the coarseness of the "Honorable" Chao) is so individualized that the educational level of the characters recedes into the background and is no longer the main factor, as it was in Li Pao-chia's *Exposure of the Official World*. As a result, the satire itself becomes all the more forceful.

Some Conclusions

In the 1920s Lu Hsün, one of the few authors who laid the foundation for modern Chinese literature, played an extraordinarily crucial and complex role. He opposed those who would subvert the cultural heritage, although the epigonists and the nationalists—those who would steer art back into the old rut—became his chief enemies. "Although the new ideas have never made much headway in China, many old fogies—young ones too—are already scared to death and have started ranting about national culture. 'China has many good things,' they assure us. 'To chase after what is new instead of studying and preserving the old is as bad as renouncing our ancestral heritage.' Of course, it carries enormous weight to trot out our ancestors to make a point; but I cannot believe that before the old jacket is washed and folded no new one must be made."[1]

Under such conditions, it would have been difficult to avoid certain extremes. The writer, for example, condemned all the poets after the T'ang dynasty,* and V. V. Petrov is correct in stating that "this clearly was an unjust attitude toward those in the post-T'ang era, such as Hsin Ch'i-chi, Lu Yu, Ku Yen-wu, and Huang Tsun-hsien, who fostered the best traditions of Chinese poetry."[2] But here we observe something curious. Though Lu Hsün deprecated the art of his immediate predecessors (including Huang Tsun-hsien and T'an Ssu-t'ung), his own poetry had much in common with theirs.[3] However interesting this problem may be, I have not dealt with it in this monograph. Poetry was not Lu Hsün's special-

---

*This condemnation was, however, far from total. Lu Hsün, for example, much admired the poetry of Kung Tzu-chen (1792-1841), among other premodern Chinese poets.—C.J.A.

ty; nor is it the place to search for his basic artistic achievements.

My primary interest has been the problem of tradition versus innovation in Lu Hsün's works, and particularly his fiction, where he made the greatest contribution to literature. Lu Hsün's attitude toward traditional fiction was, however, even harsher than his attitude toward poetry:

> Sometimes Chinese poetry talks about the suffering of the lower classes. Painting and fiction, on the other hand, describe them as if they could never be happier, living "in ignorant bliss at the behest of the Emperor," as if they were flowers or birds. . . .
> Because I grew up in the city in a large family and studied the precepts of the classics, I too regarded the working masses as flowers and birds. . . .
> Only later, when I read several works by foreign authors, especially those of Russia, Poland, and the small Balkan countries, did I realize that there were many people in the world who shared the fate of our toiling masses, and that some writers were protesting and fighting against this.[4]

This quotation does not accurately reflect developments in Chinese literature, though it does indicate clearly what the decisive factors in Lu Hsün's literary career were. Of course, it is couched in the very broadest of terms, and many of Lu Hsün's statements, including what he did in practice, contradict this devasting assessment of traditional fiction. The writer prized such novels as *The Dream of the Red Chamber* and *The Scholars* highly, and he noted several positive features of the novel of exposure as well. It is even possible that the greatest influence on Lu Hsün's style was not the Confucian classics, the official or unofficial histories, classical poetry, or the T'ang novella, but "the traditional *pai-hua* novel."[5]

At this point, one conclusion seems inevitable. The concept of tradition, as used here, should embrace not only what the writer admitted consciously, but whatever became part of his work unconsciously, without his even being aware of it, plus all that his works shared in common with other Chinese writers due to the similarities in their careers or the demands made upon them. While studying literary influences resulting from direct contact, should we not also investigate so-called "typological" features? From the standpoint of literary history it matters little whether Lu Hsün consciously thought about one or the other feature of the novel of exposure when he rejected it, imitated it, or created something similar in his own works. And incidentally, in this instance one can at least state with confidence that Lu Hsün *did* study the works of his predecessors, as his treatises on the history of Chinese fiction testify.

The relationship between Lu Hsün's work and the novel of exposure serves as a basic illustration of the link between realistic literature and the literature of enlightenment, albeit under unique circumstances, when the retarded development of Chinese art began to accelerate and much of what had just been accomplished already seemed outmoded. Perhaps this historical analysis, though far from error free, will prove of interest to a number of sinologists. The nineteenth and particularly the early twentieth century contributed much that was beneficial to Chinese literature; and here again it should be pointed out, that "modern times" had both a negative and a positive influence on Lu Hsün. Had the novel of exposure, the modern school of poetry, or colloquial drama been nonexistent at the turn of the century, the authors of contemporary literature would have found it incomparably more difficult to accomplish their aesthetic aims. And in turn, the accomplishments of a predecessor like Lu Hsün place a heavy burden on those who wish to follow.

Appendix:
Titles of Lu Hsün's Works

Bad Luck (II)
Hua-kai chi hsü-pien

    *In Memory of Miss Liu Ho-chen (1926)
    Chi-nien Liu Ho-chen

    *How "The True Story of Ah Q" Was Written (1926)
    A Q cheng chuan te ch'eng-yin
    Pričiny sozdanija "Podlinnoj istorii A-k'ju"

A Brief History of Chinese Fiction
Chung-kuo hsiao-shuo shih lüeh
Kratkaja istorija kitaiskoj prozy

    Works discussed in Lu Hsün's Brief History of Chinese Fiction:

    After the Disaster
    Chieh yü hui
    Pepelišča

    The Amazing Rumors of a Blind Man's Lies
    Hsia p'ien ch'i wen
    Udivitel'nye sluxi o vran'e slepca

    Ballad of the Great Incident of 1900
    Keng-tzu kuo-pien t'an-tz'u
    Sobytija 1900 goda

    The Bookworm
    T'an-shih
    Istorija knižnogo červja

    Cases of Lord P'eng
    P'eng kung-an
    Dela sud'i Pèna

Works discussed in Lu Hsün's Brief History of Chinese Fiction:

Cases of Lord Shih
Shih kung-an
Dela sud'i Si

A Crime Involving Nine Lives
Chiu ming ch'i yüan
Ubijstvo devjati

Dream of the Green Chamber
Ch'ing lou meng
Son v sinem tereme

Dream of the Red Chamber
Hung lou meng
Son v krasnom tereme

Exposure of the Merchants' World
(Shang-chieh hsien-hsing chi)

Exposure of the Official World
Kuan-ch'ang hsien-hsing chi
Naše činovničestvo

Exposure of the Teaching World
(Hsüeh-chieh hsien-hsing chi)

Exposure of the Women's World
(Nü-chieh hsien-hsing chi)

Five Younger Gallants
Hsiao wu i
Mladšie pjatero blagorodnyx

The Flower and the Moon
Hua yüeh hen
Sledy cvetov i luny

A Flower in an Ocean of Sin
Nieh hai hua
Cvety v more zla

Flowers in the Mirror
Ching hua yüan
Cvety v zerkale

The Gallant Maiden
Erh-nü ying-hsiung chuan
Povest' o detjax-gerojax

Works discussed in Lu Hsün's Brief History of Chinese Fiction:

The History of Pain
T'ung shih
Istorija stradanij

Lives of Shanghai Singsong Girls
Hai-shang hua lieh-chuan
Cvety na more

Living Hell
Huo ti-yü
Živoj ad

A Mirror of Theatrical Life
P'in-hua pao-chien
Dragocennoe zercalo ocenki cvetov

Miscellany Within and Without the Universe
Liu-ho nei-wai suo-yen
Melkie slova iz uezda Ljuxe

Modern Times
Wen-ming hsiao shih
Kratkaja istorija civilizacii

The Nine-tailed Tortoise
Chiu-wei kuei
Devjatixvostye čerepaxi

Notes of the Yüeh-wei Hermitage
Yüeh-wei ts'ao-t'ang pi-chi
Zapiski iz Xižiny nabljudajuščego melkoe

Random Notes from Shanghai
Sung yin man lu
Zapiski Sunczjanskogo otšel'nika

A Rustic's Idle Talk
Yeh-sou p'u-yen
Otkrovennye slova nerazumnogo starca

The Scholars
Ju-lin wai-shih
Neoficial'naja istorija konfuciancev

A Sea of Woe
Hen hai
More skorbi

Works discussed in Lu Hsün's Brief History of Chinese Fiction:

A Sequel to Five Younger Gallants
Hsü hsiao wu i
Prodolženie mladšix pjati blagorodnyx

Seven Heroes and Five Gallants
Ch'i-hsia wu-i
Sem' xrabryx pjatero blagorodnyx

Strange Events of the Last Twenty Years
Erh-shih nien mu-tu chih kuai hsien-chuang
Strannye sobytija za dvadcat' let

Strange Tales of Electricity
Tien-shu ch'i-t'an
Udivitelnyj rasskaz ob električestve

Suppression of the Rebels
Chieh Shui-hu i-ming t'ang-k'ou
Istorija usmirenija banditov

Three Heroes and Five Gallants
San-hsia wu-i
Troe xrabryx, pjatero blagorodnyx

The Three Kingdoms
San-kuo chih
Troecarstvie

The Travels of Lao Ts'an
Lao Ts'an yu-chi
Putešestvie Lao Canja

The Water Margin
Shui-hu chuan
Rečnye zavodi

Collection of Uncollected Works
Chi-wai chi
Sbornik ne vošedšego v sborniki

    The Spartan Spirit (1903)
    Szu-pa-ta chih hun
    Spartanskij dux

    On Radium (1903)
    Shuo jih
    O radii

    †Mourning for Mr. Fan (1912)
    Ai Fan chün san chang
    Oplakivaju g-na Fanja

Appendix to the Collection of Uncollected Works
Chi-wai chi shih-i

> The Past (1911)
> Huai-chiu
> Byloe
>
> Inscription on My Portrait (1903)
> Tzu-t'i hsiao-hsiang
> Nadpis' na sobstvennom portrete
>
> An Outline of Chinese Geology (1903)
> Chung-kuo ti-chih lüeh-lun
> Korotko o geologii Kitaja
>
> Against Evil Voices (1908)
> P'o o-sheng lun
> Protiv zlobnyx golosov
>
> Introducing *The Bell of Yüeh* (1912)
> Yüeh-to ch'u-shih tz'u
> K vyxodu v cvet "Jueskogo kolokola"
>
> Proposal for the Dissemination of the Arts (1913)
> Ni po-pu mei-shu i-chien shu
> Proekt rasprostranenija iskusstv

Supplement One to the Collection of Uncollected Works
Chi-wai chi shih-i fu-lu i

> Notes of a Warrior (1898)
> Chia chien-sheng tsa-chi
> Zapiski Voina
>
> Plant Sketches (1898)
> Shih-hua tsa-chih
> Zametki o rastenijax

Essays of Chieh-chieh-ting (II)
Ch'ieh-chieh-t'ing tsa-wen erh-chi

> *On Satire (1935)
> Lun feng-tz'u
> O satire
>
> *What is Satire? (1935)
> Shemma shih 'feng-tz'u'?
> Čto takoe satira

Essays of Chieh-chieh-ting (III)
Ch'ieh-chieh-t'ing tsa-wen mo-pien

    *Some Recollections of Chang Tai-yen (1936)
    Kuan-yü T'ai-yen hsien-sheng erh san shih
    Koe-čto o Čžan Taj-jane

    *A Few Matters Connected with Chang Tai-yen (1936)
    Yin T'ai-yen hsien-sheng erh hsiang-ch'i te erh san shih
    Iz vospominanij o Čžan Taj-jane

The Grave
Fen
Mogila

    A Chapter from the History of Science (1907)
    K'e-hsüeh-shih chiao-p'ien
    Glava iz istorii nauki

    On Extremes in Culture (1907)
    Wen-hua p'ien chih lun
    O krajnostjax v kul'ture

    On the Power of Demoniac Poetry (1907)
    Mo-lo shih-li shuo
    O sile demoničeskoj poèzii

    †What Happened to Nora After Her Departure (1923)
    No-la tsou hou tsen-yang

    *Some Notions Jotted Down by Lamplight (1925)
    Teng-hsia man-pi

Hesitation
P'ang-huang
Bluždanija

    *Soap
    Fei-tsao
    Mylo

    The Eternal Lamp
    Ch'ang-ming teng
    Svetil'nik

    An Example
    Shih-chung
    Na pozor

The Historical Development of Chinese Fiction
Chung-kuo hsiao-shuo te li-shih te pien-ch'ien
Istoričeskaja evoljucija kitaiskoj prozy

Hot Air
Je feng

> *Random Thoughts (57)—Murderers of the Present (1919)
> Hsien-tai te t'u-sha-che
> Ubijcy sovremennosti

> No Need for 'Corrections' (1924)
> Wang wu 'chiu cheng'
> Ne nado ispravlenij

Mixed Dialects
Nan-ch'iang pei-tiao chi
Severnye pesni na južnyj lad

> How I Came to Write Stories
> Wo tsen-ma tso ch'i hsiao-shuo lai
> Kak ja načal pisat'

Old Tales Retold
Ku-shih hsin-pien
Starye legendy po-novomu

> Beyond the Frontier
> Ch'u-kuan
> Za zastavu

> Pu Chou Mountain
> Pu Chou shan
> Gora Bučžou

>> Mending Heaven
>> Pu t'ien
>> Počinka nebosvoda

Outcry
Na-han
Klič

> *Diary of a Madman
> K'uang-jen jih-chi
> Zapiski sumasšedšego

*Kung I-chi
K'ung I-chi
Kun I-czi

*Medicine
Yao
Lekarstvo

*Tomorrow
Ming-t'ien
Zavtra

*A Small Incident
I-chien hsiao shih
Malen'koe proisšestvie

The Story of Hair
T'ou-fa te ku-shih
Rasskaz o volosax

*Storm in a Teacup
Feng-po
Volnenie

*My Old Home
Ku-hsiang
Rodina

*The True Story of Ah Q
A Q cheng-chuan
Podlinnaja istorija A-k'ju

The Dragon Boat Festival
Tuan-wu chieh
Prazdnik leta

†The White Light
Pai-kuang
Blesk

The Rabbits and the Cat
T'u ho mao
Kroliki i koška

The Ducks' Comedy
Ya te hsi-chü
Utinaja komedija

The Village Opera
She-hsi
Derevenskoe predstavlenie
Sel'skij prazdnik

Semi-Frivolous Talk
Chun feng-yüeh t'an

    It's Hard to be Stupid (1933)
    Nan te hu-t'u
    Trudno byt' glupym

Supplement to the Complete Works of Lu Hsün
Lu Hsün ch'uan-chi pu-i

    Preface to *Neglected Ancient Tales* (1912)
    Ku hsiao-shuo kou-ch'en hsü
    Predislovie k 'Zabytym drevnim rasskazam'

Three Leisures
San hsien chi
Tri bezdel'nika (Triždy bezdel'nik)

    The Evolution of Roughs
    Liu-mang te pien-ch'ien
    Evoljucija xuligana

Translations

    Expedition to the North Pole
    Pei-chi t'an-hsien chi
    Ekspedicii k Severnomu poljusu

    From the Earth to the Moon (1903)
    Yüeh-chieh lü-hsing
    S zemli na lunu

    Journey to the Center of the Earth
    Ti-ti lü-hsing
    Putešestvie k centru zemli

    Short Stories from Abroad (1920)
    Yü-wai hsiao-shuo chi
    Sbornik inostrannyx rasskazov

    A Sourcebook of Chinese Economics (1908)
    Polnoe sobranie svedenij po kitaiskoj ėkonomike

Unpublished Works

    On Foreign Literature (1914)
    I yü wen t'an
    Ob inostrannoj literature

    Wild Grass
    Yeh-ts'ao
    Dikie travy

    Revenge
    Fu-ch'ou
    Mest'

*Included in the *Selected Works of Lu Hsün*, 4 vols. (Peking: Foreign Languages Press, 1956-1960).
†See *Silent China, Selected Writings of Lu Xun*, ed. and trans. Gladys Yang (London: Oxford University Press, 1973).

Notes

INTRODUCTION

[1] Ts'ao Ching-hua, *Hua* (Flowers) (Peking: Tso-chia ch'u-pan she, 1962), pp. 131-132.

[2] Chou Shu-jen, *Lu Hsün ch'üan-chi* (Complete Works of Lu Hsün), compiled by the Lu Hsün memorial committee, 20 vols. (Shanghai: Lu Hsün ch'üan-chi ch'u-pan she, 1938), VII, 445-447.

[3] B. A. Vasil'ev, "Inostrannoe vlijanie v kitajskoj literature epoxi imperializma (Foreign Influence in Chinese Literature in the Epoch of Imperialism), *Trudy instituta vostokovedenija Akademij Nauk*, I (1932), p. 86.

[4] *Lu Sin', 1881-1936, sbornik statej i perevodov posvjaščennyj pamjati velikogo pisatelja sovremennogo Kitaja* (Lu Hsün, 1881-1936, a collection of articles and translations devoted to the memory of the great contemporary Chinese writer) (Moscow and Leningrad: AN SSSR, 1938), pp. 5-6.

[5] M. Kessel' [Castle?], "Vyšli na russkom jazyke" (New Publications in Russian), *Inostrannaja literatura*, VII (1938), 195.

[6] Vera Vladimirovna Vishnyakova-Akimova, *Two Years in Revolutionary China, 1925-1927*, trans. Steven I. Levine (Cambridge, Mass.: Harvard University Press, 1971), pp. 30-31.

[7] I. S. Lisevich, "Izučenie kitajskoj literatury v SSSR: uspexi i perspektivy" (The Study of Chinese Literature in the USSR: Successes and Perspectives), *Velikij oktjabr' i razvitie sovetskogo kitaevedenija* (Moscow: "Nauka" Publishers, 1968), p. 114.

[8] Alexander A. Fadeev, "Vsemirnoe značenie kitajskoj kul'tury," *Sobranie sočinenij*, ed. E. F. Knipovich, V. M. Ozerov, and K. A. Fedin (Moscow: State Publishing House, 1960), IV, 573-575. This speech was condensed in *Pravda* (October 7, 1949) and reprinted in complete form in *Literaturnaja Gazeta*.

[9] R. V. Vyatkin, "Synology" [sic], *Fifty Years of Soviet Oriental Studies* (Brief Reviews), Institute of the Peoples of Asia, AN SSSR (Moscow: "Nauka" Publishers, Central Department of Oriental Literature, 1968), p. 6.

[10] Gustav Glaesser, "Chinese Literature in a Russian Study," *East and West*, VIII, No. 3 (October 1957), 312.

[11] Cited by Roger Swearingen, "Asian Studies in the Soviet Union," *Journal of Asian Studies*, XVII (1958), 516.

[12] *Ibid.*, pp. 524-525.

[13] Kawakami Kyūjū, "Roshiya Sovieto ni okeru Chugoku bungaku kenkyu" (Research on Chinese Literature in Soviet Russia), *Jinbun kenkyu* (Otaru Shōdai), XXVII (January 1964), 19.

[14] L. D. Pozdneeva, *Lu Sin': žizn' i tvorčestvo*, (1881-1936) (Lu Hsün: His Life and Works, 1881-1936) (Moscow: Moscow State University, 1959), p. 198.

[15] *Ibid.*, p. 243.

[16] V. Semanov, "V. Sorokin, Formirovanie mirovozzrenija Lu Sinja," *Problemy vostokovendenija*, No. 6 (1959), 203.

[17] The author informs me that this work, or an extract from it, is also being translated for publication in England.

[18] *Silent China, Selected Writings of Lu Xun*, ed. and trans. Gladys Yang (New York: Oxford University Press, 1973), pp. 153-154.

[19] Chow Tse-tsung, *The May Fourth Movement, Intellectual Revolution in Modern China* (Stanford: Stanford University Press, 1967), pp. 341-342; Jerome B. Grieder, *Hu Shih and the Chinese Renaissance* (Cambridge, Mass.: Harvard University Press, 1970), pp. 315-318.

[20] Benjamin I. Schwartz, *In Search of Wealth and Power: Yen Fu and the West* (Cambridge, Mass.: Harvard University Press, 1964).

[21] C. Brandt, "The French-Returned Elite in the Chinese Communist Party," *Economic and Social Problems of the Far East* (Hong Kong: Hong Kong University Press, 1962), pp. 229-238.

[22] E. R. Hughes, *The Invasion of China by the Western World* (New York: Macmillan, 1938), pp. 116-117.

[23] William A. Nitze and E. Preston Dargan, *A History of French Literature* (New York: Henry Holt, 1938), p. 234.

[24] Lu Hsün, *A Brief History of Chinese Fiction*, trans. Yang Hsien-yi and Gladys Yang (Peking: Foreign Languages Press, 1959), p. 372.

[25] Chow Tse-tung, *The May Fourth Movement*, p. 342.

[26] *Selected Works of Lu Hsün*, trans. Yang Hsien-yi and Gladys Yang, 4 vols. (Peking: Foreign Languages Press, 1956-60), II, 307-308.

[27] Jaroslav Průšek, "A Confrontation of Traditional Oriental Literature with Modern European Literature in the Context of the Chinese Literary Revolution," *Literary History and Literary Criticism*, Acta of the Ninth Congress of the International Federation for Modern Languages and Literature, ed. Leon Edel (New York: New York University Press, 1964), p. 174.

[28] *Ibid.*, p. 175 *et passim*.

AUTHOR'S NOTE

[1] Ozaka Tokuji, *A History of the New Literature Movement in China, From Hu Shih to Lu Hsün* (Chugoku shin bungaku undo shi, Go Teki kara Ro Jin e) (Tokyo, 1957); and V. V. Petrov, *Lu Hsün* (Moscow, 1960).

[2] Kuo Mo-jo, *Historic Personalities* (Li-shih jen-wu) (Shanghai, 1949), pp. 161-173.

[3] Chou Ch'i-ming, *Lu Hsün's Youth* (Lu Hsün te ch'ing-nien shih-tai) (Peking, 1957), pp. 76-80.

⁴ Ch'eng Fang-wu, "Criticism of *Outcry*" ("Na-han" te p'ing-lun), in the collection *On Lu Hsün* (Lu Hsün lun) (Shanghai, 1930), p. 223. [In the Tokyo reprint of this collection (Daian, 1968) the words "at the very least" do not appear.—C.J.A.]

⁵ Li Pao-chia (1867-1906) and Liu O (1857-1909) were well-known Chinese novelists and philosophes (*prosvetiteli*).

⁶ Ch'ien Hsing-ts'un, *Contemporary Chinese Writers* (Hsien-tai Chung-kuo wen-hsüeh tso-chia) (Shanghai, 1928), pp. 2, 6, 7. The *New Citizen* or *New People's Miscellany* (Hsin-min ts'ung-pao) was a journal published in Japan in the years 1902-[1907] by the prominent Chinese reformer Liang Ch'i-ch'ao.

CHAPTER ONE

¹ See, for example, Chou Ch'i-ming, *Lu Hsün's Youth*, p. 76, and V. F. Sorokin, *The Formation of Lu Hsün's World Outlook* (Moscow, 1958), p. 11 [hereafter the latter will be abbreviated *Lu Hsün's World Outlook*].

² For further details, see Chapter II.

³ Chou Hsia-shou, *Lu Hsün's Home* (Lu Hsün te ku-chia) (Shanghai, 1952), p. 94.

⁴ Lu Hsün, *Selected Works*, 4 vols. (Moscow, 1954-56), III, 46.

⁵ Chou Ch'i-ming, *Lu Hsün's Youth*, p. 56.

⁶ Lu Hsün, *Complete Works* (Lu Hsün ch'üan-chi) (Peking, 1957-59), III, 33 [*Selected Works* (English), II, 118].

⁷ Shiga Masatoshi, "Research on Lu Hsün's Translations," *Tenri University Bulletin* (Tenri daigaku gakuho), No. 7 (1956), p. 91.

⁸ This was the title given to the Chinese translation of Huxley's *Evolution and Ethics* by Yen Fu. The translation was first published in 1897 in the Tientsin newspaper *The National Herald* (Kuo-wen pao).

⁹ Lu Hsün, *Selected Works* (Russian), III, 60.

¹⁰ Chu Cheng, *A Short Biography of Lu Hsün* (Lu Hsün chuan-lüeh) (Peking, 1956), p. 14.

¹¹ Jaroslav Průšek, "Lu Hsün the Revolutionary and the Artist," *Orientalistische Literaturzeitung*, No. 55 (1960), p. 232.

¹² Lu Hsün, *Complete Works*, II, 268, 452. The journal was published by Chinese students in Japan from 1900 to 1903.

¹³ Chou Hsia-shou, *The Characters in Lu Hsün's Fiction* (Lu Hsün hsiao-shuo li te jen-wu) (Shanghai, 1955), p. 269; Chou Ch'i-ming, *Lu Hsün's Youth*, p. 78.

¹⁴ The Hundred Days' Reform was from July 11 to September 21, 1898. During this time the Kuang-hsü emperor, on the advice of K'ang Yu-wei, undertook reforms that were abolished after the reactionary coup of the dowager empress Tz'u-hsi. See S. L. Tikhvinsky, *K'ang Yu-wei and the Reform Movement in China* (Moscow, 1959).

¹⁵ Lu Hsün, *Selected Works* (Russian), III, 140.

¹⁶ Lu Hsün, *Complete Works*, VI, 451 [*Selected Works* (English), IV, 273].

¹⁷ Ho Chia-huai, *Lectures on the Works of Lu Hsün* (Lu Hsün tso-p'in chiang-hua) (Wu-han, 1959), p. 1; Chu T'ung, "Lu Hsün's Early Ideas and Struggles

(1902-1909)" in *Wen-shih-che* (The Literary Historian), No. 10 (1956), p. 1; Huang Sung-k'ang, *Lu Hsün and the New Culture Movement of Modern China* (Amsterdam, 1957), p. 31 [hereafter abbreviated *Lu Hsün and the New Culture Movement*]; L. D. Pozdneeva, *Lu Hsün: His Life and Works* (1881-1936) (Moscow, 1959), pp. 31-32 *et passim*.

[18] See V. V. Petrov, *Lu Hsün*, p. 22.

[19] Lu Hsün, *Selected Works* (Russian), III, 60.

[20] *Ibid.*, p. 61.

[21] See the articles "Foreign Literature in China" and "Japanese Fiction in China" in the collection *From the History of Nineteenth-Century Literary Relations* (Moscow, 1962).

[22] Oda Takeo, *A Biography of Lu Hsün* (Lu Hsün chuan) (Shanghai, 1949), p. 17.

[23] The Warrior (Chia Chien-sheng) was one of Lu Hsün's early pseudonyms.

[24] The clearest and at the same time most traditional of these fragments is cited in V. F. Sorokin's *Lu Hsün's World Outlook*, pp. 20-21.

[25] Lu Hsün, *Complete Works*, VII, 709.

[26] Both of these articles were published in the newspaper *Su-pao* (1903), which was soon banned by the authorities. K'ang Yu-wei's *Letter on Revolution* refers to "A Letter to the Chinese Merchants of North and South America," wherein K'ang Yu-wei declared that China was in need of a constitution and not revolution.

[27] Wang Shih-ching, *Lu Hsün, His Life and Works* (Lu Hsün, t'a-te sheng-p'ing ho ch'uang-tso) (Peking, 1958), p. 61; Chu Cheng, *A Short Biography of Lu Hsün*, p. 18; Huang Sung-k'ang, *Lu Hsün and the New Culture Movement*, p. 31; and others.

[28] Lu Hsün, *Selected Works* (Russian), I, 56 (see also p. 51 *et passim*).

[29] These translations came out in separate editions from 1903 to 1909.

[30] Hsü Shou-shang, *The Lu Hsün That I Knew* (Wo so-jen-shih-te Lu Hsün) (Peking, 1954), pp. 74-75.

[31] Chou Ch'i-ming, *Lu Hsün's Youth*, pp. 78-79.

[32] "New Rome" was a well-known play by Liang Ch'i-ch'ao. Here Lu Hsün is mistaken. The poems by Byron to which he refers were cited by Liang Ch'i-ch'ao in his tale "The Future of the New China" (1902).

[33] The *tz'u* genre is comprised of poems with lines of unequal length (as opposed to the more orthodox *shih* genre, which includes poems with lines of equal length).

[34] Lu Hsün, *Complete Works*, I, 317.

[35] Chou Ch'i-ming, *Lu Hsün's Youth*, p. 80.

[36] Lu Hsün, *Complete Works*, VII, 9.

[37] *Ibid.*, p. 14.

[38] *Ibid.*, pp. 11, 16.

[39] Landscape descriptions in the story are laconic and purposeful. "At first light the morning sun shown on the rocks and illuminated the drops of blood there that were still moist, as if to testify how brutal yesterday's battle had

been." Clear, precise similes are widely used. The Persians go over the hill "like an enormous snake sliding down into a ravine." The sound of voices is "like a wind storm."

[40] Depending on the size of the work in question the translation for this genre will be either "tale" [*povest'*] or "novel" [*roman*].

[41] Lu Hsün, *Collected Translations* (Lu Hsün i-wen chi) (Peking, 1958), I. 3.

[42] *Ibid.*, p. 4.

[43] However, there is no basis for stating that "it was primarily because of Lu Hsün's translations" that the works of Verne "became known to the Chinese reader" (see Hui An, pseudonym of T'ang T'ao, "Jules Verne" in *T'u-shu yüeh-pao*, No. 1, 1957, p. 26). Jules Verne was often translated in China in the early twentieth century.

[44] Lu Hsün, *Collected Translations*, I, 41.

[45] Ibid. L. D. Pozdneeva agrees (see *Lu Hsün: His Life and Works*, p. 50).

[46] The translation has not been preserved and, therefore, neither the author of the work nor the precise title can be established. The dating is adopted from "Chronology of Lu Hsün's Works" (*Complete Works*, X, 356).

[47] Lu Hsün, *Letters* (Shu-chien) (Peking, 1952), II, 671.

[48] *Ibid.*

[49] I do not agree with V. F. Sorokin's conclusion that in his translations "Lu Hsün paid greatest attention to the complexity of the style" and that is why the author "put the dialogue in *pai-hua*, which is similar to colloquial speech" (see V. F. Sorokin, *Lu Hsün's World Outlook*, p. 26).

[50] Lin Ch'en, *Research on Lu Hsün's Activities* (Lu Hsün shih-chi k'ao) (Shanghai, 1955), pp. 1-15; and L. D. Pozdneeva, *Lu Hsün: His Life and Works*, pp. 37-39.

[51] Novels by H. Rider Haggard. The Chinese translations date from 1905 to 1906. See A Ying, *Bibliography of Late Ch'ing Drama and Fiction* (Wan-ch'ing hsi-ch'ü hsiao-shuo mu) (Shanghai, 1957), pp. 118, 163 [hereafter entitled *Bibliography*].

[52] 1906 and 1907. See A Ying, *Bibliography*, pp. 125, 138.

[53] 1908. See *ibid.*, p. 155.

[54] Chou Ch'i-ming, *Lu Hsün's Youth*, pp. 78, 79.

[55] Chou Hsia-shou, *Lu Hsün's Home*, p. 348.

[56] Lu Hsün, *Selected Works* (Russian), III, 141, 142.

[57] Hsü Shou-shang, *Impressions of My Late Friend Lu Hsün* (Wang-yu Lu Hsün yin-hsiang chi) (Peking, 1953), pp. 10, 12. See also Chou Hsia-shou, *Lu Hsün's Home*, p. 303.

[58] For details see V. V. Petrov, *Lu Hsün*, pp. 31, 39; and V. F. Sorokin, *Lu Hsün's World Outlook*, pp. 37, 44.

[59] Lu Hsün, *Complete Works*, I, 178.

[60] *Ibid.*, p. 203.

[61] *Ibid.*, pp. 202-203.

[62] *Ibid.*, p. 197.

[63] Ch'en Ming-shu, *In Defense of the Militant Traditions of Lu Hsün* (Pao-wei

Lu Hsün te chan-tou ch'uan-t'ung) (Tientsin, 1959), pp. 254, 294 [hereafter entitled *In Defense of Lu Hsün*].

[64] See *Wen-hsüeh p'ing-lun* (Literary Criticism), No. 3 (1963), pp. 86-88 and 90-92.

[65] Ozaka Tokuji, *A History of the New Literature Movement in China*, pp. 46, 48.

[66] Lu Hsün, *Complete Works*, VII, 243.

[67] An allusion to the "war song" and the "school song" of the pseudo-reformer Chang Chih-tung (1837-1909), who exposed the "degradation" of the Indians and the Poles, "forgetting" the servile position of his own country.

[68] Lu Hsün, *Complete Works*, I, 196.

[69] See V. F. Sorokin, *Lu Hsün's World Outlook*, pp. 25-26.

[70] Lu Hsün, *Selected Works* (Russian), IV, 199.

[71] Lu Hsün, *Collected Translations*, I, 581, 582. Ozaka Tokuji (*A History of the New Literature Movement in China*, p. 47) compares this figure to the one hundred thousand copies of Liang Ch'i-ch'ao's journal *New Fiction*, which sold out completely.

[72] Lu Hsün, *Collected Translations*, I, 581.

[73] See A Ying, *Bibliography*, p. 89.

[74] For details on realistic trends in the article "On the Power of Demoniacal Poetry," see Ou-yang Fan-hai's *Lu Hsün's Books* (Lu Hsün te shu) (Hong Kong, 1948), pp. 69, 76-78; Ch'en Ming-shu, *In Defense of Lu Hsün*, p. 256.

[75] Lu Hsün, *Collected Translations*, I, 149-150.

[76] See V. F. Sorokin, *Lu Hsün: His Life and Works*, pp. 63-65; and *A Brief History of Chinese Translations* (Chung-kuo fan-i wen-hsüeh chien-shih) (Peking, 1960), p. 30. In this last work, for example, "Silence" is interpreted as a genuinely anticlerical short story.

[77] V. F. Sorokin, *Lu Hsün's World Outlook*, p. 55.

[78] See Lu Hsün, *Selected Works* (Russian), II, 122-123; Lu Hsün, *Complete Works*, I, 204; and Chou Ch'i-ming, *Lu Hsün's Youth*, pp. 130-132.

[79] Lu Hsün, *Colleceted Translations*, I, 184.

[80] *Ibid.*

[81] V. M. Garshin, *Sočinenija* (Moscow, 1955), p. 3.

[82] W. Garschin [V. M. Garshin], *Der Narr* (Vienna and Leipzig, 1904); W. M. Garschin, *Die rote Blume und andere Novellen* (Leipzig, 1906).

[83] Lu Hsün, *Collected Translations*, I. 171.

[84] L. Andrjejew [L. Andreev], *Die Lüge, Ausgewälte Erzählungen* (Dresden and Leipzig, 1902). We were able to accurately establish that this was the source of the Chinese translation by comparing it with other translations.

[85] L. Andreev, *Complete Works* (St. Petersburg, 1913), p. 51.

[86] Lu Hsün, *Collected Translations*, I, 152.

[87] V. M. Garshin, *Sočinenija*, p. 4.

[88] See A Ying, *A History of Late Ch'ing Fiction* (Wan-ch'ing hsiao-shuo shih) (Peking, 1955), p. 187.

⁸⁹ See Hsü Kuang-p'ing, "A Short Preface," in Lu Hsün, *Complete Works* (Shanghai, 1948), II, 187.

⁹⁰ Ching Sung (Hsü Kuang-p'ing), "Lu Hsün Prior to the *Hsin-hai* Revolution," in Sun Fu-yüan, *A Few Facts about Mr. Lu Hsün* (Lu Hsün hsien-sheng erh-san shih) (Shanghai, 1949), p. 53.

⁹¹ Lin Ch'en, "Lu Hsün and the Southern Society" in *Kuang-ming jih-pao*, September 26, 1961.

⁹² Lu Hsün, *Complete Works*, VII, 255.

⁹³ Shen P'eng-nien, *A Bibliography of Research Materials on Lu Hsün* (Lu Hsün yen-chiu tzu-liao pien-mu) (Shanghai, 1958), p. 138.

⁹⁴ Lu Hsün, *Complete Works*, VII, 256.

⁹⁵ *Ibid.*

⁹⁶ *Supplement to the Complete Works of Lu Hsün* (Lu Hsün ch'üan-chi pu-i) (Shanghai, 1948), p. 3.

⁹⁷ "They say it [i.e., fiction—C.J.A.] is comprehensible even to nearly illiterate peasants and easily remembered, but it is only the discourses of simpletons and madmen" (*ibid.*, p. 2).

⁹⁸ Legends "cannot be regarded as mere vehicles for the dissemination of certain ideas" (*ibid.*, p. 3).

⁹⁹ *Ibid.*, p. 260.

¹⁰⁰ For a translation of this story see *Far Eastern Almanac* (Vostočnyj al'manax), No. 4 (Moscow, 1961). [See also William A. Lyell, Jr., *Lu Hsün's Vision of Reality* (Berkeley, University of California Press, 1976), pp. 315-328.—C.J.A.]

¹⁰¹ L. D. Pozdneeva, *Lu Hsün: His Life and Works*, p. 83.

¹⁰² Lu Hsün, *Complete Works*, VII, 258.

¹⁰³ *Ibid.*

¹⁰⁴ *Ibid.*, p. 264.

¹⁰⁵ *Hsiao-shuo yüeh-pao* (Fiction Monthly), Vol. 4, No. 1 (1913), p. 7.

¹⁰⁶ *Ibid.*, p. 25 ff.

¹⁰⁷ In addition to the remarks of Yün Shu-chüeh see, for example, Wang T'ung-chao, "First Impressions of Lu Hsün's Short Stories," in *Wen-i yüeh-pao* (Literature and Art Monthly), No. 10 (1956), pp. 15-16.

¹⁰⁸ Lu Hsün, *Complete Works*, I, 268.

¹⁰⁹ For details on the contents of the paper see Cheng Huang, "Lu Hsün During the *Hsin-hai* Revolution and Shaohsing Youth," *Chieh-fang jih-pao* (Liberation Daily), October 14, 1956.

¹¹⁰ See *ibid.*; Lu Hsün, *Diary* (Jih-chi), Vol. I (Peking, 1959), pp. 5-43 ff.

¹¹¹ Lu Hsün, *Diary*, I, 42.

¹¹² *Ibid.*, p. 14; Lu Hsün, *Selected Works* (Russian), III, 76-77.

¹¹³ Ou-yang Fan-hai, *Lu Hsün's Books*, p. 95.

¹¹⁴ Lu Hsün, *Diary*, I, 6. In a traditional Chinese performance there were often several short plays performed.

¹¹⁵ See Lu Hsün, *Diary*, I, 31, 82.

¹¹⁶ *Ibid.*, pp. 7, 22, 31, 67 ff.

¹¹⁷ *Ibid.*, pp. 14, 71; Lu Hsün, *Collected Translations*, X, 9-51.

¹¹⁸ Lu Hsün, *Complete Works*, VII, 272.

¹¹⁹ Ou-yang Fan-hai, *Lu Hsün's Books*, p. 69.

¹²⁰ Lu Hsün, *Complete Works*, VII, 271.

¹²¹ *Ibid.*, pp. 271-272.

¹²² Lu Hsün, *Complete Works*, VII, 273. Later on the writer mentions three such one-sided theories which exaggerate the cognitive, ethnic, or economic value of art.

¹²³ "Frescoes and statues. These are kept in Buddhist or Taoist temples, and are sometimes the products of outstanding artists. Lately, under the pretext of eradicating superstition they have been mercilessly destroyed. Their authorship should be clarified and they should be protected in every way possible" (see Lu Hsün, *Complete Works*, VII, 275).

¹²⁴ *Ibid.*, pp. 274-275.

¹²⁵ *Ibid.*, pp. 275-276.

¹²⁶ Lu Hsün, *Diary*, I, 7, 9, 10.

¹²⁷ Wang Shih-ching, *Biography of Lu Hsün* (Lu Hsün chuan) (Harbin, 1949), p. 75; L. D. Pozdneeva, *Lu Hsün* (Moscow, 1957), p. 94.

¹²⁸ See Lu Hsün, *Diary*, I, 97-312.

¹²⁹ *Ibid.*, pp. 95, 111, 121, 240.

¹³⁰ *Ibid.*, pp. 95, 107-108, 121, 240.

¹³¹ Lu Hsün, *Diary*, I, pp. 95, 97, 110; Chou Hsia-shou *Lu Hsün's Home*, p. 369. Lu Hsün's preface is preserved, though not in its entirety.

¹³² The writer's own words (Lu Hsün, *Complete Works*, I, 153).

¹³³ *Supplement to the Complete Works of Lu Hsün*, p. 6. [It was Lu Hsün who translated the poems, but Chou Tso-jen, his brother, who wrote the introduction. See *Lu Hsün nien-p'u* (Chronology of Lu Hsün), 2 vols. (Ho-fei: Anhui jen-min ch'u-pan-she, 1979), I, 117.—C.J.A.]

¹³⁴ Lu Hsün, *Diary*, I, 112. The journal was published in Tientsin and its goal was to use Yüan Shih-k'ai in the interests of the liberals. See Ko Kung-chen, *A History of Chinese Journalism* (Chung-kuo pao-hsüeh shih) (Peking, 1955), p. 189.

¹³⁵ Nowhere in Chinese libraries have I found issues that came out later than June 1914.

¹³⁶ Chou Hsia-shou, *Lu Hsün's Home*, pp. 308, 422.

¹³⁷ Lu Hsün, *Complete Works*, IX, 283. After the revolution Chang Ping-lin once again found himself in prison. Lu Hsün secretly visited his teacher and even persuaded him to end his hunger strike, which, under the reign of terror, might have led to nothing more than his death (see Lin Ch'en, *Research on Lu Hsün's Activities*, p. 18).

¹³⁸ Lu Hsün, *Diary*, I, 176, 183, 187, 203, 264. It is curious that prior to December 1915 Lu Hsün went to the meetings of the Society regularly (once a week, sometimes twice), but later he only went once a year, as if he no longer believed that the society could be of any use.

¹³⁹ For example: "chestnut leaves, like drops of rain, flutter past my window"

or "tiny snow flakes, like bits of willow fluff, lie on the frozen branches" (see Lu Hsün *Diary*, I, 23, 42).

[140] Huang T'ing-chien (1045-1105), well-known poet and essayist.

[141] T'an Hsien (1832-1901), poet and collector of ancient verses in the *tz'u* genre.

[142] Hu Ping, *Notes for the Study of Lu Hsün* (Lu Hsün yen-chiu cha-chi) (Shanghai, 1958), p. 129.

[143] Lu Hsün, *Diary*, I, 94.

[144] *Ibid.*, p. 263.

[145] *Hsin ch'ing-nien*, Vol. I, No. 4; Vol. II, Nos. 2, 3, 4; Vol. III, Nos. 1, 2.

[146] Ch'ien Hsüan-t'ung, "A Letter to Ch'en Tu-shiu," *Hsin ch'ing-nien*, III, No. 6; *Letters*, p. 11.

[147] Liu Fu (Liu Pan-nung), "Reply to Wang Ching-hüan," *Hsin ch'ing-nien*, IV, No. 3; *Letters*, p. 276.

[148] See Hu Shih, "Tentative Suggestions for the Reform of Chinese Literature," *Hsin ch'ing-nien*, II, No. 5; Ch'en Tu-hsiu, "On the Literary Revolution," *Ibid.*, No. 6 *et passim*.

[149] See Lu Hsün, *Diary*, I, pp. 263, 305, 307, 309, 310 *et passim*.

[150] Ch'ien Hsüan-t'ung, "Letter to Ch'en Tu-hsiu," *Hsin ch'ing-nien*, III, No. 6; *Letters*, p. 11.

[151] Ch'en Tu-hsiu, "Reply to Ch'ien Hsüan-t'ung," *Hsin ch'ing-nien*, III, No. 6, p. 12.

[152] For example, he advised others not to read Chinese books at all but to engage in the popularization of Western literature (see Ch'ien Hsüan-t'ung, "Letter to Ch'en Tu-hsiu," III, No. 6; *Letters*, pp. 10, 11).

[153] *Ibid.*, pp. 10, 15, 19, 20; *Hsin ch'ing-nien*, IV, No. 1; *Letters*, p. 81; No. 2, pp. 121-123, 140-141.

[154] There is some indirect evidence for this. In one of his linguistic works published in *New Youth*, Ch'ien Hsüan-t'ung refers directly to the opinion of Chou Shu-jen (Lu Hsün's real name). He could only have obtained such an opinion from an oral discussion, because at that time Lu Hsün had not written any works on language.

[155] Pseudonym of Ch'ien Hsüan-t'ung.

[156] Meaning the copying of ancient inscriptions.

[157] Lu Hsün, *Selected Works* (Russian), I, pp. 58, 59. [There are some emendations in this quote. The Russian text clearly says, "Despite my former convictions, I cannot renounce my hopes." But the word "former" is not in the original Chinese. The sentence "I certainly could not use my evidence that there would definitely not be (hope), to refute his evidence that there might" is deleted either from the original translation, the citation, or both. Of course the Yangs' translation (I, 6) hedges on the wording here also. Even so, the parallelism "definitely not be" (*pi-wu*) vs. "might be" (*k'e-yu*) is quite clear. —C.J.A.]

[158] This is the figure cited by Wang Shih-ching (*Biography of Lu Hsün*, p. 75) and L. D. Pozdneeva (Lu Hsün, p. 94) in reference to Lu Hsün's silence as an artist. However, Lu Hsün never restricted his creative works to *belles lettres*.

[159] Ou-yang Fan-hai, *Lu Hsün's Books*, p. 87.

CHAPTER TWO

[1] Lu Hsün, *Complete Works*, III, 85, 465.

[2] *Ibid.*, I, 363, 540.

[3] *Ibid.*, III, 397, 556.

[4] *Ibid.*, pp. 354, 537-538. [Compare *Selected Works* (English), II, 335.]

[5] *Ibid.*, V, 370, 548-549. [This is a rather free version of the original.—C.J.A.]

[6] *Ibid.*, III, 224.

[7] *Ibid.*, IV, 21-22.

[8] Lu Hsün, *Diary*, II, 1137.

[9] Lu Hsün, *Complete Works*, I, 466; VI, 321, 597; IX, 302, 352.

[10] *Ibid.*, III, 421.

[11] Kuo Mo-jo, *Historic Personalities*, p. 295.

[12] T'ang T'ao, *Learning from Lu Hsün* (Hsiang Lu Hsün hsüeh-hsi) (Shanghai, 1953), pp. 135-136.

[13] Mao Ch'en, "Modern, Classical, and Foreign Literature," in *Wen-i pao* (Literature and Art News), No. 8 (1959), p. 9.

[14] Lu Hsün, *Selected Works* (Russian), II, 29.

[15] *Ibid.*, III, 127.

[16] *Ibid.*, p. 147.

[17] Lu Hsün, *Selected Works* (Russian), II, 128. K'ang Yu-wei expressed this "idea" in *Notes on Belgrade, the Capital of Serbia*. [Compare *Selected Works* (English), III, 276.]

[18] Lu Hsün, *Complete Works*, IV, 308.

[19] *Ibid.*, III, 225.

[20] *Ibid.*, VI, 248.

[21] *Ibid.*, I, 235; III, 10 *et passim*.

[22] *Ibid.*, V, 434. [Quoted with modifications from *Selected Works* (English), IV, 86.]

[23] In a letter to T'ang T'ao on April 19, 1935, Lu Hsün said that he still considered this book "not bad" (*ibid.*, X, 232).

[24] Chou Hsia-chou, *The Characters in Lu Hsün's Fiction*, pp. 30-31.

[25] Lu Hsün, *Complete Works*, VI, 134.

[26] *Ibid.*, III, 30, 306; V, 21; VII, 393; IX, 384.

[27] *Ibid.*, I, 318 [*Selected Works* (English), IV, 266-270; 271-276].

[28] See Lu Hsün, *Selected Works* (Russian), III, 140-151 [*Selected Works* (English), IV, 266-276].

[29] Sung Yün-ping, "I Remembered Chang T'ai-yen on the Jubilee of Lu Hsün," *People's Daily* (October 13, 1956).

[30] [See also "Some Reflections of Chang T'ai-yen" in *Selected Works* (English), IV, 266-270.—C.J.A.]

[31] Lu Hsün, *Complete Works*, IX, 294.

[32] *Ibid.*

³³ See Lu Hsün, *Complete Works*, IX, 387 (commentary); V, 434, 563 (commentary).
³⁴ *Ibid.*, pp. 299, 535.
³⁵ Wang Yao, "On the Historical Relationships between Lu Hsün and Classical Literature" in *Wen-i pao* (Literature and Art News), No. 19 (1956), p. 17.
³⁶ Lu Hsün, *Complete Works*, III, 80; IV, 424-425.
³⁷ Lu Hsün, *Diary*, I, 684, 888-889, 911.
³⁸ Lu Hsün, *Complete Works*, I, 317; III, 366; IV, 60; VI, 189.
³⁹ *Ibid.*, IV, 108 (see p. 188 for a similar quotation). [Compare *Selected Works* (English), IV, 46.]
⁴⁰ The Russian translation of this article mistakenly gives another novel, *Journey to the Center of the Earth*, which Lu Hsün also translated.
⁴¹ Lu Hsün, "Hailing the Literary Ties Between China and Russia," *Selected Works* (Russian), II, 98. [See "China's Debt to Russian Literature," *Selected Works* (English), III, 180-184.—C.J.A.]
⁴² *Ibid.*, I, 134.
⁴³ Lu Hsün, *Complete Works*, I, 293, 540; V, 199, 517. [See also *Selected Works* (English), III, 295-296; and Chow Tse-tsung, *The May Fourth Movement, Intellectual Revolution in Modern China* (California: Stanford University Press, 1967), pp. 66-68.—C.J.A.]
⁴⁴ *Ibid.*, IV, 87, 89-90; V, 199. According to L. D. Pozdneeva (*Lu Hsün: His Life and Works*, p. 30), in his later years the writer's attitude toward Lin Shu was purely negative. As a matter of fact, he distinguished between Lin Shu's early works, which were progressive, and those that came later on.
⁴⁵ Lu Hsün, *Complete Works*, VII, 515.
⁴⁶ Apparently he is referring to the unfinished translation by Yang Tzu-lin and Pao Kung-ni in the journal *Li-hsüeh* for 1901. See A Ying, *Bibliography*, p. 129.
⁴⁷ A translation by Lin Shu and Wei Yi, 1905, 2 vols. See A Ying, *Bibliography*, p. 129. The annotators of the *Complete Works* (IV, 533) have evidently made a mistake in dating this as 1913.
⁴⁸ Lu Hsün, *Complete Works*, IV, 231. [Compare *Selected Works* (English), III, 117.]
⁴⁹ *Ibid.*, I, 375. [Compare *Selected Works* (English), II, 25.]
⁵⁰ Ch'ü Ch'iu-po, *Works* (Ch'iu-po wen-chi) (Peking, 1954), II, 919.
⁵¹ See Lu Hsün, *Selected Works* (Russian), IV, 20-22.
⁵² Lu Hsün, *Complete Works*, IV, 309; V, 380.
⁵³ Various Chinese transcriptions of the name Shakespeare. Yen Fu mentioned Shakespeare (stressing the vividness of his characters) in the "Introduction" to the translation of Huxley's *Evolution and Ethics*. Liang Ch'i-ch'ao called Shakespeare a great writer in the prologue to his play "New Rome."
⁵⁴ Lu Hsün, *Complete Works*, V, 450, 567.
⁵⁵ *A Brief History of Chinese Translations*, p. 11.
⁵⁶ *Changes and Developments in the Chinese Prose Since the May Fourth Movement* (Wu-szu i-lai han-yü shu-mien yü-yen te pien-ch'ien ho fa-chan) (Peking, 1959), p. 77.

[57] *A Brief History of Chinese Translations*, pp. 9-11 and 18-25.

[58] T'ang T'ao, "Lu Hsün and Theatrical Art," *Wen-i yüeh-pao* (Literature and Art Monthly), No. 10 (1956), pp. 44-45, and other works.

[59] *History of Chinese Literature* (Chung-kuo wen-hsüeh shih) (Peking, 1959), IV, 420.

[60] Ou-yang Fan-hai, *Lu Hsün's Books*, p. 222.

[61] In the notes to the Russian translation the meaning of these words is interpreted, without sufficient justification, to mean the urban "commercial theater."

[62] Lu Hsün, *Selected Works* (Russian), I, 212.

[63] Lu Hsün, *Complete Works*, III, 274 (for a similar quote, see IX, 100).

[64] *Ibid.*, V, 464, 571-572 [*Selected Works* (English). IV. 17].

[65] *Ibid.*, VI, 104-106, 547

[66] Lu Hsün, *Diary*, I, 495-496 *et passim*.

[67] Lu Hsün, *Selected Works* (Russian), I, 216-226.

[68] Yen Chia-yen, "The Village Opera" in *Yü-wen hsüeh-hsi* (The Study of Language), No. 8 (1959), p. 23.

[69] Lu Hsün, *Selected Works* (Russian), II, 167. [Quoted from *Selected Works* (English), III, 279-280.]

[70] *Ibid.*, III, 33-40, 82, 167-174.

[71] *Ibid.*, p. 35.

[72] *Ibid.*, p. 36.

[73] Lu Hsün, apparently, borrowed it from Shaohsing drama. See Hsü Chin, "Lu Hsün and Shaohsing Theatre," *People's Daily* (September 6 and 7, 1956); Lu Hsün, *Complete Works*, I, 489 (commentary).

[74] Hsü Chin, "Lu Hsün and Shaohsing Theatre," p. 3.

[75] Lu Hsün, *Complete Works*, IV, 265.

[76] *Ibid.*, V, 272, 531-532.

[77] T'ien Han, "Paths and Perspectives in the Development of Chinese Drama," *The Fifty-Year Movement for Colloquial Drama in China: A Collection of Historical Materials* (Chung-kuo hua-chü yün-tung wu-shih nien shih-liao chi) (Peking, 1958), pp. 4-5.

[78] A Ying, "A Brief History of Chinese Fiction," *Wen-i pao* (Literature and Art News), No. 20 (1956), p. 31.

[79] See Lu Hsün, *Complete Works*, VIII, 345.

[80] See Liao-chai, *Stories of Strange People* (Rasskazy o ljudjax neobyčajnyx), translated with a preface and commentary by V. M. Alexeev (Moscow, 1937); P'u Sung-ling, *The Fox's Sorcery: Strange Tales* (Lis'i čary. Strannye istorii), trans. V. M. Alexeev (Moscow, 1959).

[81] Lu Hsün, *Complete Works*, VIII, 176. [See Lu Hsün, *A Brief History of Chinese Fiction*, trans. Yang Hsien-yi and Gladys Yang (Peking: Foreign Languages Press, 1959), p. 277, hereafter cited as *Brief History* (Yang). — C.J.A.]

[82] *Ibid.*

⁸³ *Ibid.*, p. 346 [*Brief History* (Yang), p. 434].

⁸⁴ *Ibid.*, p. 179 [*Brief History* (Yang), p. 286].

⁸⁵ *Ibid.*, p. 213 [*Brief History* (Yang), p. 334].

⁸⁶ See, for example, Liu Ta-chieh, *History of the Development of Chinese Literature* (Chung-kuo wen-hsüeh fa-chan shih), 3 vols. (Shanghai, 1958), III, 349-350.

⁸⁷ See Lu Hsün, *Complete Works*, VIII, 211-212.

⁸⁸ Lu Hsün, *Selected Works* (Russian), II, 9. [Quoted from *Selected Works* (English), II, 43. Semanov translates (Yang's) "cultured gentlemen" (*ya-jen*) as "aesthetes." I have added the Chinese for the last few words in the quotation, because otherwise it would be impossible to capture the flavor of the original. —C.J.A.]

⁸⁹ Literally "like a girl." Later on Lu Hsün points out that the sequence of heroes in this genre was somewhat different.

⁹⁰ Lu Hsün, *Complete Works*, VIII, 216. [*Brief History* (Yang), p. 338. The single quotation marks around 'beauties' are my addition. —C.J.A.]

⁹¹ *Ibid.*, p. 351.

⁹² Ch'en Tse-kuang, "Correctly Determining the Place of *A Flower in an Ocean of Sin* in the History of Chinese Literature," *A Collection of Articles on Ming and Ch'ing Fiction* (Ming-ch'ing hsiao-shuo yen-chiu lun-wen chi) (Peking, 1959), p. 417 [hereafter abbreviated "Correctly Determining the Place of *A Flower in an Ocean of Sin*"].

⁹³ Lu Hsün, *Complete Works*, VIII, 220. [Compare *Brief History* (Yang), p. 345.]

⁹⁴ *Ibid.*, I, 477.

⁹⁵ *Ibid.*, p. 473.

⁹⁶ A novel by Yü Ta (?—1884). [Compare *Brief History* (Yang), p. 440.]

⁹⁷ Lu Hsün, *Complete Works*, VIII, 352.

⁹⁸ Lu Hsün singles out this detail, something new in Chinese literature, by putting quotation marks around the phrase "*la yang-ch'e*" (literally "to pull a foreign carriage").

⁹⁹ Lu Hsün, *Complete Works*, VIII, 224. Here we encounter for the first time Lu Hsün's distaste for what he calls "exaggeration" (*k'ua-chang*). For more details on this see the first chapter, devoted to the early twentieth-century novel of exposure.

¹⁰⁰ Chiang Jui-tsao, *A Collection of Statements on Fiction* (Hsiao-shuo k'ao-cheng), 3 vols. (Shanghai, 1957), I, 221.

¹⁰¹ Lu Hsün, *Complete Works*, V, 447-448.

¹⁰² In the latter part of Kuang-hsü (1875-1907) or the middle of the first decade (1900-1910) of the twentieth century.

¹⁰³ *The Nine-Tailed Tortoise* (Chiu-wei kuei), a novel by Chang Chün-fang. It first came out in 1906.

¹⁰⁴ Lu Hsün, *Complete Works*, VIII, 352 [Quoted with changes from *Brief History* (Yang), pp. 440-441.]

¹⁰⁵ Novels of the fourteenth century. Lu Hsün, *Collected Works*, VIII, 227.

[106] That is, when they were far from rebellious designs.

[107] Lu Hsün, *Complete Works*, VIII, 227. [Quoted with minor changes from *Brief History* (Yang), p. 355.]

[108] *Ibid.*, pp. 228-229.

[109] See Hu Shih, *Works* (Hu Shih wen-ts'un), 3rd ed. (Shanghai, n.d.), VI, p. 746.

[110] Liu Ta-chieh, *History of the Development of Chinese Literature*, III, 352-353; *Lectures on Chinese Literature* (Chung-kuo wen-hsüeh chiang-hua) (Peking, 1959), III, 329 ff.

[111] Lu Hsün, *Complete Works*, VIII, 228.

[112] *Ibid.*, p. 231 [Quoted from *Brief History* (Yang), p. 362. I have corrected the awkward grammar.—C.J.A.]

[113] *Ibid.*, p. 234.

[114] Hu Shih, *Works*, VI, 166-200.

[115] Lu Hsün, *Complete Works*, V, 195.

[116] See Lu Hsün, *Collected Translations*, X, 329.

[117] Lu Hsün, *Complete Works*, IV, 123-124. [Quoted from *Selected Works* (English), III, 51 with a minor variation. The term "roughs" (*liu-min*) should probably be translated "roughnecks" or "ruffians," although "roughs" apparently conveys the same meaning to the British.—C.J.A.]

[118] *Lectures on Chinese Literature*, III, 329 ff.

[119] Lu Hsün, *Complete Works*, VIII, 237. [Quoted from *Brief History* (Yang), p. 370.]

[120] *Ibid.*

[121] *Ibid.*, p. 239 [Quoted with a minor change from *Brief History* (Yang), p. 372. The term "urban population" is a complete fabrication—C.J.A.].

[122] *Ibid.* Several contemporary researchers (Liu Ta-chieh, *History of the Development of Chinese Literature*, p. 361) maintain that Lu Hsün gave the title "novel of exposure" to early twentieth-century fiction as a sign of approval. Others cite only the positive portions of the above statement; see Liu Shou-sung, *The History of Modern Chinese Literature, a Preliminary Draft* (Chung-kuo hsin wen-hsüeh shih ch'u-kao), 2 vols. (Peking, 1956), II, 333-334 ff. [hereafter cited as *History*].

[123] Lu Hsün, *Complete Works*, VIII, 240. [See *Brief History* (Yang) p. 374.]

[124] Lu Hsün *Complete Works*, VIII, 240-241. [Quoted with minor corrections from *Brief History* (Yang), p. 375.]

[125] The author's *Lectures on Chinese Literature* (III, 403) only compound this injustice.

[126] As well as several other contemporary critics (see, for example, Liu Shou-sung, *History*, II, 336).

[127] Lu Hsün, *Complete Works*, VIII, 241-243. [Quoted from *Brief History* (Yang), pp. 375-377. Semanov's translation is basically the same, with only minor variations.—C.J.A.]

[128] Chiang Jui-tsao, *Collection of Statements on Fiction*, II, 585.

[129] Lu Hsün, *Complete Works*, VIII, 244. Chou Kuei-sheng, *Notes from a*

Modern Hermitage (Hsin-an pi-chi), quoted in Lu Hsün, *Extracts from Old Sources on Fiction* (Hsiao-shuo chiu-wen ch'ao) (Peking, 1953), p. 143. The authors of the *Lectures on Chinese Literature* (III, 391) were hardly the first to level this charge against Wu Wo-yao. A different approach is taken by Liu Shou-sung (*History*, II, 337), who calls Lu Hsün's comment "an exceptionally just criticism." [The passage is quoted, with minor grammar corrections, from *Brief History* (Yang), p. 379. Semanov's translation reads something like this: "It is said that Wu Wo-yao's character was utterly inflexible, and that he was unwilling to submit to anyone. Eventually, he became broken and ruined; and so his works are full of anger.... Unfortunately, in descriptions he often gives way to such malice that he distorts reality. This considerably weakens the effect of his work on the reader, turning it into a chain of 'stories' ('gossip' in the Yang translation) purely for the amusement of idlers." The word "stories" does have italics (i.e., quotation marks) in the orginal text.—C.J.A.]

[130] Lu Hsün, *Selected Works* (Russian), II, 371. Translated precisely according to the original (V.S.) (*Complete Works*, VI, 258) [*Selected Works* (English), IV, 167-169, 183].

[131] Cheng Chen-to, *Research on Chinese Literature* (Chung-kuo wen-hsüeh yen-chiu), 3 vols. (Peking, 1957), III, 1199-1200.

[132] Lu Hsün, *Complete Works*, VIII, 307. [Quoted from *Brief History* (Yang), p. 382.]

[133] See Chang Pi-lai, "The Reactionary Character of *The Travels of Lao Ts'an* and the Reactionary Position of Hu Shih as Shown in His Evaluation of This Novel," *Jen-min wen-hsüeh* (People's Literature), No. 3 (1955) [hereafter cited as "The Reactionary Character of *The Travels of Lao Ts'an*"]; *Lectures on Chinese Literature*, III, 330-334.

[134] Hu Shih, preface to Liu O's *The Travels of Lao Ts'an* (Lao Ts'an yu-chi) (Shanghai, 1924), pp. 22-24.

[135] *Ibid.*, p. 28. It is curious that Chang Pi-lai, who takes issue with Hu Shih for his errors ("The Reactionary Character of *The Travels of Lao Ts'an*"), came to a similar conclusion.

[136] Lu Hsün, *Complete Works*, VIII, 309. [Contrast *Brief History* (Yang), pp. 384-385: "The first chapter serves as a prelude, and it is said that sixty more will follow. The story starts with a scholar named Chin Chun who comes in first in the palace examination and goes on to describe the last thirty years of the Ch'ing dynasty; it was probably intended to end with the 1911 revolution but was left unfinished after twenty chapters."—C.J.A.]

[137] See, for example, Chiang Jui-tsao, *Collection of Statements on Fiction*, I, 220.

[138] *Ibid.*, II, 572.

[139] *Ibid.*, I, 221; II, 572.

[140] Ch'en Tse-kuang, "Correctly Determining the Place of *A Flower in an Ocean of Sin*," 410-426.

[141] Lu Hsün, *Complete Works*, VIII, 248. [Compare *Brief History* (Yang), p. 385.]

[142] *Ibid.*, VIII, 333.

[143] Lu Hsün, *Selected Works* (Russian), II, 379. [Quoted from *Selected Works* (English), IV, 183.]

[144] [But, Lu Hsün states specifically: "Innuendo and subtlety are essential in satirical writing. If the author exaggerates or puts the case too bluntly, his work loses its literary value. But later novelists did not pay enough attention to this, with the result that after *The Scholars* we can say there was no real satire" *Brief History* (Yang), p. 436.—C.J.A.]

[145] For a correct understanding of Lu Hsün's criticism one should take into account that in the twenties and thirties he also had a harsh opinion of his own early works. See Lu Hsün, *Selected Works* (Russian), IV, 198; *Complete Works*, I, 153-154; *Letters*, II, 671.

CHAPTER THREE

[1] Chu T'ung, *The Ideas and Struggle of the Young Lu Hsün*, p. 5.

[2] (Shen) Yen-ping (Mao Tun), "Reading *Outcry*" in *On Lu Hsün* (Lu Hsün lun), p. 181.

[3] Sun Ch'ang-hsi, "The Originality of Lu Hsün's Short Stories," *Hsin-hua yüeh-pao* (New China Monthly), No. 1 (1954), p. 236.

[4] Ch'eng Fang-wu, "Criticism of *Outcry*" in *On Lu Hsün*, pp. 230-232.

[5] Chang Ting-huang, "Mr. Lu Hsün" in *On Lu Hsün*, p. 136. [I have corrected the error in the Russian text so that "*shuang-ch'eng chi*" reads "*shuang-p'ing chi*" ("A Tale of Twin Chessboards").—C.J.A.]

[6] [See *Selected Works* (English), III, 230: "For instance, as to why I wrote, I still felt, as I had a dozen years earlier, that I should write in the hope of enlightening my people, for 'humanity,' and of the need to better it. I detested the old habit of describing fiction as 'entertainment,' and regarded 'art for art's sake' as simply another name for passing the time" ("How I Came to Write Stories"). The word "philosophe" is derived from the Chinese "*ch'i-meng chu-i che.*"—C.J.A.]

[7] Compare "The Biography of Hung Chün," from "A Survey of Ch'ing History" (Ch'ing shih kao) in Tseng P'u, *A Flower in an Ocean of Sin* (Nieh-hai hua) (n.p., 1936).

[8] Chu T'ung, *An Analysis of Lu Hsün's Works* (Lu Hsün tso-p'in te fen-hsi) (Shanghai, 1953), I, 107.

[9] V. F. Sorokin, *Lu Hsün's World Outlook*, pp. 127-128.

[10] For other examples, see the story "Tomorrow."

[11] See Lu Hsün, *Complete Works*, IV, 4, 495.

[12] Sun Fu-yüan, *A Few Facts about Mr. Lu Hsün*, p. 24.

[13] Shen P'eng-nien, *A Bibliography of Research materials on Lu Hsün*, p. 192.

[14] Chu T'ung, *An Analysis of Lu Hsün's Works* (Shanghai, 1953), II, 95.

[15] See Lu Hsün, *Selected Works* (Russian), II, 222-223 ff.

[16] *Ibid.*, I, 130. [See also *Selected Works* (Yang), I, 75.]

[17] L. D. Pozdneeva, *Lu Hsün: His Life and Works*, p. 243.

[18] V. F. Sorokin, *Lu Hsün's World Outlook*, p. 101. V. V. Petrov also says that the novel of exposure "did not touch on the problems of the peasantry in a semicolonial, semifeudal China" (Lu Hsün, p. 60). True, the authors of the novel of exposure did not focus on the peasant problem, but one cannot say that they did not even touch upon it.

[19] Lu Hsün, *Selected Works* (Russian), I, 63. [A quotation from "Diary of a Madman." See *Selected Works* (English), I, 10.—C.J.A.]

[20] Hu Ping, *Notes for the Study of Lu Hsün*, p. 44.

[21] See, for example, I chün, "Brief Notes on Lu Hsün's Short Stories," *Shou-hu*, No. 1 (1960), p. 187.

[22] See V. F. Sorokin, *Lu Hsün's World Outlook*, p. 102.

[23] Ou-yang Fan-hai, *Lu Hsün's Books*, pp. 188-189. Li Hsi-fan, "On 'The True Story of Ah Q'" in *Hsin chien-she* (New Construction), No. 4 (1956), p. 23 ff.

[24] L. D. Pozdneeva, *Lu Hsün: His Life and Works*, p. 148.

[25] P'ing Hsin, *The Great Popular Writer Lu Hsün* (Jen-min wen-hao Lu Hsün) (Shanghai, 1947), p. 62.

[26] Lu Hsün, *Complete Works*, I, 314.

[27] Of course there were early twentieth-century novelists who regarded any kind of uprising with hostility—Liu O, for example.

[28] "The hall was crammed full. It seemed as though dragons were writhing, tigers lashing out with their paws, swallows chirping, and orioles singing" (ch. 17).

[29] For more details, see V. F. Sorokin, *Lu Hsün's World Outlook*, p. 129.

[30] *Ibid.*

[31] Lu Hsün himself wrote about the historical basis for "Storm in a Teacup" (*Complete Works*, VI, 151).

[32] See, for example, Jef Last, *Lu Hsün, Dichter und Idol* (Frankfurt am Main and Berlin, 1959), p. 55. See also Liu Chun-jo's article "The Heroes and Heroines of Modern Chinese Fiction: From Ah Q to Wu Tzu-hsü," in *The Journal of Asian Studies*, XVI, No. 2 (1957), pp. 201-211.

[33] Wang Hsi-yen, *A Great Man and a Great Writer* (Wei-ta te jen ho wei-ta te tso-chia) (Shanghai, 1954), p. 56.

[34] Lu Hsün later devoted many of the stories in the collection *Hesitation* to family problems.

[35] Lu Hsün, *Complete Works*, VI, 190.

[36] V. F. Sorokin, *Lu Hsün's World Outlook*, p. 106.

[37] Chao Ching-shen, "Lu Hsün and Chekhov" in *Wen-hsüeh chou-pao* (Literary Weekly), No. 8 (1929), p. 564 ff. Lu Hsün essentially maintained this line of thinking, even later on. In the collection *Hesitation*, for example, he touches on the theme of love, but not its passion, only the dissapointment that remains afterward.

[38] Lu Hsün, *Selected Works* (Russian), I, 206.

[39] *Ibid.*

[40] See the works of Hsü Ch'in-wen, L. D. Pozdneeva, V. F. Sorokin, et al. Among Soviet authors these stories were first analyzed by V. V. Petrov (*Lu Hsün*, pp. 141-145).

[41] See, for example, Tseng P'u, *A Flower in an Ocean of Sin*.

[42] See Li Pao-chia, *Exposure of the Official World*.

[43] Buddhism in its pure form provided the philosophical basis for Su Man-shu's novel (*The Lone Swan*) and short stories.

[44] Lu Hsün, *Collected Translations*, III, 284.

[45] Lu Hsün, *Selected Works*, II, 95. [This is a well-known quotation from the "Preface to Outcry." The quotation from the Russian *Selected Works* reads "following the orders . . . of the revolution's avante-guarde"—which is undoubtedly an interpolation. The Chinese is *"t'ing chiang ming-ling."* See *Selected Works* (English), I, 6.—C.J.A.]

[46] *Ibid.*, I, 59. [Quoted from *Selected Works* (English), I, 6. The Russian quotation is "Just as I added a wreath to the grave of Yü-erh in the story 'Drug,' so in the story 'Tomorrow' I *deleted* the widow Shan's dream in which she saw her son" (italics added). A literal translation of the last portion of the passage would read "I did not say that Fourth Shan's wife would not ultimately see her son in a dream." The Yang translation is more precise.—C.J.A.]

[47] Hsü Ch'in-wen, *An Analysis of Outcry ("Na-han" fen-hsi)* (Peking, 1957), p. 35 (see also I-chün, "Brief Notes on Lu Hsün's Short Stories," p. 184).

[48] B. Krebsová, *Lu Sün. Sa vie et son oeuvre* (Prague, 1953), p. 73 (see also V. V. Petrov, *Lu Hsün*, p. 86).

[49] J. Chinnery, "The Influence of Western Literature on Lu Xün's 'Diary of a Madman,'" *Bulletin of the School of Oriental and African Studies*, No. 2 (1960), p. 31.

[50] See Chien Ming and Ch'ien Ho, "Erroneous Tendencies in the Study of Lu Hsün," *Vostočnyj Al'manax* (Moscow, 1957), p. 31.

[51] Lu Hsün, *Complete Works*, VI, 190.

[52] See Lu Hsün, *Selected Works* (Russian), I, 81.

[53] See, for example, the collection *On Lu Hsün* compiled in 1930.

[54] Among contemporary progressive critics, the Czech sinologists B. Krebsová (*Lu Sün. Sa vie et son oeuvre*, pp. 97, 108, 111) and J. Průšek (*Die Literatur des befreiten China und ihre Volkstraditionen* [Prague, 1955], pp. 106, 187, and "Subjectivism and Individualism in Modern Chinese Literature," *Archiv Orientalni* [1957], p. 264) basically emphasize the pessimistic tone in Lu Hsün's works. Unfortunately B. Krebsová sometimes goes to an extreme and extends this "pessimism" to all of Lu Hsün's works.

[55] Sun Fu-yüan, "The May Fourth Movement and the 'Diary of a Madman,'" in *Hsin chien-she* (New Construction), Vol. 4, No. 2 (1951), p. 17.

[56] Lu Hsün, *Complete Works*, IX, 18.

[57] See Wang Hsi-yen, *A Great Man and a Great Writer*, p. 52; Aiura Takashi, "A Peculiarity of Lu Hsün's Short Stories in 'Medicine,'" *Chugoku bungaku ho* (Bulletin of Chinese Literature), No. 10 (1959) pp. 127-128, 131 *et passim*.

[58] Lu Hsün, *Complete Works*, I, 332.

[59] This was the writer's intention (see Chou Hsia-shou, *The Characters in Lu Hsün's Fiction*, p. 64). It is a pity this detail was not fully explained in the Russian translation and that the letter "Q" appears only in transcription ("kju").

[60] L. D. Pozdneeva, *Lu Hsün: His Life and Works*, 192.

[61] [See John L. Bishop, "Some Limitations of Chinese Fiction," *Far Eastern Quarterly*, XV (1955-56), 239-247. See also my article "A Survey of English Language Criticism of the *Shui-hu chuan*," in *Tsing Hua Journal of Chinese*

Studies, VII, 2 (August 1969), pp. 102-119.—C.J.A.]
[62] V. F. Sorokin, *Lu Hsün's World Outlook*, p. 111.
[63] Lu Hsün, *Complete Works*, I, 362.
[64] L. D. Pozdneeva, *Lu Hsün: His Life and Works*, p. 209.
[65] V. F. Sorokin, *Lu Hsün's World Outlook*, p. 141.
[66] L. D. Pozdneeva, *Lu Hsün: His Life and Works*, p. 210.
[67] Lu Hsün, *Selected Works* (Russian, I, 100). [Compare *Selected Works* (English), I, 50. Note that the Russian translation, like the original, conveys the ideal of interior monologue.—C.J.A.]
[68] *Ibid.* [Quoted from *Selected Works* (English), I, 50.]
[69] V. F. Sorokin, *Lu Hsün's World Outlook*, p. 162.
[70] See Hsü Ch'in-wen, "Lu Hsün and Classical Literature," *Wen-i yüeh-pao* (Literature and Art Monthly), No. 10 (1956), p. 50.
[71] Lu Hsün, *Selected Works* (Russian), II, 125. [Quoted from *Selected Works* (English), III, 232. Minor changes have been made to accord with the Russian.]
[72] *Ibid.*, I, 75 [Quoted with a minor change from *Selected Works* (English), I, 23.]
[73] See Lu Hsün, *Complete Works*, I, 81. In the Russian translation of "The True Story of Ah Q" (*Selected Works*, I, 145) this detail is omitted.—V.S.
[74] Chu T'ung, *An Analysis of Lu Hsün's Works*, I, 165.
[75] Hsü Ch'in-wen, *An Analysis of Outcry* ("*Na-han*" *fen-hsi*) (Peking, 1957), p. 77. [For the complete story see William A. Lyell, Jr., *Lu Hsün's Vision of Reality* (Berkeley: University of California Press, 1976), pp. 153-155, 31-32. —C.J.A.]
[76] Chou Hsia-shou, *Lu Hsün's Home*, pp. 42-44, 48-49.
[77] Jun-t'u, for example. Se Chu T'ung, *An Analysis of Lu Hsün's Works*, I, 117.
[78] Lu Hsün, *Complete Works*, VI, 423.
[79] Lu Hsün, *Selected Works* (Russian), II, 124.
[80] *Ibid.*, I, 157. [Quoted from *Selected Works* (English), I, 104.]
[81] Chu T'ung, *An Analysis of Lu Hsün's Works*, II, 107.
[82] [Quoted with minor changes from *Selected Works* (English), I, 75. The Russian translation (*Selected Works*, I, 130) substitutes the word "dream" for "hope." "A dream is not something which exists or which may never be...."
—C.J.A.]
[83] [Quoted with a minor change from *Selected Works* (English), I, 49-51.]
[84] L. D. Pozdneeva, *Lu Hsün: His Life and Works*, p. 138.
[85] See Ch'uan Tao, "On 'Medicine,'" *Yü-wen hsüeh-hsi* (The Study of Language and Literature), No. 9 (1959), p. 10.
[86] [See C. T. Hsia, *A History of Modern Chinese Fiction, 1917-1957* (New Haven: Yale University Press, 1961) pp. 34-36.—C.J.A.]
[87] Chu T'ung, *An Analysis of Lu Hsün's Works*, II, 108.
[88] Wu Pen-hsing, *The Study of Literature* (*Wen-hsüeh tso-p'in yen-chiu*) (Shanghai, 1954), pp. 145-155; Ma Han-hua, "The Structure of 'My Old Home'" in *Yü-wen hsüeh-hsi* (The Study of Language and Literature),

No. 10 (1956), pp. 16-17 ff.

[89] Tan Yen-i, *Lu Hsün's Lectures in Sian* (Lu Hsün chiang-hsüeh tsai Hsi-an) (Wuhan, 1957), p. 37.

[90] Ho Chai-huai, "An Experimental Analysis of 'A Small Incident,'" *Yü-wen hsüeh-hsi* (The Study of Language and Literature), No. 10 (1959), p. 22.

[91] Ou-yang Fan-hai, *Lu Hsün's Books*, pp. 156-160, 202-203. [See also Chi-chen Wang, "What's the Difference?" in *Contemporary Chinese Stories* (New York: Columbia University Press, 1944), pp. 181-189—C.J.A.]

[92] B. Krebsová, *Lu Sün. Sa vie et son ouevre*, p. 82.

[93] Lu Hsün, *Selected Works* (Russian), I, 186. [See Chi-chen Wang, *Contemporary Chinese Stories*, p. 182.]

[94] *Ibid.*

[95] V. V. Petrov, *Lu Hsün*, p. 148.

[96] Ou-yang Fan-hai, *Lu Hsün's Books*, p. 190.

[97] V. F. Sorokin, *Lu Hsün's World Outlook*, p. 163.

[98] *Ibid.*, p. 173 [*Selected Works* (English), I, 128].

[99] Lu Hsün, *Selected Works* (Moscow, 1945), p. 152 [*Selected Works* (English), II, 307].

[100] Lu Hsün, *Complete Works*, V, 36.

[101] *Ibid.*, IV, 435.

[102] *Ibid.*, III, 284 [*Selected Works* (English), II, 311].

[103] *Ibid.*, p. 50.

[104] Lu Hsün, *Selected Works* (Russian), II, 124.

[105] Lin Ch'en, *Research on Lu Hsün's Activities*, p. 21.

[106] Wu Pen-hsing, *The Study of Literature*, p. 136.

[107] Chu T'ung, *An Analysis of Lu Hsün's Works*, II, 73.

[108] Lu Hsün, *Selected Works* (Russian), I, 181. [Compare *Selected Works* (English) I, 134.]

[109] Wu Pen-hsing, *The Study of Literature*, p. 112.

[110] Lu Hsün, *Selected Works* (Russian), I, 75-76. [Quoted in part from *Selected Works* (English), I, 23-24.]

[111] *Ibid.*

[112] T'ang T'ao, "On Lu Hsün's 'A Small Incident,'" *A Collection of Articles on Lu Hsün's Works* (Lu Hsün tso-p'in lun-chi) (Peking, 1957), p. 128.

[113] Lu Hsün, *Selected Works* (Russian), I, 100-101. [Quoted from *Selected Works* (English), I, 49-51.]

[114] Lu Hsün, *Complete Works*, I, 104. In the Russian translation (*Selected Works*, I, 170) the words "frightening thing" ["cause for alarm" in the above translation] have been changed to "annoyance," and this weakens the artistic effect. [See *Selected Works* (English), I, 120.—C.J.A.]

[115] Quoted from *Selected Works* (English), I, 8-21.

[116] Lu Hsün, *Selected Works* (Russian), I, 88. [Quoted from *Selected Works* (English), I, 37.]

[117] *Ibid.*, p. 90. [Quoted from *Selected Works* (English), I, 39.]

[118] *Ibid.*

[119] L. D. Pozdneeva, *Lu Hsün: His Life and Works*, pp. 216-217.

CONCLUSION

[1] Lu Hsün, *Selected Works* (Russian), II, 18. The last sentence of the translation is an emendation of the original (V.S.). Lu Hsün, *Complete Works*, I, 276. [Quoted from *Selected Works* (English), II, 78).]

[2] V. V. Petrov, "Lu Hsün and Chinese Poetry," *Research Notes of Leningrad State University* (Učenye zapiski LGU), series on Oriental Sciences, No. 7 (1958), p. 92.

[3] It is sufficient to compare the poems that V. V. Petrov cited with those of Huang Tsun-hsien and T'an Ssu-t'ung, published in *Far Eastern Almanac* (Vostočnij al'manax) No. 1 (Moscow, 1957), pp. 85-95.

[4] Lu Hsün, *Complete Works*, VIII, p. 632, cited in V. F. Sorokin, *Lu Hsün's World Outlook*, p. 100.

[5] Wang Yao, *Lu Hsün and Chinese Literature* (Lu Hsün yü Chung-kuo wen-hsüeh) (Shanghai, 1952), p. 38.

Bibliography

Aiura, Takashi. "A Peculiarity of Lu Hsün's Short Stories in 'Medicine,'" *Chugoku bungaku ho* (Bulletin of Chinese Literature), No. 10 (1959).

Alber, C. J. "A Survey of English Language Criticism of *Shui-hu chuan*," *Tsing Hua Journal of Chinese Studies*, VII, 2 (August 1969), 102-119.

Andreev, L. *Polnoe sobranie sočinenie* (Complete Works). St. Petersburg, 1913.

Andrjejew (Andreev), L. *Die Lüge, Ausgewählte Erzählungen* (The Lie: Selected Narratives). Dresden and Leipzig, 1902.

Bishop, John L. "Some Limitations of Chinese Fiction," *Far Eastern Quarterly*, XV (1955-56), 238-247.

Chang, Pi-lai. "Lao Ts'an yu-chi te fan-tung-hsing ho Hu Shih tsai *Lao Ts'an yu-chi* p'ing-chia chung suo piao-hsien te fan-tung cheng-chih li-ch'ang" (The Reactionary Character of *The Travels of Lao Ts'an* and the Reactionary Position of Hu Shih as Shown in His Evaluation of the Novel), *Jen-min wen-hsüeh* (People's Literature), No. 3 (1955).

Chang, Ting-huang. "Lu Hsün hsien-sheng" (Mr. Lu Hsün), *Lu Hsün lun* (On Lu Hsün). Shanghai: [Pei-hsin shu-chü], 1930, 129-144.

Chao, Ching-shen. "Lu Hsün and Chekhov," *Wen-hsüeh chou-pao* (Literary Weekly), No. 8 (1929).

Ch'en, Ming-shu. *Pao-wei Lu Hsün te chan-tou ch'uan-t'ung* (In Defense of the Militant Traditions of Lu Hsün). Tientsin, 1959.

Ch'en, Tse-kuang. "Cheng-ch'üeh ku-chi *Nieh-hai hua tsai* Chung-kuo chin-tai wen-hsüeh shih shang te ti-wei" (Correctly determining the Place of *A Flower in an Ocean of Sin* in the History of Chinese Literature), *Ming-ch'ing hsiao-shuo yen-chiu lun-wen chi* (A Collection of Articles on Ming-Ch'ing Fiction). Peking, 1959.

Ch'en, Tu-hsiu. "Reply to Ch'ien Hsüan-t'ung," *Hsin ch'ing-nien* (New Youth), III, No. 6 (August 1, 1917).

Cheng, Chen-to. *Chung-kuo wen-hsüeh yen-chiu* (Research on Chinese Literature). 3 vols. Peking: [Tso-chia ch'u-pan she], 1957.

Ch'eng, Fang-wu. "'Na-han' te p'ing-lun" (Criticism of *Outcry*), *Lu Hsün lun* (On Lu Hsün). Shanghai: [Pei-hsin shu-chü], 1930.

Cheng Huang. "Lu Hsün During the Hsin-hai Revolution and Shaohsing Youth," *Chieh-fang jih-pao* (Liberation Daily), October 14, 1956.

Chiang, Jui-tsao. *Hsiao-shuo k'ao-cheng* (A Collection of Statements on Fiction). 3 vols. Shanghai: [Ku-tien wen-hsüeh ch'u-pan she, 2nd ed.], 1957.

Ch'ien, Hsing-ts'un (A Ying). "A Brief History of Chinese Fiction," *Wen-i pao* (Literature and Art News), No. 20 (1956).

_____. *Hsien-tai Chung-kuo wen-hsüeh tso-chia* (Contemporary Chinese Writers). Shanghai, 1928.

_____. *Wan-ch'ing hsiao-shuo shih* (A History of Late Ch'ing Fiction). Peking: [Tso-chia ch'u-pan she, rev. ed.], 1955.

_____. *Wan-ch'ing hsi-ch'ü hsiao-shuo mu* (Bibliography of Late Ch'ing Drama and Fiction). Shanghai: [Wen-i lien-ho ch'u-pan she], 1957.

Ch'ien, Hsüan-t'ung. "A Letter to Ch'en Tu-hsiu," *Hsin ch'ing-nien* (New Youth), III, No. 6 (August 1, 1917).

Chien Ming and Ch'ien Ho. "Ošibočnye tendencii v izučenii proizvedenij Lu Sinja" (Erroneous Tendencies in the Study of Lu Hsün), *Vostočnij al'manax* (Far Eastern Almanac). No. 1 (Moscow, 1957).

Ching Sung (Hsü Kuang-p'ing). "Lu Hsün Prior to the Hsin-hai Revolution," in Sun Fu-yüan, *Lu Hsün hsien-sheng erh-san shih* (A Few Facts about Mr. Lu Hsün). Shanghai, 1949.

Chinnery, J. "The Influence of Western Literature on Lu Xün's 'Diary of a Madman,'" *Bulletin of the School of Asian and African Studies*, XXIII, No. 2 (1960), 309-322.

Chou, Ch'i-ming (Chou Tso-jen). *Lu Hsün te ch'ing-nien shih-tai* (Lu Hsün's Youth). Peking: [Chung-kuo ch'ing-nien ch'u-pan she], 1957.

Chou, Hsia-shou (Chou Tso-jen). *Lu Hsün hsiao-shuo-li te jen-wu* (The Characters in Lu Hsün's Fiction). Shanghai: [Shanghai ch'u-pan kung-szu], 1955.

_____. *Lu Hsün te ku-chia* (Lu Hsün's Home). Shanghai: [Shanghai ch'u-pan kung-szu], 1952.

Chou, Shu-jen (Lu Hsün). *A Brief History of Chinese Fiction*. Translated by Yang Hsien-yi and Gladys Yang. Peking: Foreign Languages Press, 1959.

_____. *Hsiao-shuo chiu-wen ch'ao* (Extracts from Old Sources on Fiction). Peking, 1953.

_____. *Lu Hsün ch'üan-chi* (Complete Works of Lu Hsün). 10 vols. Peking, 1957-59.

_____. *Lu Hsün ch'üan chi pu-i* (Supplement to the Complete Works of Lu Hsün). Shanghai, 1948.

_____. *Lu Hsün i-wen chi* (Collected Translations of Lu Hsün). Peking, 1958.

_____. *Lu Hsün nien-p'u* (Chronology of Lu Hsün). Compiled by the Lu Hsün nien-p'u editorial committee of Shanghai Normal College and Fu-tan University, 2 vols. Ho-fei: An-hui jen-min ch'u-pan-she, 1979.

_____. *Selected Works of Lu Hsün*. Edited and translated by Yang Hsien-yi and Gladys Yang. 4 vols. Peking: Peking Foreign Languages Press, 1956-60.

_____. *Shu-chien* (Letters). 2 vols. Peking, 1952.

_____. *Sobranie sočinenij* (Selected Works). 4 vols. Moscow: Goslitizdat, 1954-56.

Chou, Tso-jen. *Lu Hsün hsiao-shuo li te jen-wu* (The Characters in Lu Hsün's Fiction). Shanghai: [Shanghai ch'u-pan kung-szu], 1955.

Chow, Tse-tsung. *The May Fourth Movement, Intellectual Revolution in Modern China*. Stanford, Calif.: Stanford University Press, 1967.

Chu Cheng. *Lu Hsün chuan-lüeh* (A Short Biography of Lu Hsün). Peking: [Tso-chia ch'u-pan she], 1956.

Ch'ü, Ch'iu-po. *Ch'iu-po wen-chi* (Collected Essays of Ch'ü Ch'iu-po). Peking, 1954.

Chu T'ung. *Lu Hsün tso-p'in te fen-hsi* (An Analysis of Lu Hsün's Works). 2 vols. Shanghai: [Tung-fang shu-tien], 1953-54.

_____. "Lu Hsün's Early Ideas and Struggles (1902-1909)," *Wen-shih-che* (The Literary Historian), No. 10 (1956).

Ch'uan Tao. "On 'Medicine,'" *Yü-wen hsüeh-hsi* (The Study of Language and Literature), No. 10 (1959).

Chung-kuo fan-i wen-hsüeh chien-shih (A Brief History of Chinese Translations). Peking, 1960.

Chung-kuo wen-hsüeh shih (The History of Chinese Literature). 4 vols. Peking, 1959.

Garshin, V. M. *Sočinenija* (Works). Moscow, 1955.

_____. *Der Narr* (The Fool). Vienna and Leipzig, 1904.

_____. *Die rote Blume und andere Novellen* (The Red Flower and Other Novellas). Leipzig, 1906.

Ho, Chia-huai. "An Experimental Analysis of 'A Small Incident,'" *Yü-wen hsüeh-hsi* (The Study of Language and Literature), No. 10 (1959).

_____. *Lu Hsün tso-p'in chiang-hua* (Lectures on the Works of Lu Hsün). Wu-han: [Ch'ang-chiang wen-i ch'u-pan she], 1959.

Hsia, C. T. *A History of Modern Chinese Fiction, 1917-57*. New Haven: Yale University Press, 1961.

Hsiao-shuo yüeh-pao (Fiction Monthly). Vol. IV, No. 1 (1913).

Hsin ch'ing-nien (New Youth). Vol. IV, No. 1.

Hsü Chin. "Lu Hsün and Shaohsing Theatre," *Jen-min jih-pao* (The People's Daily), September 6 and 7, 1956.

Hsü, Ch'in-wen. "Lu Hsün and Classical Literature," *Wen-i yüeh-pao* (Literature and Art Monthly), No. 10 (1956).

_____. "*Na-han*" *fen-hsi* (An Analysis of *Outcry*). Peking: [Chung-kuo ch'ing-nien ch'u-pan she], 1957.

Hsü, Shou-shang. *Wang-yu Lu Hsün yin-hsiang chi* (Impressions of My Late Friend Lu Hsün). Peking: [Jen-min wen-hsüeh ch'u-pan she], 1953.

_____. *Wo-so-jen-shih te Lu Hsün* (The Lu Hsün That I Knew). Peking: [Jen-min wen-hsüeh ch'u-pan she], 1954.

Huang, Sung-k'ang. *Lu Hsün and the New Culture Movement of Modern China*. Amsterdam: Djambatan, 1957.

Hui An (T'ang T'ao). "Jules Verne," *T'u-shu yüeh-pao* (Library Monthly), No. 1 (1956).

Hu Ping. *Lu Hsün yen-chiu cha-chi* (Notes for the Study of Lu Hsün). Shanghai: [Hsi wen-i ch'u-pan she], 1958.

Hu Shih. "Wen-hsüeh kai-liang ch'u-i" (Tentative Suggestions for the Reform of Chinese Literature), *Hsin ch'ing-nien* (New Youth), II, No. 5 (January 1917), 7-23.

_____. *Hu Shih wen-ts'un* (The Collected Essays of Hu Shih). 3rd ed. Shanghai, [n.d.].

I Chün, "Brief Notes on Lu Hsün's Short Stories," *Shou-hu*, No. 1, (1960).

Ko, Kung-chen. *Chung-kuo pao-hsüeh shih* (A History of Chinese Journalism). Peking, 1955.

Krebsová, B. *Lu Sün, Sa vie et son oeuvre*. Prague: Académie Tschécoslovaque des Sciences, 1953.

Kuo, Mo-jo. *Li-shih jen-wu* (Historic Personalities). Shanghai, 1949.

Last, Jef. *Lu Hsün, Dichter und Idol* (Lu Hsün, Poet and Idol). Frankfurt am Main and Berlin: Metzner, 1959.

Li, Hsi-fan. "On 'The True Story of Ah Q,'" *Hsin chien-she* (New Construction), No. 4 (1956).

Lin Ch'en. *Lu Hsün shih-chi k'ao* (Research on Lu Hsün's Activities). Shanghai: [K'ai-ming shu-tien], 1955.

_____. "Lu Hsün and the Southern Society," *Kuang-ming jih-pao* (Kuang-ming Daily), September 26, 1961.

Liu, Chun-jo. "The Heroes and Heroines of Modern Chinese Fiction: From Ah Q to Wu Tzu-hsü," *Journal of Asian Studies*, XVI, No. 2 (1957), 201-211.

Liu Fu (Liu Pan-nung). "Reply to Wang Ching-hsüan," *Hsin ch'ing-nien* (New Youth), IV, No. 3.

Liu O. *Lao Ts'an yu-chi*, with a preface by Hu Shih. Shanghai, 1924.

Liu, Shou-sung. *Chung-kuo hsin wen-hsüeh shih ch'u-kao* (The History of Modern Chinese Literature, A Preliminary Draft). 2 vols. Peking: [Tso-chia ch'u-pan she], 1956.

Liu, Ta-chieh. *Chung-kuo wen-hsüeh chiang-hua* (Lectures on Chinese Literature). Peking, 1959.

_____. *Chung-kuo wen-hsüeh fa-chan shih* (History of the Development of Chinese Literature). 3 vols. Shanghai: [Ku-tien wen-hsüeh ch'u-pan she], 1958.

Ma, Han-hua. "The Structure of 'My Old Home'" *Yü-wen hsüeh-hsi* (The Study of Language and Literature), No. 10 (1956).

Mao Ch'en. "Modern, Classical and Foreign Literature," *Wen-i pao* (Literature and Art News), No. 8 (1959).

Oda, Takeo. *Lu Hsün chuan* (A Biography of Lu Hsün). Translated by Fan Ch'üan. Shanghai: [K'ai-ming shu-tien, 6th ed.], 1949.

Ou-yang, Fan-hai. *Lu Hsün te shu* (Lu Hsün's Books). Hong Kong: [Hua-mei t'u-shu kung-szu], 1948.

Ozaka, Tokuji. *Chugoku shin bungaku undo shi, Go Teki kara Rojin e*. (A History of the New Literature Movement in China, from Hu Shih to Lu Hsün). Tokyo, 1957.

Petrov, V. V. *Lu Sin': očerk žizni i tvorčestva* (Lu Hsün: A Survey of His Life and Works). Moscow: Gosudarstvennoe izdatel'stvo xudožestvennoj literatury, 1960.

_____. "Lu Hsün and Chinese Poetry," *Učenye zapiski LGU* (Research Notes of Leningrad State University), series on Oriental Sciences, No. 7 (1958).

P'ing Hsin. *Jen-min wen-hao Lu Hsün* (The Great Popular Writer Lu Hsün). Shanghai: [Hsin wen-i ch'u-pan she], 1947.

Pozdneeva, L. D. *Lu Sin'* (Lu Hsün). ("Žizn' zamečatel'nyx ljudej.") Moscow: Molodaja gvardija, 1957.

_____. *Lu Sin': žizn' i tvorčestvo, (1881-1936)* (Lu Hsün: His Life and Creative Works, 1881-1936). Moscow: Moscow State University, 1959.

Průšek, Jaroslav. *Die Literatur des befreiten China und ihre Volkstraditionen* (The Literature of Liberated China and Its Folk Traditions). Prague: Artia, 1955.

_____. "Lu Hsün the Revolutionary and the Artist," *Orientalistische Literaturzeitung* (Oriental Bibliographical News), No. 55 (1960), 229-236.

_____. "Subjectivism and Individualism in Modern Chinese Literature," *Archiv Orientalni*, XXV, No. 2 (1957), 251-286.

P'u, Sung-ling. *Lis'i čary. Strannye istorii* (The Fox's Sorcery, Strange Tales). Translated by V. M. Alexeev. Moscow, 1959.

_____. *Rasskazy o ljudax neobyčajnax* (Stories of Unusual People). Translated with a preface and commentary by V. M. Alexeev. Moscow: AN SSSR, 1937.

Semanov, V. I. "Inostrannaja literatura v Kitae..." (Foreign Literature in China), *Iz istorii literaturnyx svjazej XIX veka* (From the History of Nineteenth-Century Literary Relations). Moscow, 1962.

_____. "Japonskaja proza v Kitae..." (Japanese Prose in China), *Iz istorii literaturnyx svjazej XIX veka* (From the History of Nineteenth-Century Literary Relations). Moscow, 1962.

Shen, P'eng-nien. *Lu Hsün yen-chiu tzu-liao pien-mu* (A Bibliography of Research Materials on Lu Hsün). Shanghai: [Shanghai wen-i ch'u-pan she], 1958.

(Shen), Yen-ping (Mao Tun). "Tu 'Na-han'" (Reading *Outcry*), *Lu Hsün lun* (On Lu Hsün). Shanghai: [Pei-hsin shu-chu], 1930, 182-189.

Shiga, Masatoshi. "Research on Lu Hsün's Translations," *Tenri daigaku gakuho* (Tenri University Bulletin), No. 7 (1956).

Sorokin, V. F. *Formirovanie mirovozzrenija Lu Sinja: ranjaja publicistika i sbornik "Klič"* (The Formation of Lu Hsün's World Outlook: Early Publicism and the Collection *Outcry*). Moscow: Izdatel'stvo vostočnoj literatury, 1958.

Sun, Ch'ang-hsi. "The Originality of Lu Hsün's Short Stories," *Hsin-hua yüeh-pao* (New China Monthly), No. 1 (1954).

Sun, Fu-yüan. "The May Fourth Movement and the 'Diary of a Madman,'" *Hsin chien-she* (New Construction), IV, No. 2 (1951).

_____. *Lu Hsün hsien-sheng erh-san shih* (A Few Facts about Mr. Lu Hsün). Shanghai, 1949.

Sung, Yün-ping. "I Remembered Chang T'ai-yen on the Anniversary of Lu Hsün," *Jen-min jih-pao* (The People's Daily), October 13, 1956.

Tan, Yen-i. *Lu Hsün chiang-hsüeh tsai Hsi-an* (Lu Hsün's Lectures in Sian). Wu-han, 1957.

T'ang T'ao. *Hsiang Lu Hsün hsüeh-hsi* (Learning from Lu Hsün). Shanghai: [P'ing-min ch'u-pan she], 1953.

_____. "On Lu Hsün's 'A Small Incident,'" *Lu Hsün tso-p'in lun-chi* (A Collection of Articles on Lu Hsün's Works). Peking, 1957.

_____. "Lu Hsün and Theatrical Art," *Wen-i yüeh-pao* (Literature and Art Monthly), No. 10 (1956).

T'ien Han. "Paths and Perspectives in the Development of Chinese Drama," *Chung-kuo hua-chü yün-tung wu-shih nien shih-liao chi* (The Fifty-year Movement for Colloquial Drama in China. A Collection of Historical Materials). Peking, 1958.

Tikhvinsky, S. L. *Dviženie za reformy v Kitae i Kan Ju-vèj* (K'ang Yu-wei and the Reform Movement in China). Moscow, 1959.

Tseng P'u. *Nieh-hai hua* (A Flower in an Ocean of Sin). [n.p.], 1936.

Vostočnyj al'manax (Far Eastern Almanac), No. 1 (Moscow, 1957), 85-95; No. 4 (1961).

Wang, Chi-chen. "What's the Difference?" *Contemporary Chinese Stories*. New York: Columbia University Press, 1944.

Wang, Hsi-yen. *Wei-ta te jen ho wei-ta te tso-chia* (A Great Man and a Great Writer). Shanghai: [Hsin wen-i ch'u-pan she], 1954.

Wang, Shih-ching. *Lu Hsün chuan* (Biography of Lu Hsün). Harbin, 1949.

_____. *Lu Hsün, t'a te sheng-p'ing ho ch'uang-tso* (Lu Hsün, His Life and Works). Peking: [Chung-kuo ch'ing-nien ch'u-pan she], 1958.

Wang, T'ung-chao, "First Impressions of Lu Hsün's Short Stories," *Wen-i yüeh-pao* (Literature and Art Monthly), No. 10 (1956), 15-16.

Wang Yao. *Lu Hsün yü Chung-kuo wen-hsüeh* (Lu Hsün and Chinese Literature). Shanghai: [P'ing-min ch'u-pan she], 1952.

_____. "On the Historical Relationship between Lu Hsün and Classical Literature," *Wen-i pao* (Literature and Art News), No. 19 (1956).

Wen-hsüeh p'ing-lun (Literary Criticism), No. 3 (1963).

Wu, Pen-hsing. *Wen-hsüeh tso-p'in yen-chiu* (The Study of Literature). Shanghai, 1954.

Wu-szu i-lai han-yü shu-mien yü-yen te pien-ch'ien ho fa-chan (Changes and Developments in Chinese Prose Since May Fourth). Peking, 1959.

Yen, Chia-yen. "The Village Opera," *Yü-wen hsüeh-hsi* (The Study of Language), No. 8 (1959).

Index

Abramson, E. M., x
Academy of Sciences, ix, xi, xii, xvi
"Adventures of Sherlock Holmes," 49
aesthetics, 5, (13), (17), (18), 19, 33-35 (nn. 122, 123), 36, 37, 43, 44, 50, 53-54, 64, 78, 103, 122
After the Disaster, 82, 85, 103, 109
"Against Evil Voices," 18, 19
Aho, J., 20
Ah Q (*see* "The True Story of Ah Q")
Aiura, Takashi, 95 (n. 57)
Alber, C. J., 97 (n. 61)
Alexeev, V. M., xxiv, 57 (n. 80)
allegory, xviii, 25-26, 76, 92, 94
Alliance Society (T'ung-meng hui), 15, 16
Amah Wu ("Ah Q"), 91
The Amazing Rumors of a Blind Man's Lies, 70, 81
An Chi, 62-63
Andreev, Leonid, 20, 21, 22-23, 30, 31, 94, 95
Artsybashev, 95
Asia, x, xii, xvi
"At a Country House" (Chekhov), 20
A Ying (*see* Ch'ien Hsing-ts'un)

Ballad of the Great Incident of 1900, 88
Barbusse, Henri, ix

The Bell of Yüeh (Yüeh-to jih pao), 31-32
"Beyond the Frontier," 48
Bishop, John L., 97 (n. 61)
A Blind Man's Lies (*see The Amazing Rumors of a Blind Man's Lies*)
Blockhead Fu (*see* Fu Mi-hsien)
Bokanenko, x
The Bookworm (T'an-shih), 58, 73
Boxer Rebellion, 4, 65, 88, 89
Brandt, C., xix (n. 21)
A Brief History of Chinese Fiction, xxi, xxv, 56-73
A Brief History of Chinese Translations, 51 (nn. 55, 57)
Buddhism, 35 (n. 123), 36, 47, 93
Byron, 10, 18, 21, 39

Caesar, 6
cannibalism, 79, 110, 117-118
Canton Uprising, 24
"The Captain's Daughter" (Pushkin), 21
Cases of Lord Peng, 64
Cases of Lord Shih, 64
Cervantes, (18), (49)
Chang Chih-tung, 19 (n. 67)
Chang Chün-fang, 61 (n. 103)
Chang Hsün, 38-39, 90
Chang Pi-lai, 70 (n. 133), 71 (n. 135)
Chang Ping-lin (Chang T'ai-yen), 3, 7, 9, 11, 15, 16, 37, 40, 46, 47-48, 82

Chang Shih-chao, 77 (n.)
Chang T'ai-yen (*see* Chang Ping-lin)
Chang Ting-huang, 77
"A Chapter from the History of Science," 17
Chao (*see* Honorable Chao)
Chao Ching-shen 91 (n. 37)
Chao Erh-pao, 60-61
Chao P'u-chai, 60-61
Chekiang, 61
Chekiang Tide (Che-chiang ch'ao), 9, 12, 20
Chekhov, Anton, vii, xvii, 20, 21, 27, 36, 86, 91 (n. 37), 115
Ch'en Ch'ü-ping, 32
Ch'en Ming-shu, 18, 21 (n. 74)
Ch'en Sen, 59
Ch'en Shih-ch'eng ("The White Light"), 83, 103
Ch'en Tse-kuang, 59, 72
Ch'en Tu-hsiu, 39 (n. 146), 40 (nn. 148, 150-152)
Cheng Chen-to, xvi, 70
Ch'eng Fang-wu, 3, 4 (n. 4), 76 (n. 4)
Cheng Huang, 32 (n. 109)
Chia (*Exposure of the Official World*), 67-68
Chia Chien-sheng (Lu Hsün), 8 (n. 23)
Chiang Chih-yu, 11, 15, 16-17
Chiang Jui-tsao, 61 (n. 100), 68 (n. 128), 71 (n. 137)
Chiang Kuan-yün (*see* Chiang Chih-yu)
Chieh and Chou, 118
Ch'ien ("Ah Q"), 100
Ch'ien Ho, 94 (n. 50)
Ch'ien Hsing-ts'un, 4 (n. 6), 15 (n. 51), 16 (nn. 52-53), 21 (n. 73), 23 (n. 88), 50 (n. 46), 56
Ch'ien Hsüan-t'ung (Chin Hsin-yi), 39, 40-41
Chien Ming, 94 (n. 50)
Chin Hsin-yi (*see* Ch'ien Hsüan-t'ung)
Chin Wen-ch'ing (Hung Chün), 71 n. 136), 72, 79 (n. 7)
Chin Yao-tsung ("The Past"), 27, 28

Chinese Communist Party (CCP), ix, xiv
The Chinese Soul, 7
Ch'ing Dynasty, 3, 4, 48, 54, 57, 58, 59, 61, 64, 65, 69, 71-72, 86
"Ching-sheng the Giant" (Lin Shu), 49
Ching Sung (*see* Hsü Kuang-p'ing)
Chinnery, J., xvi, 7, 94 (n. 49)
Ch'iu Chin, 11, 46
Ch'iu-hen, 60
Chi Yün, 5, 57-58
Chou Ch'i-ming (*see* Chou Tso-jen)
Chou Hsia-shou (*see* Chou Tso-jen)
Chou Kuei-sheng, 69
Chou Shou-chuan, 37
Chou Tso-jen, 3, 5 (n. 1), 6 (nn. 3, 5), 7 (n. 13), 10 (nn. 31, 35), 15, 16, (nn. 54, 56), 17 (n. 57), 22 (n. 78), 28 (n.), 36 (nn. 131-133), 37 (n. 136), 46 (n. 24), 52, 97 (n. 59), 103 (n. 76)
Chow Tse-tsung, xix (n. 19), xxi (n. 25), 49 (n. 43)
Chu (*After the Disaster*), 103
Chu Cheng, 7 (n. 10), 9 (n. 27)
Ch'ü Ch'iu-po, 50
Chu T'ung, 7 (n. 17), 76 (n. 1), 80, 82 (n. 14), 102 (n. 74), 103 (n. 77), 105 (n. 81), 108, 115
ch'uan-chi (*see* novella)
Ch'uan Tao, 108 (n. 85)
Ch'ü Yüan, xi
"Claire de lune" (Maupassant), 20
classical language and literature, xi, xxiii, 8, 10, 12, (14-15), 16, 20, 22-24, 28, 30, 38, 42, 49, 51, 58-59, 72, 73, 76, 77, 94, 100, 104, 109, 113-116, 118, 121
Cleopatra (Haggard), 8
Collection of Uncollected Works (Chi-wai chi), 11
colloquial (pai-hua), xi, xxii, 14-15 (n. 49), 20, 24, 39, 40, 41, 49, 55-56, 113-117, 121
Comintern, viii
Commercial Press, 15

Common Talk, 37
The Completion of the Heavens (*see Evolution and Ethics*)
Confucianism, xiv, 26, 28, 39, 45, 46, (79), 80, 91, 93, 116, 118, 121
Contrat social (Rousseau), xix, 7
Creation Society, 4
A Crime Involving Nine Lives, 11, 78, 98
Current Affairs (Shih-wu pao), 7, 49

Danow, D., xxv
Dargan, E. Preston, xxi (n. 23)
Darwin, xix
David Copperfield, 16
De l'esprit de lois (Montesquieu), xix, 7, 10
Diary from the Hall of the Extraordinary (Yueh-man-t'ang jih-chi), 38, 43
Diary from the Hall of Rebirth (Fu-t'ang jih-chi), 38
Diary (Lu Hsün), 32 (nn. 110, 111, 114), 33 (nn. 115-117), 35, 36 (nn. 128-131), 37-38 (nn. 134, 138, 139, 143, 144), 40 (n. 149), 43-44 (n. 8), 53 (n. 66)
"Diary of a Madman," xvi, 41, 48 (n. 37), 76, 77, 79, 80, 81, 84 (n. 19), 85, 86, 91, 92, 94, 95 (n. 55), 97, 110, 117-118
Dickens, viii, 21
Don Quixote, 16, 49
Dostoevsky, xxiv, 33, 36, 39
Doyle, Arthur Conan, 8
"The Dragon Boat Festival," 79, 81, 98, 110, 111
drama (*see* theater)
The Dream of the Green Chamber, 60
The Dream of the Red Chamber, 59, 62, 63, 73, 79 (n.), 121
Dreiser, Theodore, ix
"The Duck's Comedy," 76, 77, 92, 110

Dubasova, x
Dumas, A. (*fils*), 8

Eastern Europe, 18, 19, 20, 37, (121)
Editorial Section Monthly, 33
England, xvi (n. 16), xviii, 6, 8, 10, 13, 36, 49-50, 113
Enlightenment, xviii-xxi, 8, 9, 11, 13, 15, 19, 26, 28, 29, 35, 37-38, 58, 78-79, 116, 122
Enoki, Kazuo, xxvi
Eroshenko, 92
essay, xiv, xvii, xviii, xxvi, (8-9), 10, 12, 13, 19, 20, 25-26, 31, 37, 39, 42-48, 49, 54, 55, 60, 64, 75-76, 95, 113
"The Eternal Lamp," xvii, 87 (n.)
Europe, 6, 7, 8, 13, 18, 19, 23, 31, 36, 37, 39, 45, 55-56, 58, 76, 93, 115
European and American Short Stories, 37
Evolution and Ethics, 6-7, 50, 51 (n. 53)
"The Evolution of Roughs," 64
"An Example," xvii, 87 (n.)
Expedition to the North Pole, 14, 15, 16
Exposure of the Merchant's World, 66
Exposure of the Official World, 66-69, 80, 82, 83, 87, 88, 93 (n. 42), 111-112, 119
Exposure of the Teaching World, 66
Exposure of the Women's World, 66
Eydlin, L. Z., xi-xii, xv, xvi,

Fadeev, Alexander, x-xi (n. 8), xxiv
Family Chronicle from the Region of I-chou (I-chou chia-ch'eng), 38
Fan Tseng-hsiang, 43
Fang, Achilles, 114 (n.)
Fang Hsüan-ch'o, 81, 110, 111
Far East, x, xii, xv, xix
Far Eastern University (Vladivostok), x

Fat Mama Huang, 96
The Fate Which Awakens the World, 81
Fedin, K. A., xi (n. 8)
Fedorenko, N. T., xi-xii, xv
"A Few Matters Connected with Chang T'ai-yen," 47 (n. 30)
fiction (hsiao-shuo), xxii-xxiii, 5, 8, 10, 11, 12 (13), 26 (n. 97), 29, 33, (36), 42, 56-74, (76-77), 80, (91), 93, 100-101, 103-104, 109. 111, 113, 115, 116, 119, 121
Fiction Monthly (Hsiao-shuo yüeh-pao), 20, 31
Fishman, O. L., xi
Five Younger Gallants, 63-64
"Flood North of the Yangtze," 32
The Flower and the Moon (Hua yueh hen), 59-60
A Flower in an Ocean of Sin, 71-73, 78, 79, 80, 81, 82, 86, 88, 89, 91, 93 (n. 41), 98, 99, 114
Flowers in the Mirror, 5, 58-59
folklore, 5, 26 (n. 98), 35, 62
the "foreign devil" ("Story of Hair"), 110
"Four Days" (Garshin), 20, 21, 22
Fourth Shan's wife ("Tomorrow"), 84, 85, 91, 93-94 (n. 46), 106, 107
France, xvii-xxi
From the Earth to the Moon (Verne), 13, 14, 17
Fu Mi-hsien ("Blockhead Fu"), 69, 83, 96
Fu Ts'ai-yün, 72, 78
Fukien, 8
"The Future of the New China" (Liang Ch'i-ch'ao), 10 (n. 32), 94

The Gallant Maiden (Erh-nü ying-hsiung chuan), 62-63
Gamberg, V. L., x
Garshin, Vsevolod, 20, 21, 22-23
Germany, 22-23, 36, 71
Glaesser, Gustav, xii (n. 10)
Gogol, N. T., vii, 21, 29, 41, 94, 97

Gorky, vii, xii, 21, 36
The Grave, xvii
The Great World, 56
Greece, 6, 10, 11, 19, 33
Grieder, Jerome, xix (n. 19)
grotesque, 67, 68-69, 74, 76, 79, 112, 113
Gulliver's Travels, 16

Haggard, H. Rider, 8, 10, 15 (n. 51), 18, 24, 49
Han Ho-sheng, 60
Han Pang-ch'ing, 60
Hanan, Patrick, xxvi
Harbin, x
"A Happy Prince" (Wilde), 20
Heine, Heinrich, 36-37
Helen (of Troy), 11
A Hero of Our Time (Lermontov), 21
Hesitation, xvii, 77, 81, 84, 87 (n.), 91 (nn. 34, 37), 95
The Historical Development of Chinese Fiction, 57
The History of Pain, 76
Ho Chia-huai, 7 (n. 17), 110 (n. 90)
Ho Shih, 42
Ho Yü-feng, 62-63
Honan, 20
Hong Kong, x
The Honorable Chao ("Ah Q"), 83, 97, 100, 102, 115, 119
"How I Came to Write Stories," 78 (n. 6)
"How 'The True Story of Ah Q' Was Written," xxii, 113
Hsia Ching-ch'ü, 58
Hsia, C. T., 108 (n. 86)
Hsia Tseng-yu, 18, 35, 46
Hsia Yü ("Medicine"), 84, 85, 88, 89, 94-95, 100, 107-108, 118
Hsieh Wu-liang, 39
Hsin Chi-chi, 120
Hsin-hai Revolution (*see* Revolution of 1911-13)
Hsü Chin, 55 (nn. 73-74)
Hsü Ch'in-wen, 92 (n. 40), 94, 100

(n. 70), 103 (n. 75)
Hsü Hsi-lin, 32, 118
Hsü Kuang-p'ing (Ching Sung), 23 (n. 89), 24 (n. 90)
Hsü Shou-shang, 10, 11, 16, 17 (n. 57), 47
Hsüan Ting, 58
Hu Hua-jo, 83, 112
Hu Ping, 38 (n. 142), 85 (n. 20)
Hu Shih, xix (n. 19), 3 (n. 1), 39, 40 (n. 148), 52, 56, 63-64, 70-71 (n. 133), 72
Hua Ta-ma ("Medicine"), 84
hua-pen (story script), xviii, xxii-xxiii, 12, (36), 61, 65, (66), (69), (73), 109
Huang Jen, 18
Huang Sung-k'ang, xvi, 7 (n. 17), 9 (n. 27)
Huang T'ing-chien, 38
Huang Tsun-hsien, 8, 46, 75, 120 (n. 3)
Hughes, E. R., xix, xx (n. 22)
Hugo, Victor, 10, 18
Hui An (*see* T'ang T'ao)
humanism, xix
Hundred Days (*see* Reform Movement of 1898)
Hung Chün (*see* Chin Wen-ch'ing)
Huxley, A., xix, 6, 50, 51 (n. 53)

I-chun, 86 (n. 21), 94 (n. 47)
Ideological Currents and the Literature of Contemporary Russia, 36
Illustrated Fiction, 20
The Imitation Foreign Devil ("Ah Q"), 83, 91, 110
India, xiii, 18, 19
"In Exile" (Chekhov), 20
"In Memory of Miss Liu Ho-chen," xvii
Inoue, Tsutomu, 14
"Inscription on My Portrait," 9
Institute of Chinese Studies, xiii
Institute of Oriental Studies, x, xii, xiii
International Literature, viii-ix

"Introducing *The Bell of Yueh*" (*see The Bell of Yüeh*)
An Introduction to the Study of European and American Literature, 36
Irving, Washington, 16
"It's Better Not to Live" (Tokutomi, Roka), 21
"It's Hard to Be Stupid," 48
Ivanhoe, 16

"Jamiol" (Sienkiewicz), 20
Jao Han-hsien, 42
Japan, x, xiii, xix, xxiii, xxiv, xxvii, 4 (n. 6) 6, 7, 9, 10, 11, 14, 15, 16, 20, 22, 33, 36, 42, 44, 45, 51, 82, 114
Jenks, J. W., 9
Jesuits, xix
Joan Haste (Haggard), 49-50
Journey to the Center of the Earth, 13, 49 (n. 40)
Jun-t'u ("My Old Home"), 87, 96, 98, 99, 101, 103 (n. 77), 106

"Kaim and Artem" (Gorky), 21
Kang Pi, 70, 85
K'ang Yu-wei, 6, 7 (n. 14), 8, 9 (n. 26), 39, 44-46
Kao Yi-han, xxii
Kawakami, Kyujū, xiii (n. 13), xxvi
Kessel (Castle), M., ix (n. 5)
Khrushchev, xiii, xv
Knipovich, E. F., xi (n. 8)
Ko Kung-chen, 37 (n. 134)
Korolenko, 21
Kou Ts'ai, 111
Krasinski, x., 18
Krebsová, B., xvi, 94, 95 (n. 54), 110 (n. 92)
Krokodil (Crocodile), xii
Ku Yen-wu, 120
Kuang Hsü, Emperor, 7 (n. 14), 54, 61 (n. 102)
"K'ung I-chi," 79, 80-81, 82, 83, 84, 85, 87, 97, 100, 102, 106, 108, 110, 114 (n.), 116, 118

Kung Tzu-chen, 44, 120
Kung Yün-fu, 52
Kunming, x
Kuo Mo-jo, 3, 44
Kuomintang, 43
Kuprin, 36, 39

La Dame aux camélias (Dumas, fils), 8
Lamb, Charles, 51
Lang, A., 24
Last, J., xvi, 90 (n. 32)
Lee, Leo Ou-fan, xxvi
Lenin, xix
Leningrad, ix, x, xv, xvi
Lermontov, 18, 21
Les Misérables (Hugo), 18
A Letter on Freedom, 7
A Letter on Oppression (Chiu shu), 7
Levine, Steven I., x (n. 6)
Li Hsi-fan, 86 (n. 23)
Li Ju-chen, 5, 58
Li Pao-chia, 4 (n. 5), 10, 12, 30, 40, 66-68, 70, 72, 75, 79-80, 81, 82, 83, 85, 86, 87, 88, 89, 93 (n. 42), 96, 97, 100, 103, 104, 111-112, 118-119
Li Po, x
Li Tz'u-ming, 33, 38, 43-44
Li Yüan-hung, 42
Liang Ch'i-ch'ao, xx, 4 (n. 6), 7, 8, 9, 10 (n. 32), 13, 16, 17, 19, 20 (n. 71), 28, 37, 40, 45-46, 49, 50, 51, 75, 78, 94
Liao-chai (*see* P'u Sung-ling)
"Lie" (Andreev), 20, 21, 22
"The Lighthouse Keeper of Aspinwall" (Sienkiewicz), 20
Lin Ch'en, 15 (n. 50), 24 (n. 91), 37 (n. 137), 114
Lin Shu, 8, 10, 15, 16, 36, 40, 49-50, 51
Lin Yü-t'ang, 113
Lisevich, I. S., x (n. 7)
Liu Chün-jo, xvi, 90 (n. 32)
Liu Fu (Liu Pan-nung), 39
Liu Ho-chen, xiv, xviii
Liu O, 4 (n. 5), 12, 30, 66, 70-71, 72, 79, 83, 85, 88 (n. 27), 93, 94, 96, 103, 104, 105, 109
Liu Shou-sung, 65 (n. 122), 67 (n. 126), 69 (n. 129)
Liu Ta-chieh, xvi, 58 (n. 86), 63 (n. 110), 65 (n. 122)
Liu Wu-chi, xxvi, 24, 61 (n.), 77 (n.)
Liu Ya-tzu, 24, 48
Lives of Shanghai Singsong Girls (Hai-shang-hua lieh-chuan), xxv, 60-62
Living Hell, 82, 83, 87, 103, 111, 112
Lo Kuan-chung, 108
The Lone Swan (Su Man-shu), 93 (n. 43)
Lu Hsün (Chou Shu-jen), anarchist, viii, (92 n.); anti-Confucianism, xiv, 117-118; avoids eroticism, 91; *Brief History* (English), 58 (nn. 83, 84, 85), 59 (n. 90), 60 (nn. 93, 96), 61 (n.), 62 (nn. 104, 107), 63 (n. 112), 64 (n. 119), 65 (nn. 121, 122), 66 (nn. 123, 124), 67-68 (n. 127), 69 (n. 129), 70 (n. 132), 71 (n. 136), 72 (n. 141), 74 (nn. 143, 144); commemorative volume in honor of, ix, x, xi; and Chinese Communist Party, ix; compared to Chekhov, vii, xvii; compared to Dickens, viii; critical realist, xiv, 21, 28; democrat, xiv, 3, 14, 18, 54, 56, 82; enlightener (*see* philosophe); exposer, xxi-xxii, 21-22, (28), (38), (39-40), (41), (69-70), 74, 81, (86-87), 89, (90), 91, 92, 112, 113; father of modern Chinese literature, 3; hero, ix-xix; honored by Fadeev, xi; humanist, ix, xi, xiv, (xvii), xxii, 3, 21, 41, 50, 78, 92, 93, (95), 96, 98, 110; introduced to B. A. Vasilev, vii-viii; materialism, 17, 33-34 (n.), 39; as narrator, xv, 11-12, 29, 53, 83, (85), 87, 89-90 (n.), 96, 98, 100, (106-107), 109-113, (116-117); optimism, xiv, xv,

xvii, 25, 85, 87, 93-94, 95-96, 105, 109, (113); and the people, xv, xvi, xvii-xviii, 14, 17-18, 22, 25, 27, 53, 82-88, 89, 90, (91), 92, 93, 95-96, 105, 110; pessimism, xv, 21-22, 25-26, 36, 38, (46), 85-86, 88-90, 93-96 (n. 54), 105, 112-113; petit bourgeois radical, viii; philosophe, xx-xxi, 8, 9-15, 16, 17, 18, 19, 26, 28-29, 33-34, 38, 46, 51, 78, 82, (86-87), 122; realist, xiv, 20, 21, 28, 29, 33, 36, 37, 74, 79, 88, (93-96), 122; revolutionary, (ix), xiv, xv, xvii, (xix), 7, 9, 11, 15, 16, 17, 18, 24-26, (27), (30), 31-32, (36-37), (41), 46, 48, (71), 84, 85-86, 88-90, 94-95, (108); revolutionary democrat, xiv, 7, 70-71, 86; revolutionary humanist, xiv, xxii; revolutionary romanticist, xiv, 36; romanticist, 13, 18-19, 20, (27), 36, (77). 88; satirist, xiii-xiv, xvii, xxi, xxii, (30), (36-37), (38), 43, 49, 52, 55, 57, 69-70, 72, 74 (n. 144), 81, 87, (90), (91), 97, 105, 112, 113, 114, 117, 118, 119; *Selected Works* (English), xviii, xxii (n. 26), xxv, 6 (n. 6), 7 (n. 16), 41 (n. 157), 43 (n. 4), 45 (n. 17), 46 (n. 22), 47 (nn. 27, 28, 30), 48 (n. 39), 49 (n. 41), 50 (nn. 48, 49), 53 (n. 64), 54 (n. 69), 59 (n. 88), 64 (n. 117), 69-70 (n. 130), 74 (n. 143), 78 (n. 6), 83 (n. 16), 84 (n. 19), 92 (n.), 93 (n. 45), 94 (n. 46), 99 (n. 67), 100 (n. 68), 101 (nn. 71, 72), 105 (nn. 80, 82), 107 (n. 83), 112 (nn. 98, 99), 113 (n. 102), 115 (n. 108), 116 (n. 110), 117 (nn. 113, 114), 118 (nn. 115-117), 120 (n. 1), and Appendix; socialist realist, xiv; theory of art, 13, 17-18, 33-35, 69, 73-74; and theory of evolution, 7; translator, 5, 11, 12-13 (n. 43), 14-15 (n. 49), 19, 20, 21, 22-24, 36, 37, 45, 48-51, 75; youth, 5-9, 43, 44, 114; and the Yüeh Society, 24-26
Lu Jen-hsien, 111
Lu Xun (*see* Lu Hsün)
Lu Yu, 120
The Lucky Man (*Strange Events*), 99
Lyell, William, xxvi, 26 (n. 100), 103 (n. 75)

Ma Han-hua, 108 (n. 88)
Manchus, xix, (3), 7, 9, 12, 16, 31, 43, 44, 45, 46, 47, 48, 55, 57, 62, 64, 65
Mao Ch'en, 44 (n. 13)
Mao Tse-tung, xiv
Mao Tun (*see* Shen Yen-ping)
Marxism-Leninism, xiv, xv, xix
Maupassant, Guy de, 20, 39
May Fourth Movement, xix (n. 19), xxiii, 4, 42, 46, 49, 79, 80, 81, 82, 113, 115
"Medicine," 76, 79, 81, 82, 85, 88, 90, 91, 93, 94-95 (n. 57), 96, 102, 105, 107, 108, 115, 118
Mei Lan-fang, 52-53
Mei Tzu-yü, 59
Melnikov, V. I., x
"Mending Heaven," 76, 77
A Method of Reading Japanese Texts in Chinese, 45
Mickiewicz, xxiv, 18, 21
Mikoyan, Anastas, xii
Mill, J. S., xix, 10
Miller, F. xxv
Mills, Harriet, xvi, xxvi
Minister Fu Mi-hsien (*Strange Events*), 69
Minister Hsü (*Exposure of the Official World*), 68
Minister Hua (*Exposure of the Official World*), 67-68
Minister of Justice (*Exposure of the Official World*), 67
Ministry of Education, 33, 35-36, 37, 38, 39, (44), 46
A Mirror of Theatrical Life, 59-60

Miscellany Within and Without of the Universe, 57
Modern Review, xxii
Modern Times, 72, 82, 86, 88, 100, 111, (122)
Moneybags Ho the Third, 96
Montesquieu, xix-xx, 7, 9-10
Moscow, ix, x, xiii, xvi
"Mourning for Mr. Fan," 31
Mr. Meeson's Will (Haggard), 15
Mr. N ("The Story of Hair"), 46, 89-90 (n.), 99, 110
"Murderers of the Present," 58
"My Old Home," 4, 25, 76, 79, 81, 82, 83, 87, 92, 93, 96, 98-99, 101, 105, 108, 109, 110

N (*see* Mr. N)
Nada the Lily, 15
Nanking, x, 5, 6, 7, 8, 24, 32
The National Herald (Kuo wen pao), 6 (n. 8)
Neglected Ancient Tales (Ku hsiao-shuo kou-ch'en), 26, 31
New Citizen (Hsin-min ts'ung-pao), 4, 9
New Fiction (Hsin hsiao-shuo), 9, 11, 20 (n. 71), 49
New Life (Hsin sheng), 19, 20
New People's Miscellany (*see New Citizen*)
"New Rome," 10 (n. 32), 51 (n. 53)
"New Village" (Aho), 20-21
The New World, 56
New Youth (Hsin ch'ing-nien), 39, 40, 41, 77
Nietzsche, xx, 21, 87, 95
"The Nightmare" (Lin Shu), 49
Nikolaev, 89
The Nine-Tailed Tortoise (Chiu-wei kuei), 61
Nitze, William A., xxi (n. 23)
"No Need for 'Corrections,'" 60
"Notes on Literature" (Wen-i tsa-hua), 36
Notes of the Yüeh-wei Hermitage, xxv, 5, 57

"Notes of a Warrior," 8
novel, xvi, xviii, xx-xxi (France), xxiv, 10, 12, 13, 14, 20, 21, 29, 30, 36, 49, 56, 58, 59, 62, 66, 73, 76, 78, 79, 81, 82, 83, 84, 88, 90, 91, 95, 96, 98, 100-103, 104, 107-108, 109, 111, 116, 117, 118, 121; of adventure (*hsia-i*), 6, 13, (50), 57, 62-65, 78, 83, 117; of censure, xx-xxii (France), 8, 14, 27, 28-29, 56, 57, 59, 61 (n. 99), 62, 63, 65-73 (n. 122), 76, 77, 78, 79, 80, 82, 83 (n. 18), 84-85, 86-87, 88, 89, 91, 92, 93, 94, 96, 97, 98, 99, 100, 102, 103-104, 105, 106, 108, 109, 111-113, 115, 116, 117, 118, 119, 121, 122; chivalric (*see* adventure); detective (*kung-an*) (*see* adventure); erotic, 57, 58, 59-65; of erudition, 57, 58-59, 65, 66; of exposure (*see* novel of censure); of fantasy, 5, 12, 14, (19), 57-59, 63; heroic (*see* adventure); historical, 14, (17), 29, 76; imitative (*ni-ku*), 57, 69, 73; of manners (*jen-ch'ing*), 14, 57, 60-62; picaresque (*see* adventure); psychological, 62; romantic, 62, 65; of satire (*feng-tz'u*), 5, 57, 58-59, 65, 69-70, 111-113, 117; science fiction, 14, 20, 49; with a key (*see* novel of censure)
novella, xxii, 12, 57-58, 59, 104, 121
Novoselov, x

Oda, Takeo, 8 (n. 22)
Ogai, Mori, 114 (n.)
Okoneshnikova, S. M., x
Old Shuan ("Medicine"), 102
Old Tales Retold, 77, 84, 95, 113
"On Extremes in Culture," 17, 18
"On Foreign Literature" ("I yü wen t'an"), 37
On Humanism (Jen-hsüeh), 7
On Literary Trends, 36

"On the Power of Demoniacal Poetry," 17, 18, 19, 21 (n. 74), 36
"On Radium," 10, 12
"On the Relationship Between Fiction and Popular Sovereignty," 78
"On Satire," 74
Ono, Shinobu, xxvi
Oriental Institute (*see* Institute of Oriental Studies)
Oshanin, I. M., x
Outcry, vii, xiii, xv, xvii, xxi, 4, 76, 77, 79, 81, 83, 85, 87, 89, 91, 92, 93 (n. 45), 95, 98, 104, 107, 108, 110, 112, 113
"An Outline of Chinese Geology," 10
Ou-yang Fan-hai, 21 (n. 74), 32 (n. 113), 33 (n. 119), 41, 52, 86 (n. 23), 110 (n. 91), 111 (n. 96)
Ozaka Tokuji, 3, 18, 19 (n. 65), 20 (n. 71)
Ozerov, V. M., xi (n. 8)

pai-hua (*see* colloquial)
Pao Kung-ni, 50 (n. 46)
"The Past" ("Huai chiu"), 26-31
Peking, x, xi, xvii, xviii, 32, 47, 50, (52-55), 56-57, 99
Peking opera (*see* theater)
The People (*Min pao*), 16
Perlin, x
Petöfi, Sandor, 18, 21
Petrov, V. V., xiv-xv, xvii, 3, 7, 17 (n. 58), 83 (n. 18), 92 (n. 40), 94 (n. 48), 111, 120 (nn. 2, 3)
philology, xi
philosophes, xx-xxi, 4 (n. 5), 6, 7, 9-15, 16, 17, 18, 19, 26, 33, 34, 38, 44, 45, 46, 51, 58, 78, 93
P'ing Hsin, 86
"Plant Sketches," 8, 24
Plato, 6
Plushkin (*Dead Souls*), 28
Po Chü-i, x
Poe, Edgar Allen, 20

poetry, xi, xii, xxiii, 10 (n. 33), 11, 16-17, 18, 24, 25, 26, 31, 32, 33, (35), 36-37 (n. 133), 38 (nn. 140, 141), 39, 40, 42-48, 54, 75, 76, (95), 104, 120-121, 122
Poland, 19, 36, 121
Political News Society (*Cheng-wen-she*), 17
"Popular Tales" (Tolstoy), 21
Pozdneeva, L. D., xi, xiii-xiv (n. 14), xv, xvi, 7 (n. 17), 14 (n. 45), 15 (n. 50), 21 (n. 76), 28, 35, 36 (n. 127), 41 (n. 158), 49 (n. 44), 83 (n. 17), 86 (n. 24), 92 (n. 40), 94, 97 (n. 60), 98 (n. 64), 99 (n. 66), 107 (n. 84), 119
Pravda, ix, xi (n. 8)
"Preface to *Neglected Ancient Tales*" (*see Neglected Ancient Tales*)
Prefect Pao, 63
Primer of Chinese History, 46
Prince of Hsiang-yang, 63-64
Prince Serebryany, 36
Principles of Politics, 9
The Principles of Sociology (Spencer), 9
"Proposal for Dissemination of the Arts," 33-35
Průšek, Jaroslav, xvi, xxii, xxvi, 7, 28 (n.), 95 (n. 54)
Public Opinion (*Ch'ing-i pao*), 9, 45
"Pu Chou Mountain" (*see* "Mending Heaven")
Pushkin, 18, 21
P'u Sung-ling, 57

"The Rabbits and the Cat," 76, 77, 79-80, 92, 110
Random Notes from Shanghai, 5
random thoughts (*tsa-kan*), 75
realism, 20, 21, 28, 36, 37, 69, 78-79, 122
Rebirth of the People (Min-hsin jih-pao), 31
Red-eyed Ah Yi ("Medicine"), 96
reformer (*see* philosophes)
Reform Movement of 1898, 6-8

(n. 14), (9-15), (16-19), 44-48,
   49-51, 65, 89
"Reminiscences of the Past" (*see*
   "The Past")
Republic (*see also* Ministry of Education), xiv, 31, 33, 35-36, 38,
   42, 48
"Reply to K'ang Yu-wei's Letter on
   Revolution," 9
The Restoration Society (*Kuang-fu
   hui*), 9, 15
"Revenge (I)," xvii
Revolution of 1911-13, 24-35, 46,
   66-67, 71, 77, 79, 81, 82, 89, 90
Revolutionary Army (Tsou Jung), 9,
   47
Rogachev, A. P., x
Rogov, V., xv
roman à clef (*see* novel of censure)
romanticism, xix, 18-19, 20, 36, 77,
   88
Rome, 6
Rousseau, xix, 7
The Rout (Fadeev), xi
Russia (*see also* Soviet Union),
   viii, xi, xxiv, 8, 24, 36, 39, 49
   (n. 41) 52 (n. 61), 53, 71, 86,
   88, 92, 97 (n. 59), 99 (n. 67),
   105 (n. 82), 117 (n. 114), 121
A Rustic's Idle Talk (Yeh-sou p'u-
   yen), 58

Saltykov-Shchedrin, 115
Sappho, 10
Sara(*A Flower in an Ocean of Sin*),
   88
The Scholars, 66-67, 73, 74 (n. 144),
   80-81, 121
Schultz, William, xxvi
Schwartz, William, xix (n. 20)
Scott, Walter, 10
Scudéry, Madeleine de, xx-xxi
A Sea of Woe, 72
Seaton, Jerome P., xxvi
Semanov, V. I., xv, xvi, xvii, xviii, xx,
   xxi, xxiii, xxv-xxvi, 27 (n.), 29
   (n.), 52 (n.), 89 (n.)
Sendai, 9, 15, 16

A Sequel to Five Younger Gallants,
   63-64
*Series of European and American
   Short Stories*, 37
Seven Heroes and Five Gallants,
   63-64
Shakespeare, 51
Shanghai, x, xxvi, 32, 56, 61
Shaohsing, 5, 7, 31, 32, 54-55
Shaw, J. Thomas, xxiv
Shelley, 18, 21
Shen P'eng-nien, 25, 82 (n. 13)
(Shen) Yen-ping (Mao Tun), 76
Shen Yin-mo, 39
Shiga, Masatoshi, 6
shih poetry (*see* poetry)
Shih, young master (*Lives of Shang-
   hai Singsong Girls*), 61
Shih Yü-k'un, 63-64
A Short Biography of Joan (*see Joan
   Haste*)
short story, viii, ix, xiii-xiv, xv, xvi-
   xvii, xviii, xxii-xxiii, xxiv, 8, 11,
   12, 20, 21, 27, 29, 30, 39, 69,
   75, 76, 77, 80, 82, 84, 86-87,
   93, 94, 96, 97, 98, 99, 104-106,
   107, 110-111, 112-113, (116-
   117)
Short Stories from Abroad, 20, 23,
   29, 33, 39
Shuan (*see* Old Shuan or Young
   Shuan)
Sian, 56-57, 61
Siao Emi (Hsiao San), xi
Sienkiewicz, Henryk, 20, 36
"Silence" (Andreev), 20, 28-29
"Silence. A Fable" (Poe), 20, 21
Sinclair, Upton, ix
Skachkov, P. Ye., x
Sketches (Irving), 16
Slowacki, J., xxiv, 18, 21
"A Small Incident," 76, 79, 82, 87,
   93, 98, 99-100, 107, 109, 110,
   115, 117
"Soap," xiii
Society for the Promotion of National Learning, 37
Socrates, 6

"Some Notions Jotted Down by Lamplight," xvii
"Some Recollections of Chang T'ai-yen," 47
Soochow, 61
Sorokin, V. F., xiv-xv (n. 16), 5 (n. 1), 8 (n. 24), 15 (n. 49), 17 (n. 58), 19 (n. 69), 21 (n. 76), 22 (n. 77), 28, 81 (n. 9), 83 (n. 18), 86 (n. 22), 88 (n. 29), 91, 92 (n. 40), 97, 98 (nn. 62, 65), 100 (n. 69), 112 (n. 97), 121 (n. 4)
A Sourcebook on Chinese Economics, 16
Southern Society (*Nan she*), 24, 32, 37, 48
Soviet Union, vii, viii, ix, x, (xi), xii, xiii, xv, xvi, xviii, xxiii, xxv-xxvi, 49, 53
"The Spartan Spirit," 11-12, 18, 27, 29
Spencer, xix, 9
Ssu-ma Ch'ien, 12
Ssu-min ("Soap"), xiii-xiv
Stalin, ix, x, xii
Stepnyak-Kravchinsky, S., 20
Stoics, 6
"Storm in a Teacup," 27 (n.), 90, 105, 106, 112
"Story of Hair," 46, 76, 77, 89, 99, 110
"The Story of a Kopeck," 20
story script (*see hua-pen*)
Strange Events of the Last Twenty Years, 10, 29, 69-70, 79, 82, 87, 91, 99, 111
Strange Tales of Electricity, 81
successful county candidate ("Ah Q"), 116
successful provincial candidate ("Ah Q"), 83, 112, 115, 116
Su Man-shu, 10, 18, 20, 36, 39, 48, 75, 77, 93 (n. 43), 104
Sun Ch'ang-hsi, 76 (n. 3)
Sun Ch'uan-fang, 46, 47
Sun Society, 4
Sun Fu-yüan, 24 (n. 90), 82 (n. 12),

95 (n. 55)
Sun Te-ch'ing, 32
Sun Yat-sen, 9, 32, 47, 48, 71, 88
Sung Yün-pin, 47
Su-pao, 91 (n. 26)
Suppression of the Rebels, 6
Supplement to the Diary of the Hall of the Extraordinary, 44
Swearingen, Roger, xii (n. 11)
Swift, Jonathan, 16
System of Logic (Mill), 10

Tachibana, Kozen, xxvi
Tagore, 39
Takeuchi, Yoshimi, xxvi
Taiping Rebellion, 27, 56, 58
"Tale of a Broken Hairpin," 39
"A Tale on the Burning of the Sword," 77
"A Tale of Crimson Silk," 77
"The Tale of a Mad Knight" (*see Don Quixote*)
"A Tale of Twin Chessboards" (Shuang p'ing chi), 77
A Tale of Two Cities, viii
T'an Hsien, 38
T'an Hsin-p'ei, 52
T'an Ssu-t'ung, 7, 46-47, 120 (n. 3)
Tan Yen-i, 109
T'ang T'ao, 13 (n. 43), 44, 46 (n. 23), 52 (n. 58), 117
T'ao Ch'eng-chang, 32
theater, 3, 5, 32 (n. 114), 35, 42, 44, 51-56, (75), 99, 104, 113, 122
theory of evolution, xix, 7, (82)
Third Master ("The Past"), 27
Thousand and One Nights, xii
The Three Heroes and Five Gallants (San-hsia wu-i), 62, 63, 64
The Three Kingdoms, 62
T'ien Han, 56 (n. 77)
Tientsin, x
The Tiger (Chia-yin), 77
"The Tiger's Battle with the Dragon," 55
Tikhvinsky, S. L., 7 (n. 14)
Tokutomi, Roka, 21
Tokyo, 9, 15, 16

Tolstoy, A. K., 36
Tolstoy, L., 21, 39
"Tomorrow," 80, 81 (n. 10), 82, 91, 93-94 (n. 46), 98, 105, 106, 107
translations, 6, 7, 8, 9, 10, 14, 15-16, 20, 21, 37, 48-51, 75
Translation Magazine (I-shu hui-pien), 7
"Travel Notes of the Year 1911," xviii, 24-25, 31
The Travels of Lao Ts'an, 70-71, 72, 78, 80, 82, 83, 85, 87, 93, 94, 96, 103, 104 105, 109
"The True Story of Ah Q," vii-viii, xxii-xxiii, 4, 49, 55, 76, 79, 80, 83, 84, 85, 86, 87, 89, 90, 91, 93, 96-97, 99, 100, 101-102, 104-105, 106, 108, 109, 110, 111, 112, 113, 114 (n.), 115, 116, 117, 119
Ts'ao-ch'iu, 60
Ts'ao Ching-hua, vii-viii (n. 1)
Ts'ao Hsüeh-ch'in, 59, 63, 98
Tseng Kuo-fan, 43
Tseng P'u, 12, 14, 18, 20, 23, 28, 35, 66, 71-73, 78, 79, 80, 81, 86, 87, 88, 91, 93 (n. 41), 98, 99, 111, 114
Tso Chuan, 12
Tsou Jung (Tsou Yung), 9, 47
Tu Ch'in-yen, 59
T'u Shen, 57, 58
Tui Yen, 13
T'ung-ch'eng school, 6, 42
Turgenev, 21, 33, 39
T'u Shen, 57, 58
Twenty Thousand Leagues Under the Sea, 49
Tz'u Hsi, 7 (n. 14)
tz'u poetry, 10 (n. 33), 38 (n. 141), 42, 44

Ueno, Yoichi, 33
Uncle K'ang ("Medicine"), 89
United States, xx, xxiii, 13

Vasilev, B. A., vii-viii (n. 3), x, xxiv

Verne, Jules, 10, 13 (n. 43), 14, 16, 17, 20, 49, 109
"The Village Opera," 52, 53, 55, 76, 77, 80, 87, 92, 93, 98-99, 111
Vishnyakova–Akimova, Vera Vladimirovna, x (n. 6)
Vladivostok, x
Voyloshnikov, x
Vyatkin, R. V., xi (n. 9), xiii

Wang, the servant ("The Past"), 27, 30
Wang Chi-chen, 90 (n.), 110 (n. 91), 111 (n. 93)
Wang Chin-fa, 32
Wang Ching-hsuan, 39 (n. 147)
Wang Hsi-yen, 90, 95 (n. 57)
Wang K'ai-yun, 43
Wang Kuo-wei, 3, 18, 44
Wang Shih-ching, 9 (n. 27), 35, 36 (n. 127), 41 (n. 158)
Wang Shih-yen, 90
Wang T'ao, 5, 58
Wang Tung-chao, 31 (n. 107)
Wang Yao 48, 121 (n. 5)
Wang Yüan-fang, 60
"Ward No. 6" (Chekhov), 21
War Minister Huang (*Exposure of the Official World*), 67-68
The Water Margin, 6, 62, 97 (n. 61)
Wei (*The Travels of Lao Ts'ao*), 70
Wei Ch'iu-chu, 60
Wei Hsiu-jen, 59
Wei I, 50 (n. 47)
Weichuang, 90, 105
Wells, H. G., 36
Wen K'ang, 62-63
West, vii, xiii, xv, xix, xxi, 8, 14, 33, 37, 44, 45, 115
"What Happened to Nora after Her Departure?" xvii-xviii
"What is Satire?" 74
"The White Light," 79, 80-81, 82, 103
Wild Grass, xiv, xvii, 75, 77, 80, 84, 87 (n.), 95

Wilde, Oscar, 20, 39
Wiskers Wang ("Ah Q"), 102
World War II, x
Wu Ch'ang, 54
Wu Ching-tzu, 66, 80
Wu Pen-hsing, 108 (n. 88), 115 (nn. 106, 109)
Wu Wo-yao, 10-11, 29, 40, 66, 68-70, 72, 76, 78, 79, 81, 85, 87, 91, 98, 99, 103, 109, 111
Wuch'ang Uprising, 27, 32, 47

Xerxes, 11

Yakovlev, x
Yang Erh-sao, 91
Yang, Gladys, xviii (n. 18), xxiv, 85 (n. 81), see also the Appendix
Yang Hsien-yi, xxi (n. 24), xxiv
Yang Sheng ("The Past"), 27-28, 30
Yang Tzu-lin, 50 (n. 46)
"Yanko the Musician" (Sienkiewicz), 20
"Years of Silence," 35-41
Yellow Dragon, 103
Yen Chia-yen, 53-54 (n. 68)
Yen Fu, xix (n. 20), 6 (n. 8), 7, 8, 9, 10, 46, 50-51 (n. 54).
Yenan, xiv
Yi Ya, 118
Yolk, Ye. S., x
Young Shuan ("Medicine"), 107-108
Yü-erh ("Medicine"), 94 (n. 46)
Yü Ta, 60 (n. 96)
Yüan Chen, x
Yüan Shih-k'ai, 32, 36, 37 (n. 134), 38, 39, 46, 47
Yüeh Society, 24-25, 32
Yüeh Society Miscellany, 24-26, 31
Yün Shu-chüeh, 13, 30, 31 (n. 107)

For Product Safety Concerns and Information please contact our EU
representative GPSR@taylorandfrancis.com
Taylor & Francis Verlag GmbH, Kaufingerstraße 24, 80331 München, Germany

www.ingramcontent.com/pod-product-compliance
Lightning Source LLC
Chambersburg PA
CBHW052119300426
44116CB00010B/1720